Sonam,
I hope you enjoy
your read!

-Ryan

THE KNOWLEDGE-POWER PARADIGM

HOW TO LEAD LIKE A GENIUS

PRASH P. PAVAGADHI

Copyright © 2008 by Prashant P. Pavagadhi

All rights reserved. No part of this book shall be reproduced or transmitted in any form or by any means, electronic, mechanical, magnetic, photographic including photocopying, recording or by any information storage and retrieval system, without prior written permission of the publisher. No patent liability is assumed with respect to the use of the information contained herein. Although every precaution has been taken in the preparation of this book, the publisher and author assume no responsibility for errors or omissions. Neither is any liability assumed for damages resulting from the use of the information contained herein.

ISBN 0-7414-4515-8

Published by:

1094 New DeHaven Street, Suite 100
West Conshohocken, PA 19428-2713
Info@buybooksontheweb.com
www.buybooksontheweb.com
Toll-free (877) BUY BOOK
Local Phone (610) 941-9999
Fax (610) 941-9959

Printed in the United States of America

Printed on Recycled Paper

Published January 2008

DEDICATED TO

My parents, Pankaj and Nalini, for instilling
in me the principles of the knowledge-power
paradigm from an early age. Your encouragement,
love, and dedication has helped to shape my life
in so many positive ways. Thank you.

CONTENTS

	Foreword	VII
	Preface	IX
	Acknowledgements	XIV

PART I: INTRODUCTION TO THE PARADIGM

1	The Knowledge-Power Paradigm	3
2	The Right Stuff	17
3	The Right People	31
4	Timing Is Everything	45
5	Individual and Collective Action	61

PART II: COMMON ORGANIZATIONAL FAILURES & MISSED OPPORTUNITIES

6	The Knowledge-Power Success Model	75
7	Data Collection & Evaluation Feedback Loop	89
8	The Essential Role of Leadership	103
9	Decision-Making & Opportunity Cost	117
10	Industry Study: Knowledge Management in Healthcare	131

PART III: THE KNOWLEDGE-POWER PARADIGM IN PRACTICE

11	The Changing Role of Technology In Knowledge Management	149
12	1st Down & Goal: Knowledge-Power in the World of Sport	163
13	The Quality Improvement Continuum	181
14	Stepping Up to the Starting Line	193
15	One Parable & Ten Text Messages	205

Notes

FOREWORD

"KNOWLEDGE IS POWER" is a concept very familiar to the modern psyche - at least since Sir Francis Bacon first introduced it in the late 1500s. Very few people, however, have truly mastered the skills needed to translate basic knowledge into personal and professional power.

Knowledge itself does not bestow power. Success rests on many pillars, including hard work, luck, insight, and knowledge. Prash Pavagadhi introduces the 'Knowledge-Power Paradigm' to empower the reader with the skills needed to use knowledge as vehicle to attain both personal and professional success. Knowledge, properly leveraged, can empower us on many levels. Pavagadhi illustrates how the 'Knowledge-Power Paradigm' can be applied across a variety of disciplines and organizations. In science and technology, knowledge of the way our universe works can be used to not only predict but also control how a system will behave under given circumstances. In business, the 'knowledge-power paradigm' presents a road map for converting industry and domain knowledge into financial success. On a personal level, the book inspires the reader to attain higher self knowledge and aspire for success beyond traditional financial metrics.

The 'Knowledge-Power Paradigm' is effectually a discussion on achieving personal and organizational quality improvement and success through the systematic acquisition and use of knowledge. The book forces you to introspect on the quantity and quality of knowledge you currently possess about your industry, customers, organizational processes, and ultimately even yourself. Pavagadhi's use of insightful examples makes the book an enjoyable and easy read. I sincerely hope that the thoughts in this book resonate with your personal and professional mission as they have with mine.

Dr. Anita Goel, M.D., Ph.D.

Dr. Anita Goel, M.D., Ph.D.

Founder, Chairman, and CEO of Nanobiosym Diagnostics, Inc & President and Scientific Director of Nanobiosym Labs.

Physicist and physician Anita Goel, MD, PhD was recently named one of the world's "top 35 science and technology innovators under the age of 35" by MIT's Technology Review Magazine. Dr. Goel holds both a PhD in Physics from Harvard University and an MD from the Harvard-MIT Joint Division of Health Sciences and Technology (HST) and BS in Physics from Stanford University.

Dr. Goel is the President and Scientific Director of Nanobiosym Labs and the President and CEO of Nanobiosym Diagnostics, Inc. Nanobiosym Diagnostics, Inc. is the commercial arm of Nanobiosym that is developing next-generation diagnostic capabilities. Nanobiosym Labs focuses on fundamental research at the interface of Physics, Medicine, and Nanotechnology, and maximizing the global impact of this synergy, with a focus on both developed and emerging world markets.

Dr. Goel's work at Nanobiosym has been recognized by several prestigious funding awards from the United States Department of Defense agencies including Defense Advanced Research Projects Agency (DARPA), Air Force Office of Scientific Research (AFOSR) and US Dept of Energy (DOE) and US Defense Threat Reduction Agency (DTRA).

She is a Fellow of the World Technology Network, a Fellow-at-Large of the Santa Fe Institute, and an Associate of the Harvard Physics Department, and Adjunct Professor of BEYOND institute for Fundamental Concepts in Science. She serves on the Board of Trustees and Scientific Advisory Board of India-Nano, an organization devoted to bridging breakthrough advances in nanotechnology with the burgeoning Indian nanotech sector.

PREFACE

The secret of business is to know something that nobody else knows.
- ARISTOTLE ONASSIS

OBTAINING AND POSSESSING KNOWLEDGE has always been the cornerstone for success, whether applied to individual or collective ambition. The more you know, the more effective you are likely to be. My parents were always strict disciplinarians. They incessantly lectured me about the importance of acquiring an education, because having a proper education would afford me a greater opportunity to succeed in life. I, on the other hand, was not interested in education. I much preferred raising hell with my friends. I'm glad they did not give up on me. With their guidance, I got my act together, eventually.

I learned that it wasn't only about working hard, it was about acquiring knowledge and working smart. Therein lies the lesson for successful leaders; obtain and understand accurate, timely information, to form a platform for sound strategic planning and decision-making. In this book I will outline various points which underpin the workings of the knowledge-power paradigm–i.e. attaining success through superior information, and working smarter through effective application. We also will use real-world examples to highlight how these principles can greatly help goal attainment.

The Challenger space shuttle disaster in 1986 is a vivid example of what can happen when the knowledge-power paradigm breaks down. It was one of the worst tragedies in NASA's history. Until that point, only the fire in Apollo 1 came close to sheer tragedy for the space program. It was one of those "where were you when" moments in history. Many remember the day vividly. The shuttle program was working so well, and the tragedy was definitely a shock to the system for the nation. Following the disaster, President Reagan set up the Rogers Commission to investigate the cause of the accident and outline recommendations to prevent such an event from happening again.

The Rogers Commission included aviation heavyweights Neil Armstrong, Sally Ride and Chuck Yeager. Their investigation was long and thorough. The official cause of the accident was the failure of O-ring seals, which set into motion a flame leak, causing structural failure in the external tank. But the report went on to give a damning account of the role played by management and the processes that led to the launch in the first place. The report specifically pointed out that "...failures in communication...resulted in a decision to launch...based on incomplete and sometimes misleading information, a conflict between engineering data and management judgments, and a NASA management structure that permitted internal flight safety problems to bypass key Shuttle managers."[1]

The report stated that information and communication among key parties within the organization was a major source of the problem that likely contributed to the disaster. Safety concerns were brought up, and salient information was shared. But for some reason it was ignored. After the lessons of the Challenger disaster, it was believed that NASA had taken the necessary steps to improve its communication and information-sharing processes. In the wake of the Columbia disaster in 2003, however, NASA was once again criticized for getting lax with its safety protocol, allowing for "acceptable risk."[2] The investigating commission came down hard on organizational processes within NASA and its mechanisms for handling vital information and communications.

Both the Challenger and Columbia disasters outline the critical role played by information, knowledge, and communication within all organizations. These tragic examples highlight the importance of information and knowledge, and the consequences of ignoring it in such situations. Everyday, professionals across all organizations make decisions, some minor, some major, and others somewhere in-between. Therefore, successful decision-making is based on sound processes to obtain and communicate accurate, relevant and timely information, and the ability to deliver it to the right people, at the right time.

Billions of dollars ride on the decisions made by professionals, so making correct decisions is of paramount importance. Yet, how can professionals know for sure that the decisions they make will result in success? Metaphorically, it's like that overplayed movie scene where the protagonist has only seconds to defuse a ticking bomb; should he cut the red, blue or green wire? Without the right information, making that call is nothing short of a gamble that may or may not pay off. In reality there is nothing sure about any decision or strategy. But with the right information and knowledge, professionals do have the ability to tip probability in their favor. Knowledge gives rise to better understanding and insight. Successful leaders recognize this, and it is a large part of why they are successful. They effectively gather accurate information, analyze it, and in turn use their leadership skills to form sound decisions and strategies.

The purpose of this book is two-fold: (1) to share observations and experiences, and (2) to challenge you to look at the knowledge-power paradigm with the purpose of fully understanding and implementing it. At the heart of the matter is how one acquires comprehensive, reliable, relevant and timely information to execute effective decisions. Secondly, what organizational systems are required in order to become knowledgeable?

Knowledge management is a two-step process: the ability to gather/capture data and the ability to analyze data into structured, meaningful information. For example, when I leave the house today should I wear a coat? Well, that depends on the temperature outside and the forecast for the remainder of the day. Having and using accurate information helps me to make the right decision. This is a delicate yet critical equation from which professionals can benefit, once they fully understand:

Accurate Information & Knowledge = **Data Gathered** + **Data Analyzed**

Essentially, if the goal is to attain accurate information to attain knowledge, there has to be an information-data gathering stage and an information-data analysis stage. Some organizations are good at gathering data, yet fall short in analyzing it. The Challenger disaster findings confirmed that NASA management was running sophisticated data gathering systems. But part of the problem was the inability to effectively evaluate available data, and even when it was evaluated, important safety issues were ignored. In some organizations, formal data-gathering processes do not even exist; decisions are simply made through experience and assumptions. In other organizations, information is available but not communicated, and it gets lost or is completely ignored. This is hardly working smart.

Leaders often make the mistake of depending primarily on financial statements to ascertain the well-being of their division or organization. Just because profit is being made, it does not necessarily follow that profit will be sustained. While financials do offer vital information, they only paint a picture of what has already occurred, not what can be expected.

Successful leaders also judge the health of their organization through their ability to collect information from different customers who greatly affect their long-term performance and growth potential. Customers offer the greatest insight because they are the only ones who matter: without them there is no growth, no profit and no organization. Customers are the eyes that allow you to see into the very soul of your organization and also into what the future potentially holds. Use this knowledge wisely and you will be working smarter.

In a dynamic and constantly changing global economy, competition is becoming fiercer. Traditional barriers to entry and competitive advantages like price, technology and economies of scale have been eroded away. Leaders are being challenged to find new methods to succeed and stay ahead of the pack. Few organizations can boast lower prices or technological and geographical advantage for solutions. As the global economy continues to expand, customers become more savvy, understanding that they have a greater choice, and that choice is not limited to a few suppliers. The advent of the Internet has allowed for mass communication of information which has resulted in the average person becoming a more discerning and demanding buyer. The Internet and other technological advancements have also opened up massive channels so that organizations can market from anywhere in the world to huge audiences.

PREFACE

Never has there been a time when competition has been so stiff, and never has there been a time when professionals have had so much pressure to deliver.

The Knowledge-Power Paradigm, in principle, is not a new concept. It dates back many centuries and has been employed successfully by leaders in every imaginable type of organization. Its relevance today, however, is even greater than ever before. Leaders are increasingly turning to the paradigm to assist them in strategy formulation and decision-making. The paradigm is the ability to use knowledge to leverage power (success)—simple in concept, but often misunderstood in practical application. This book will explore the various considerations and assumptions that govern this paradigm. We will discuss many well-known examples to explain how the paradigm has positively affected eventual results.

The one thing that this book aims to achieve is to raise critical questions about how you can elevate your knowledge-management systems and processes to better understand your market, your organization, and the environment within which you operate. This position then becomes the essential precursor to effective decision-making and strategy execution. Examples and explorations throughout the book will offer insight as to how successful leaders, professionals and organizations have made the paradigm work for them—and how you can too.

Aristotle Onassis said, "The secret of business is to know something that nobody else knows." Knowing is better than not knowing. Knowing something and not acting upon it is a missed opportunity. One of the most valuable ways to improve performance, success and quality is to attain and effectively use knowledge to positively influence outcomes. It's not only about working hard. It's about becoming smart, through superior knowledge, and then effectively using it.

ACKNOWLEDGEMENTS

IT ISN'T EASY TO NAME EVERYBODY WHO has helped to shape your collective experience and imparted critical teachings. There have been so many people who have been responsible for helping me get a better understanding of organizations, businesses, and industries. My first significant experiences were with Xerox Corporation (UK) and the exposure I received there was second to none. I was straight out of the university and Stephen Cronin took a chance on me and was the architect for much of the exposure I gained within the organization. My first sales teachers were John Esposito and Taj Onigbanjo, among Xerox's elite salesmen, producers and trainers. Their commitment to quality and knowledge was my grounding.

In the U.S., my learning and development were enhanced through Eaton Corporation in their marketing division and then later with R.F. Technologies. The strategic, operational and executive exposure afforded to me within these two organizations was extraordinary. The likes of Paul Handle and Bob Smith opened new doors which afforded me an opportunity to grow and develop further.

Since starting *Key Elements Consulting, Inc.* and *Qualitick, Inc.*, I have had the pleasure of working with many firms, across myriad industries. Over many years and countless projects I have had the opportunity of honing the principles of the knowledge-power paradigm with CEOs, CFOs and officers who have been clients, partners and quite often friends. I thank them one and all through this book, especially Chuck, Vakesh, Rajeev, Lisa, and Jill.

Last, but by no means least I thank my family for being the rock that has protected me and encouraged me to dream big, yet reminded me to keep my feet firmly on the ground. Mum, Dad, Bijal, Mira and Samir, thank you for your love, encouragement, and support.

PART I
INTRODUCTION TO THE PARADIGM

1

THE KNOWLEDGE-POWER PARADIGM

A wise man has great power, and a man of knowledge increases strength.
- PROVERBS 24:5

FRANCIS BACON'S LATIN PROVERB, *"scientia potentia est,"* is one of the earliest known examples where the common term "knowledge is power" is found. Indeed, Bacon's proverb is more a reflection that with an improvement of an individual's knowledge there comes an increase in that individual's potential. In essence, an individual has a better chance at succeeding in life by increasing his knowledge, consequently giving rise to power. Bacon was clearly one of the earliest and most prominent advocates for individual education and development, citing its critical role in attaining maximum potential.

And, that attainment is not limited only to individuals. The rise of every great nation and empire is almost always founded on its ability to acquire and apply knowledge for maximum gain, often through strategic and militaristic advantage. The legendary Manhattan Project is an excellent example of the knowledge-power paradigm, paving the way for the U.S. to bring the Second World War to an end, while also asserting and establishing its status as a world superpower.

Intelligence reports during the late 1930s indicated that the Nazis were making significant strides towards developing an enriched uranium (nuclear) bomb. The basis of developing such a bomb lay in Albert Einstein's famous $E=MC^2$ equation. However, Einstein initially did not believe that developing a nuclear bomb, through the release of massive amounts of atomic energy, was easily attainable, definitely not during his lifetime. In fact it was one of Einstein's friends, Leo Szilard, who figured out a theoretical way for a nuclear bomb to be developed. He visited Einstein in July of 1939 to urge him to write a letter to President Roosevelt communicating the urgency of joining the race to research and develop a working nuclear bomb. This famous letter was the catalyst that triggered the Manhattan Project, the detonation of atomic bombs over Nagasaki and Hiroshima, as well as the subsequent Cold War and the resulting arms race. Einstein later reflected on writing this letter as being one of the few regrets in his life.

Following President Franklin Delano Roosevelt's receipt of the letter, the U.S. embarked upon the single largest engineering project in its history: to win the race to produce the first ever nuclear weapon. The project's chief engineer, J. Robert Oppenheimer, a brilliant physicist, was tasked with developing the most powerful weapon known to man. At a cost of $2 billion ($20 billion in today's money) and employing no less than 130,000 people, the first nuclear bomb was tested in the barren desert near Alamogordo, New Mexico in 1945. That successful test was quickly followed by the detonation of the first nuclear bombs over the Japanese cities of Hiroshima and Nagasaki.

This vivid display of scientific knowledge led to power over the Japanese, which resulted in an immediate and unconditional Japanese surrender. It was also the precursor to the Cold War and the Space Race, when political brinkmanship revolved around three key pursuits: (1) the quest for knowledge, (2) pushing the boundaries of mathematics and science, and (3) dominance over rival nations. Many commentators have since reflected that vast technological advancements during the latter half of the 20th century could only have happened in a Cold War political environment, where the intense rivalry between two adversaries acted as the mechanism which advanced the boundaries of human knowledge and understanding.

1.1 Differing Aspects of the Knowledge-Power Paradigm

Joseph Campbell asserted that historical development of many towns and cities, especially in Europe, can be traced back through the dominant buildings that constitute their skylines. During the Middle Ages, it was common for churches to be the most imposing and tallest building within the center of cities, towns and villages. This was by no means accidental but rather by design–it highlighted the importance placed upon religion by society during that period. Over time, churches were dwarfed and superseded by governmental and judicial buildings, and finally in modern society, we find that the most magnificent, dominant buildings in city centers are those which represent business and commerce. These social and spatial development observations reflect changes in revered sources of knowledge and power over centuries–from religion to politics and then ultimately to commerce.

The knowledge-power paradigm has undoubtedly played a critical role in societal development over time. The emergence of each one of these types of organizations–religious, political, and commercial–was enabled by the development of spiritual, scientific, militaristic and economic knowledge, and the ability to effectively communicate that knowledge. Today, in business and commerce, we find the knowledge-power paradigm used by strategists to drive home the potential of gaining a competitive advantage through the acquisition and successful application of knowledge. For example, you may possess significant market knowledge, to which your competition may not be privy, effectively creating an important competitive advantage. However, this really begs some important questions: What is knowledge? How does it differ from 'data', 'information' and 'wisdom'? If leaders across all industries suddenly acquire knowledge, does that automatically give rise to power? Can the knowledge-power paradigm be planned for in a strategic manner by leaders?

Many pages in numerous books have been dedicated to outlining how knowledge-power can effectively be used. Do a quick search online or just browse the business shelves of your local book store, and you can see how extensively the topic is documented. So an obvious question is, "why are so many industries, businesses and decision-makers still not effectively using nor leveraging this paradigm to improve performance and productivity, which can ultimately lead to success?" Is it cynicism regarding the validity of the paradigm? Perhaps leaders feel that the maxim does not apply to them?

Is the problem that, although they agree that the paradigm is essential to success, perhaps they really don't know where to start and how to apply it?

Whatever the reason, the following chapters will highlight the inner understanding and practical workings of the knowledge-power paradigm, and producing a clearer awareness of the conditions required for it to effectively work. This book will also outline a strategic planning-success model that defines the most critical aspect of information collection and evaluation, and how that relates to goal planning and execution.

Accelerated technological innovation plays a central role in the knowledge-power paradigm for managers and decision-makers, regardless of industry or organizational size. Some of the most successfully applied knowledge-power paradigm models will be illustrated, among these the importance of applying the knowledge-power paradigm in healthcare will be outlined in great detail. In essence, this book will instill a greater confidence to investigate and implement processes to assist in the measurement and evaluation of gathered data, and how that gathered data forms the basis of knowledge, which can be used effectively to attain greater success.

1.2 Data, Information, Knowledge and Wisdom

One of the most obvious assumptions of the knowledge-power paradigm is that we know the exact meaning of the terms "knowledge" and "power." Within the process of strategy and decision-making, terms like "data," "information" and "wisdom" can easily be mistaken for "knowledge." In reality, each has a specific meaning and influence in the grander scheme of the knowledge-power paradigm and it is critical that the varying definitions are known and understood.

It may seem that the definition of "data," "information" and "knowledge" is pretty much the same thing. However, subtle differences in their meaning has widespread implications for management and successful decision-making. Consider this example: Marie is a marketing manager with Pluggo, Inc. and she wishes to get feedback from her customers as to their thoughts about the service provided by her company. With good intentions, Marie implements a customer survey program where her customers are asked to fill out a feedback form and deposit it into a ballot box at the entrance of her office. In a short period of time, the ballot box is filled up, and Marie finds hundreds of completed surveys containing data relating to customer service experiences. This is great news for her as she now has a tool that can help her get a better understanding of Pluggo's strengths and weaknesses, thus, helping her make better strategic planning decisions.

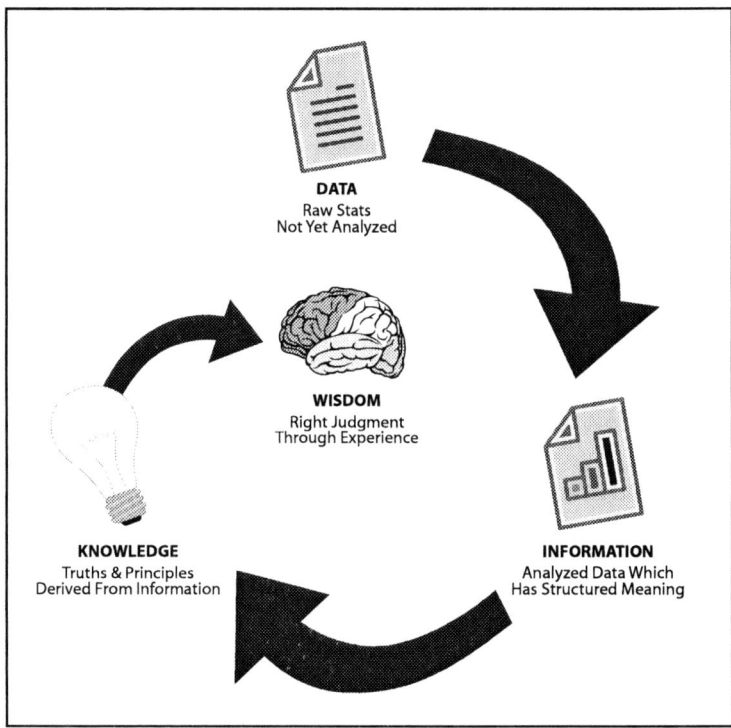

Figure 1.1 - The Knowledge Hierarchy

It takes Marie some time but she manages to input the feedback from the surveys into a spreadsheet. What she finds are several areas in which Pluggo can immediately improve its service and several areas where Pluggo performs extremely well and should be left as is. So at what point does Marie have true data, information, and knowledge?

Figure 1.1 illustrates the Knowledge Hierarchy, which helps us to understand the subtle differences between data, information, knowledge and wisdom. **Data**—the plural for the Latin "datum"—are raw statistics that have little or no structure, and drawing meaning from them can only come from structured analysis. In Marie's case, data is represented in all of the completed surveys. While the surveys contain important statistics, they don't have structured meaning until she is able to analyze them.

Information is the product of analyzed data which has structured and ordered meaning. In simple terms, Marie only derived information from her surveys when she was able to input the data into a spreadsheet to gain understanding from it. The information she derived outlined a sample of the negative and positive aspects of the service that Pluggo, Inc. had provided.

Knowledge and information are often mistaken for being one and the same. The difference here is very subtle: **Knowledge** is the truth or principle that is gleaned from information, which in turn is assembled from gathered data. Marie now has information that tells her that Pluggo's customers are very happy with their signing-in process during their visit. Upon investigation, she deduces that it was the friendly and efficient manner in which Jim, the sign-in supervisor, treated the customers that resulted in excellent satisfaction levels. Therefore, the knowledge Marie was able to garner was: Jim was doing a fantastic job in dealing with customers at the sign-in desk, which resulted in a positive reflection for Pluggo.

So how does "wisdom" fit into all of this? Wisdom is not easily defined and it often means different things to different people. In terms of leadership and decision-making, **wisdom** is defined as right judgment through experience. Wisdom often evokes images of experienced elders with glasses who impart wise words to help us along the way of solving life's problems. In business terms, wisdom often comes with experience and know-how, but the challenge that leaders face is a constantly changing business environment. So what was deemed as "wisdom" yesterday may not necessarily qualify as "wisdom" today. For that reason, the wise stay wise when they recognize that they need to stay abreast of the latest information and knowledge. A good example of this is the daily briefing that the U.S. president receives first thing every morning. He recognizes that his decision-making hinges on the wisdom of judgment he applies to the information he is given, and that has the potential to affect billions of people around the world. Therefore, it is critical that the information he receives is comprehensive, reliable, relative and timely to the decisions he is expected to make.

It is written in the Old Testament that God came to Solomon in a dream and offered him anything he wanted. Solomon asked for "an understanding heart to judge..."[1] and he was granted his wish because of God's pleasure at

Solomon's non-materialistic nature. Solomon understood that the key to success and power over his people was the wisdom to decipher between right and wrong. This wisdom stood him in good stead and he was revered as a great leader for it. The expression, "the wisdom of Solomon," is a direct reference to this story. The purpose of such stories is to instill understanding within us to follow the same path they illustrate—the path of applying knowledge through accurate information, which results in greater success (power). In the business sense, leaders who have a greater understanding (knowledge) can apply it to garner better results (power).

1.3 Success and Power

We have discussed the importance of a common understanding of the terms data, information, knowledge, and wisdom in order to fully understand one side of the knowledge-power paradigm. It is just as important for us to have a clear understanding of the other side of the equation, i.e. the terms and the relationship behind "power" and "success"—two similar terms with subtle differences in meaning.

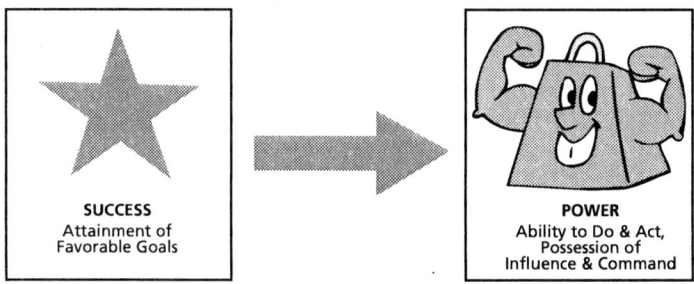

Figure 1.2 - The Success-Power Principle

Success is the achievement of specific goals and **power** is the ability to manipulate one's environment to achieve specific goals. One uses power to achieve success and success contributes to an increase in power. Success often leads to greater success. This specific relationship is illustrated in Figure 1.2. Success that gives rise to power can be said to have a direct relationship to it. Conversely, power is unlikely to exist without the presence of some kind of related success. Going back to the example of the Manhattan Project, that success came from building the first nuclear bomb and consequently using it against the Japanese to bring World War II to an end.

THE KNOWLEDGE-POWER PARADIGM

The success of the project gave rise to power which allowed the U.S. to influence and command the unconditional surrender of the Japanese. However, in the absence of success there can be little or no power.

Transferred to the world of leadership and decision-making, in terms of the knowledge-power paradigm, knowledge fosters success and success leads to power. If Marie at Pluggo, Inc. had all the knowledge she needed to improve organizational performance, but was unable to execute effective changes, then her knowledge would not lead to success. However, if she responded successfully to the knowledge she attained then her success would provide her with power.

1.5 Knowledge=Power

The knowledge-power paradigm is a delicate equation which seems simplistic on the surface. But by digging deeper, a better understanding can successfully be applied in the field of business management and decision-making. Figure 1.3 summarizes the relationships that help the 'knowledge = power' equation to work.

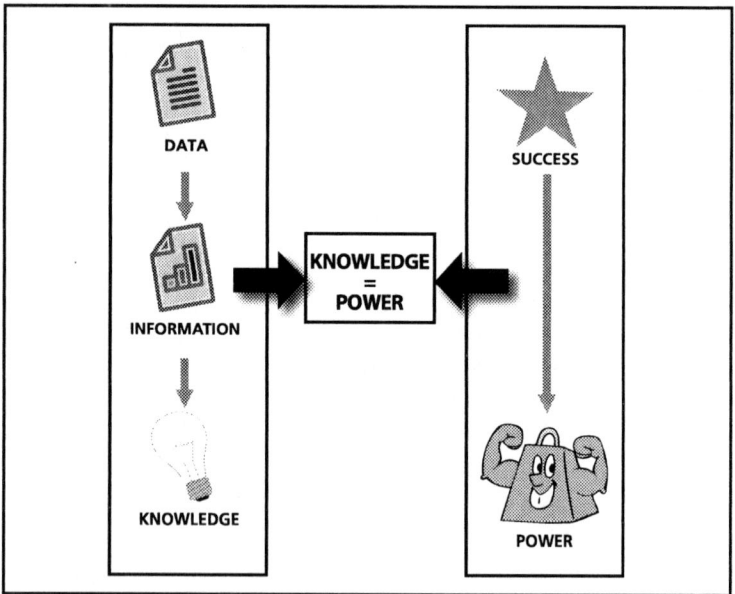

Figure 1.3 - Key Elements of the Knowledge-Power Paradigm

Accordingly, 'knowledge=power' is a function of a leader and an organization's ability to effectively collect and evaluate data to glean information, and then establish principles in the form of knowledge. On the flip side of the equation, derived knowledge gives rise to the successful attainment of set goals which increases the leader's influence, command and power. As a result, these relationships are sequential. They cannot easily be attained by just hard work; a tried and trusted methodology must be implemented to attain the 'knowledge=power' premise.

Organizations have faced many challenges in making the knowledge-power paradigm work, especially those organizations which, because they are not large in size, have limited resources. Many of the largest Fortune 500 organizations attain a thorough knowledge of the market's reaction to the introduction of potential product and services. Why? Because not knowing the probability of success of a new product or service, can have serious implications on organizational performance and thus bottom line. Therefore, prior to engaging in major decision-making, where vast resources are invested in the development and release of proposed products/services, organizations will carry out extensive information gathering initiatives, mainly via market research. Market research allows for the capture of data, information and knowledge which helps forecast anything–from product design to performance viability in the market. Knowledge can be priceless in the hands of smart leaders and influential decision-makers, as it significantly reduces risk and increases sound decision-making, and resource allocation. And when applied properly it often leads to working smarter, not harder.

Then, again, hundreds of thousands of small businesses across the U.S. do not have the resources, nor the luxury, which large organizations possess to help them apply the knowledge-power paradigm at this level. The vast resources required to make it work are simply not available, and quite often they have to make some tough decisions based on "feel", "gut instinct" and plain old "experience." However, things are changing. The playing field is becoming more level, small firms are beginning to enjoy the same knowledge-power benefits that large firms have enjoyed for decades.

The environment we operate in, the environment of business and commerce, has always been dynamic in nature, and things change often and at times dramatically. Technology continues to have a fundamental and permanent influence on how we work and the processes we employ. This same technology has advanced to the point where the knowledge-power paradigm can now be employed by small organizations, where it is no longer a luxury afforded to only a few. In effect, what this means is that leaders and decision-makers, irrespective of organization size or scarcity of resources, can manage and make sound decisions based upon the knowledge-power paradigm, thus empowering and emancipating them. But overcoming this lack of resources does not precipitate a certain rush to use the principles of the knowledge-power paradigm. To fully understand the benefits of this paradigm a shift in leadership thinking is needed, coupled with a willingness to adapt and change from methods currently being employed in the decision-making process. Furthermore, leaders must be willing to embrace this change and adopt the use of technology to yield accurate information, which paves the way to success, power, increased entry barriers, and a real competitive advantage.

1.5 The Four Basic Conditions

Understanding the definition and workings of the knowledge-power paradigm is simply not enough to succeed. There are certain conditions that govern the knowledge-power paradigm. Each of these conditions has to be satisfied for the paradigm to work. They cannot be satisfied in an "either/or" fashion. They have to be fully present, and only then can the paradigm work and yield success. So what are the conditions?

A. The Right Information. Gleaned information must be accurate, reliable and correct. If I have a map that marks the spot where I can find buried treasure, it can lead to success and power if, and only if, the map is accurate and correct. Therefore, information must be complete, timely, reliable and relative.

B. The Right Person. Knowledge is only useful and capable of leading to power if it's in the hands of the right person(s). If an organization's market research outlines factors that will help develop the next generation of its product, then it is critical that such knowledge be communicated to the leaders, decision-makers, and development team. However, if the knowledge is not passed onto people who can execute appropriate decisions then the knowledge becomes useless. Therefore, it is imperative that leaders ensure that accurate information flows to the right person(s) so that it can be evaluated and used.

C. The Right Time. As the old adage goes, "timing is everything." If knowledge is acquired too early or too late then it is likely to have a negative impact on the knowledge-power paradigm. Good examples of such occurrences are products/services that are often labeled "well before their time" or products and services that are "a day late and a dollar short." But can knowledge be obtained too early? Science is littered with such examples. Einstein's $E=MC^2$ as a precursor to the atomic bomb can be considered knowledge before its time because he never believed that an atomic bomb could practically be built, even though it was possible in theory. But only a few years after his famous equation the race to build the first atomic bomb was on. An example of something similar in the business world is that of the Xerox Star software program. The Xerox Star was the precursor to Apple Macs and Microsoft Windows - employing a graphical user interface, icons, a mouse, folders, documents, email, networked computing and print servers. Xerox was unable to sell its acquired knowledge at the time, mainly due to the high cost of the software and hardware on offer. However, later on Apple and Microsoft built their vast empires on that very technology. Xerox's knowledge was truly well ahead of its time.

D. The Right Action. Refers to an individual or organization's ability to carry out the right actions once information has been acquired, and that the actions are deemed timely. Incorrect or inappropriate actions lead to failure and the equation will not work. Appropriately applying what is known is just as critical as the knowledge itself.

None of the aforementioned conditions work independently. They are totally dependent on each other. When each and every one of the conditions is met, the knowledge-power paradigm can be successfully applied. The following chapters of Part 1 of the book will explore the importance of each of these conditions in greater detail and their implications on leaders and decision-makers.

1.6 The 'Knowledge Economy'
The modern U.S. economy has often been referred to as the 'knowledge

THE KNOWLEDGE-POWER PARADIGM

economy.' It is also known as the 'information society' based on 'knowledge workers.' The concept of the knowledge economy was developed by the well known business guru, Peter Drucker. The basic premise of Drucker's knowledge economy theorem is that companies operating across numerous industries (like IT, communications, software and educational institutions) achieve leadership status through the accumulation of knowledge. Their knowledge, effectively applied, catapults them ahead of their competitors. 'Knowledge' capability is an asset which can be viewed by an organization as a product in and of itself, and also as a corporate asset, though it is often difficult to attach a particular financial value to it. That's why we often see firms valued well above their total asset value.

Drucker's knowledge economy concept was first explored in the mid 1960's, and while it makes complete sense, it was not until decades later that it was adopted by mainstream organizations. The chief reason for this, in all probability, was the acceleration and advancement of technology, which created organic entities whose main asset was software—a semi-tangible, knowledge-based product which often led to improvements in organizational productivity. One of the best known examples of this type of organic entity is Microsoft, an organization whose initial product offering (software) was basically internal knowledge of software coding translated into a friendly graphical user interface (GUI) for the widespread use of IBM computers.

In retrospect the 'knowledge economy' can be traced back decades, and Coca-Cola, Xerox, and NASA can be cited as good examples of organizations that assumed a leadership position through possessing knowledge that other organizations did not have and could not easily get their hands on. Though knowledge-based companies have existed for centuries, the explosion of technologically knowledge-based organizations did not occur until the back-end of the 20th century.

One of the benefits associated with the emergence of knowledge-based companies is the radical thinking and organizational development that often influences and challenges traditional non-knowledge-based organizations. Traditional non-knowledge-based companies hawkishly watched how these new 'information society' organizations operated and flourished. They adopted many of the practices of companies like Microsoft, Cisco, and Sun Microsystems and discovered how knowledge-based ideas and thinking worked for them. At the core of this emergence was the knowledge-power paradigm, a powerful tool which reduced inefficiencies and improved the probability of success.

As the 'knowledge economy' develops and progresses into the 21st century, we are likely to see an expansion of small, nimble, organizations adopting emerging technologies to successfully navigate and penetrate all types of markets. The 'knowledge economy' does not apply only to industries that are technology based but also non-technology-based industries operating in the manufacturing and service economy. They are changing and succeeding with the knowledge-power paradigm as their blueprint for success.

We have only begun to scratch the surface of the knowledge-power paradigm. In the following chapters, we will dig deeper into understanding the paradigm and outline specific examples of how the paradigm has worked for other individuals, organizations, and nations.

2
THE RIGHT STUFF

There is only one good, knowledge, and one evil, ignorance.
- SOCRATES

ACQUIRING THE RIGHT INFORMATION is one of the key requirements within the knowledge-power paradigm. Tales of successes and failures have been well documented in the pages of history books, and reflected in these outcomes are triumphant knowledge acquisition and failure to acquire *pertinent* knowledge. In this chapter we will explore the paramount importance of attaining pertinent knowledge, as one of the conditions that must be met for the success of the knowledge-power paradigm. Furthermore, we will discuss the significance of knowledge availability. Is it possible to have too much knowledge?

2.1 Success and Failure - A Thin Dividing Line
It is often said that the margin between success and failure is very thin. Statistics pertaining to performance in professional sports suggest that the difference between success and failure is often lower than one percent. Similarly, in the world of leadership and decision-making, the gap between failure and success is becoming increasingly narrow. We live in times when

bringing a product or service to market can be done more quickly than ever, rendering even smaller the window of opportunity when a distinct product advantage may be attained. At the other end of the spectrum are price and cost advantages. With markets saturated with competitors, a low cost of production becomes a prerequisite for entry. Consequently, the traditional factors that govern competitive advantage (product and price) do not apply in the same manner they once did. So what are the new battle rules which determine competitive advantage for organizations? What helps to differentiate organizations from their rivals and make good on the goal of long-term quality and growth?

The 'knowledge economy' and the growth of the 'knowledge worker' suggest that knowledge has become not just an emerging battleground but a key battleground, where levels of success and failure are determined. Corporate espionage, lawsuits between rival organizations, and antitrust suits that pertain to knowledge seem to be more common in business. The emergence of tighter employee agreements, which include 'golden handcuffs' and stricter non-compete language, also point to organizations embracing the 'knowledge worker' as a key asset and, conversely, a potential liability if lost to competitors.

This trend is further revealed in the finding of a Wharton Business School study that "companies are struggling to attract and retain talented executives."[1] The study was compiled by McKinsey & Company using data collected from 77 U.S. companies across various industries and surveys of more than 400 corporate officers and 6,000 executives. The study's conclusion states, "what we found should be a call to arms for corporate America. Companies are about to be engaged in a war for senior executive talent that will remain a defining characteristic of their competitive landscape for decades to come." In addition, the study also found that "most companies are ill-prepared, and even the best are vulnerable."

In a speech delivered at Harvard University in 1994, business strategist and guru Peter F. Drucker commented on his vision for the 'knowledge worker' and the 'knowledge economy.' Drucker believed that knowledge learning is applicable to employees at all ages, especially through the means of "the new learning technologies." Drucker went on to state that the performance of people, firms, industries and countries would be more and more dependent upon "acquiring and applying knowledge" as a key competitive factor "for the performance, if not the survival of the individual organization; or of an industry, and for a country."[2] He termed this the 'knowledge society' and he predicted that it would be far more competitive than any we have seen to date mainly due to knowledge being widely accessible, so "there are no excuses for nonperformance."

Drucker outlined how the 'knowledge worker' would influence the competitiveness of organizations as early as 1994, and the recent McKinsey & Company study describes the challenges that modern organizations are facing in attracting and retaining 'knowledge workers.' Not only is the stream of knowledge assets in short supply, but the scarcity of supply also points to issues with the quality of knowledge.

2.2 Knowledge Accuracy

In *The Art of War*, the author Sun Tzu articulates his thoughts and beliefs on successful military strategies and tactics. Even though this work dates back to the 6th century BCE, *The Art of War* is a timeless piece that has influenced the likes of Napoleon, General Douglas MacArthur, and Mao Zedong. Our modern day battlefields are business markets, and generals planning strategies for success can be found in corporate board rooms. Therefore, many of the teachings from Sun Tzu apply metaphorically to organizations and officers. *The Art of War* was initially adopted in the corporate setting by Japanese companies and then by other organizations worldwide. Sun Tzu's treatise has become the definitive metaphoric guide to business strategy for many modern day board room generals.

> *"Know the enemy and know yourself; in a hundred battles you will never be in peril. When you are ignorant of the enemy, but know yourself, your chances of winning or losing are equal. If ignorant both of your enemy and yourself, you are certain in every battle to be in peril."*[3] - The Art of War, Sun Tzu

This quote is one of the most revered maxims in *The Art of War*. Sun Tzu expresses the importance of having accurate knowledge about yourself and also about your rival(s). He also goes on to explain that only having knowledge of your strengths and weaknesses and no such knowledge of your enemy's leaves the outcome in a state of balance, essentially a 50-50 scenario. Furthermore, he writes, the worst scenario is having no knowledge about yourself or your enemy, in which case "you are certain in every battle to be in peril." Knowledge in the face of an enemy is arguably the best weapon a general can have. All quantities are known, nothing is left to chance and strategies are formed which govern the theater of war and ultimately its outcome.

The Battle of Little Bighorn is a classic example in American history of a disastrous defeat where inaccurate and insufficient information resulted in a massacre. The battle was led by General Custer against the Nez Pierce tribe of Native Americans; the mission was to return the tribe to their reservation. Events leading up to the battle, and during the battle, highlight the scarcity and inaccuracy of information, upon which poor assumptions and decisions were made. One such assumption made by Custer was that the Native Americans would flee if hit with strong force. As the battle unfolded, it became very clear that this was grossly incorrect as it was based both on inaccurate information and a limited understanding of the Nez Pierce.

Undoubtedly, the most decisive mistake Custer made was not having accurate information regarding the sheer number of Nez Pierce warriors in the camp. It is reported that Custer knew that he was outnumbered but did not have knowledge as to the exact number, which was an approximate ratio of 3-to-1. In the words of Sun Tzu, "when you are ignorant of the enemy, but know yourself, your chances of winning or losing are equal." Custer compounded the problem of inaccuracy and lack of information, however, by impulsively rushing into battle, even when his orders were to locate the Nez Pierce and wait for reinforcements. In retrospect, the battle's outcome was a foregone conclusion and the massacre that Sun Tzu could have predicted was acted out as one would expect, in total defeat for Custer.

The Battle of Little Bighorn is metaphorically played out over and over again in business markets on a regular basis. Leaders implement and execute strategies with partial and inaccurate data, knowing little about themselves, their customers and even less about their competitors. Not only are business results held in the balance, but often organizations go into battle in "peril." As previously mentioned, accurate information is not always easy to come by and there is also the limiting factor of resources. However, the lesson that leaders can learn is the critical importance of evaluating how internal and external information is obtained and the accuracy of that information. Is the information sufficient to make successful decisions? Do I know enough about my customers and my competitors? How can I do what I do better?

If knowledge can be described as an engine, then the oil that flows through it is communication, allowing the engine's power to be put to work effectively and efficiently. Meaningful knowledge is mostly gathered and used through proficient methods of communication. For example, if my goal were to know what customers thought about a product or service I provide to them, then I would have an important decision to make as there are many different methods available for gathering data, information and knowledge. Some of the most common data gathering methods employed by organizations include:

- **Surveys**-by phone, mail, fax, and email.

- **Informal,** unstructured, direct conversation with a small population of customers.

- **Round Tables** that feedback from a small sample of customers who may or may not represent a sample cross-section of all customers.

- A formalized, full-blown **Market Research Program** (MRP) that polls the opinions and thoughts of customers.

The aforementioned methods all have varying levels of value, mainly due to the effectiveness of communication and the resources available to capture accurate information. Nonetheless, effective two-way communication is one of the essential methods of acquiring knowledge.

This essentially applies to any leader, whether in a battle scenario or in an organizational setting. A demonstration of the impact of knowledge and communication can be directly applied to the example of General Custer: would Custer have attacked the Nez Pierce village if he had accurate information about how hopelessly outnumbered he was? Probably not, and as often is the case, hindsight is 20-20. In modern warfare the first step that is normally taken as a precursor to a ground assault is to knock out the enemy's communication systems, blocking their attempts to relay information and essentially leaving them blind. Sun Tzu states the importance of knowing your enemy, but if the enemy does not have the ability to see you and communicate vital information, you are cutting off an essential supply of knowledge that they can use to hurt you. The reverse principle also applies: the more you know about your environment, your target, and yourself, the greater the chances of success.

A good case in point is the battle plan drawn up for Operation Desert Storm during the first Gulf War in 1991. Before any army set foot on the battlefield, the coalition forces ordered more than 1,000 air sorties over Kuwait and Iraq each day. One of the main objectives was to destroy and disable critical command and communication facilities. The initial sorties over Iraq and Kuwait were spearheaded by Stealth bombers that had the capability to fly undetected thereby successfully completing their missions. By design, the strategy severely dented Iraq's ability to gain knowledge about enemy activities, and what information Iraq did possess, regarding changes within the theater of war, were not easily communicated. In essence, the allies dramatically reduced Iraq's power to wage war by reducing information-flow, through disabling Saddam Hussein's forces ability to communicate.

The principle of gathering accurate information to attain power has been around since prehistoric times. The business of prehistoric man was survival and only the fittest (and smartest) succeeded in that business. The ones who survived were the ones who developed the most effective survival techniques. Basically, those who had the best knowledge about the movement of their prey and knowledge to develop effective hunting implements as well as those who adopted the correct technique of hunting in packs succeeded. Even prehistoric man depended on gathered and applied information to prosper and survive.

Fast forward several thousand years and the principle applies more than ever in business. Nowhere is knowledge regarded and revered more than on Wall Street, the hub of American business and commerce. Every year, billions upon billions of stocks are traded through the various markets where you can buy and speculate on almost anything. Speak to anybody who happens to have even a passing interest in the markets and they will tell you that when buying and selling stocks the investor is effectively buying the potentiality of stocks, not necessarily the stocks' present value, but their potential value. In other words, the smart investor buys and sells stocks based on his best knowledge of how stocks will perform in the future. Therefore, economists and business strategists place great interest in the value of the DOW, Nasdaq and S&P indices. These indices are an aggregate of all the various stocks that comprise them, and the fluctuation of these indices can be viewed as an indicator of the overall health of the economy. If acquired and perceived knowledge is one factor that drives the potential of individual stocks, one can easily deduce that the performance of stocks in the whole economy, worth trillions of dollars, is influenced to some degree by pertinent knowledge obtained by investors. Pertinent knowledge is the one variable of which investors cannot have enough. It drives intricate strategies, and its completeness and timeliness often determine levels of success and failure.

The knowledge-power paradigm, in terms of classic Americana, is portrayed perfectly in the tragic story of Bud Fox in Oliver Stone's Oscar winning movie, "Wall Street" (1987). Fox is an up and coming stockbroker who idolizes, and is later mentored by, corporate raider Gordon Gekko. Fox's quest is to move up in the cut throat world of Wall Street and acquire the kind of power his mentor possesses. While the movie is purely dramatic fiction, perhaps even a flight of fancy, the importance placed on attaining valuable information and knowledge as the driving force to success is represented throughout. The extent to which Fox went to obtain knowledge about potential investments was incredible, and the measures he takes to obtain it exemplifies the importance of knowledge that separates success from failure. Fox is told early on by Gekko, "the most valuable commodity I know of is information."[4] Thus begins Fox's journey of obtaining valuable information, following his prey like a reporter follows his leads, obtaining information by every method possible, legal and illegal.

In the late 1990s the U.S. markets, especially the Nasdaq, surged on the crest of the new wave of "dot com" technology companies. Figure 2.1 shows the steady growth of the Nasdaq stock market through the mid 70s and 80s. However, take a close look at the sharp rise in the index towards the late 1990s. Not only did the index performance experience a meteoric rise in a space of 3 years but the sheer volume of trading jumped up, too. What was the reason behind such an unprecedented growth? How did the knowledge-power paradigm play an important role in such an occurrence?

The 1990s were heady days in technology and it almost seemed like anybody with a PC, internet access and a technology-based idea could succeed in the new economy. There are legendary tales of incredible stock movement for companies like Cisco, Amazon and Yahoo! Almost anyone whose business was technology-based, experienced unprecedented stock price inflation. Figure 2.2 illustrates the sharp rise in the stock price of

THE KNOWLEDGE-POWER PARADIGM

Amazon.com in the late 1990's and its subsequent devaluation and readjustment.

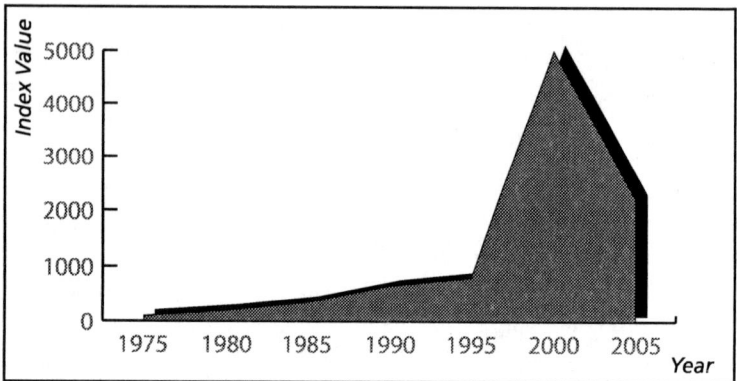

Figure 2.1 - A Historical Performance of the Nasdaq Stock Market

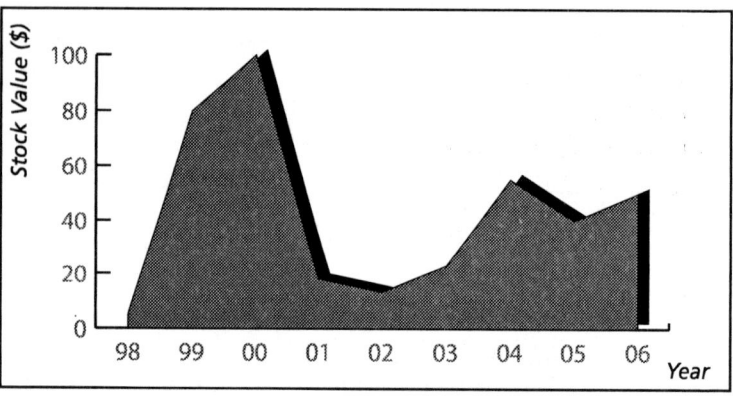

Figure 2.2 - A Historical Stock Performance of Amazon.com

Knowledgeable analysts were flabbergasted because they were experiencing something that they had never seen before; company valuations defied the standard tried and tested formulas that had stood the test of time across the markets. That is, these "dot com" companies were valued in the millions and billions when their total assets only totaled a fraction of that valuation. Furthermore, the standard 'price to earnings' (P/E) formulas, were clearly not representative of the actual stock prices.

So what was going on? Why was this occurring?

The knowledge-power paradigm and the 'knowledge economy' principle can help us understand some of the reasons behind the rise and eventual fall of the technology boom of the late 1990's. The partial explanation can be broken down into two categories; incorrect information and false assumptions.

First, let's consider the role of incorrect information. There seemed to be widespread belief that the emergence of the internet and breakthroughs in communications made the World Wide Web (WWW) the bold new frontier for business. Not since the Industrial Revolution and the post-war boom had new business opportunity presented itself in this manner. However, one of the assumptions of the knowledge-power paradigm that has to be satisfied in order for it to work, is the acquisition of accurate information. The broad belief that the Internet commerce boom was the next big thing was in fact wholly inaccurate for many technology-based organizations. Scores of these companies advocated seemingly plausible business models, they raised incredible venture capital, and upon reflection it became very clear that much of it was unworkable and the promise of growth was, in many cases, nothing but a pipe dream. Invariably, the "bubble" burst in 2000 and markets came crashing down from the heady highs of the previous two years.

The second factor was false assumptions. The 'knowledge economy' is a working and thriving paradigm today, but in the late 1990's, with the absence of a rational P/E ratio to help define stock prices, it was assumed that the organizational knowledge would make up the shortfall. The 'knowledge worker' is without a doubt the biggest and most important asset of many companies, and in some cases such workers may go some way in defining stock prices. Nonetheless the widespread justification of disparate P/E figures through the 'knowledge worker,' the 'knowledge economy,' and knowledge as capital was a false assumption that was implied within the business model of many 'dot com' companies.

In spite of the aforementioned explanations there were numerous technology companies that defied the odds of the 'dot com' boom/bust period and thrive in today's market. They were the ones who accumulated meaningful knowledge and adapted to the changing market conditions to build robust business principles, strong P/E ratios and, most importantly, profitable growth. They have embraced the potential of the knowledge-power paradigm to take leadership positions and redefine American corporate culture, from the way we work to the way we conduct business today.

2.3 Factors Affecting the Gathering of Accurate Information

We have discussed the important principal of attaining accurate information and its role in attaining success. But even when organizations have the intention of acquiring information how do they know that what they are acquiring is accurate and pertinent? The acid test seems to be whether the information acquired passes the scrutiny of being applied to decision-making and strategy. Does applying gathered information to strategy help attain success? The only drawback to this assertion seems to be the likely failure that may be experienced if the acquired information is inaccurate. In the proceeding examples we have seen the disastrous consequences of inaccurate information in varying forms, from battlefields to corporate boardrooms. But how can accurate information-gathering be used in other fields like healthcare or businesses that depend on sales and marketing?

Dr. Albert Newton runs a small medical practice in Tampa, Florida where he can see up to 250 patients every week. During a normal week Newton refers many of his patients out for radiological exams like MRI, CT, mammography, bone density, x-ray and ultrasound. The one thing that he is mindful of is the serious liability he takes on when referring patients out. If the radiology report for any of his patients is not returned to him, and a patient happens to have a serious condition, then Newton could be heading for serious medical and litigation trouble. This issue is further compounded by the fact that he only keeps hard copy notes of all the exams that he has referred out, so if there ever came a day when he needed to know the status of every referred exam, for a given period of time, he would be in a serious bind. The only way Newton could currently overcome the problem situation would be to close the practice down and start trawling through all of the patient records to determine which patients were referred out and when it occurred.

The liability in such cases is high, which is a problem that many physicians share across the U.S., and there have been instances where physicians and hospitals have paid a heavy penalty when such simple and accurate information is not being tracked. In such a situation the solution for Newton would be to employ a system that could easily fit into his practice which would gather accurate and up-to-date patient referral information that he could easily retrieve, if and when needed. Unlike the profitable benefits that the knowledge-power paradigm yields for many other organizations, here is a case where accurate information helps to improve quality and performance in an environment where more is at stake than just profitable growth, e.g. litigation trouble.

Therefore, the key factors which govern the capture and use of accurate knowledge are summarized as follows:

A. Methodology - There has to be a set methodology that is easy to implement which enables data/information/knowledge to be captured.

B. Timing - The method used to capture information must be efficient, where the information and knowledge gathered is effectively communicated and delivered within a reasonable timeframe. Accurate information is only good if it has not gone beyond its "shelf life."

C. Asking the Right Questions - If information sought from other parties is critical than what is being probed has to directly relate to the type of answer you are looking for. Organizations often capture inaccurate information because the questions being asked are inadequate or inappropriate. Therefore, is the element being measured appropriate to the information being sought?

D. Communication Media Employed - We know that communication of data and information is critical within the knowledge-power paradigm. However, does the communication medium affect efficiency and accuracy? There are many examples of organizations that check for quality of service from customers but employ inefficient mediums, which results in inaccurate and untimely information. Examples include the deployment of customer surveys long after the product/service experience, and employment of slow communication mediums like the mail and phone, which creates unnecessary delay in knowledge acquisition.

E. Information Access - Information can only be useful and accurate if it gets into the hands of the right people who can make best use of it.

F. Dedicated Resources - Are the resources dedicated to capturing accurate information sufficient to the needs of the organization? Quite often organizations seek accurate information without dedicating the required resources to achieving the goal.

G. Process Integration - Does the methodology and communication channels employed integrate into the established processes of the organization? Or are wholesale changes required to make it work? The methods employed are more likely to yield meaningful results when they effectively fit into existing processes, as the people who form parts of the process are more likely to accept simple changes. Dramatically disturbing the existing process often leads to inaccurate information or even a complete system breakdown within the information-gathering process, as people generally do not adapt to dramatic changes to the way they normally work.

2.4 What Can Be Achieved With Accurate Information?

Business in the modern economy is about attaining profitable growth while consistently offering quality products and services. Conversely, in increasingly competitive markets, where replication and true competitive advantage is hard to attain, organizations are constantly searching for the long-term edge over rivals. Progressive companies find that elusive edge through building a bank of accurate information that is not easily replicable by rivals. This accurate information bank allows for sound decision-making, strategic planning and process execution. The different types of knowledge that these organizations seek include:

- **Product Knowledge** - What options are available to allow my product to take a competitive or leadership position in the market?

- **Service Knowledge** - For the service that is being offered, what are the things we do well and what are the things we can do better?

- **Customer Knowledge** - What aspects of the product and service do customer's like, dislike and wish they were offered? How does their decision-making process work? What is important to them during their decision-making process? Knowledge that can also be gathered with regards to trend data, for example, demographics, buying habits, age, gender yields much insight which organizations can use to determine marketing strategy.

- **Competitive Knowledge** - How are competitors (including industry leaders) performing? What are their strengths and weaknesses? What opportunities can be gleaned from such knowledge, and how does this form part of the strategic decision-making process?

- **Industry Knowledge** - Where is the industry heading? Who are the main players? How is technology going to change? Is legislation going to affect future business? What are the barriers to entry?

- **Benchmarking Knowledge** - Outside of the organization's industry who are the leaders that an help improve my performance? That is, how can the organization benefit from benchmarking for best practices?

- **Human Asset Knowledge** - If employees are the 'knowledge workers' what are trends inside and outside of the organization? What are the areas of shortfall in skill set? Which human resource areas need to be protected for continued long-term success?

- **Process Knowledge** - Where are the 'bottlenecks' within the essential processes of the organization? What are the repercussions of these 'bottlenecks?' How can essential processes be streamlined and improved for optimal performance.

- **Marketing Knowledge** - Gone are the days when price and product gave a long-term advantage to organizations. Marketing offers organizations the ability to create significant separation from competitors. Therefore, what knowledge can be acquired to aid marketing practices and create a business advantage in the long-term?

Upon obtaining pertinent knowledge for many of the aforementioned categories it is essential that knowledge is effectively communicated to various decision-makers within the organization. It is also essential that knowledge is shared with all stakeholders who can affect the decision-making process and not just the decision-makers. Figure 2.3 illustrates how these varying categories go towards helping make consistent and successful decisions. Therefore, once acquired, pertinent knowledge should be shared, dissected, understood and used (where appropriate) to form sound strategic, developmental and operational decisions.

There is another pitfall that should be mentioned at this point, most, if not all, organizational environments are in a constant state of change and flux—in fact the only thing that is permanent is impermanence. This presents another strong argument for organizations to implement strong information-gathering and communication processes, because what we think

THE KNOWLEDGE-POWER PARADIGM

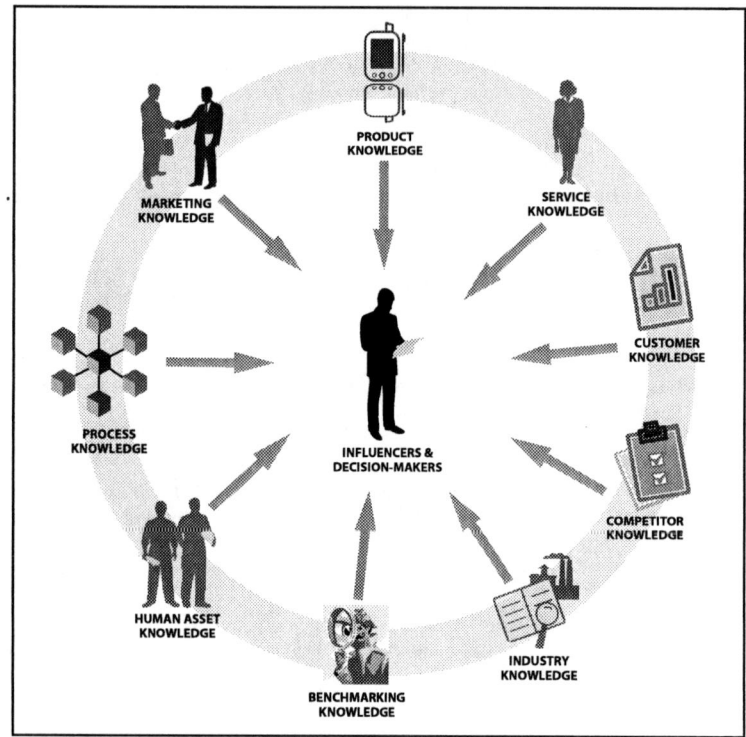

Figure 2.3 - Knowledge Categories & Use

is accurate today may be inaccurate tomorrow. Organizations at the top of their game often place a great deal of emphasis on collecting information and knowledge, and they continue to collect it on a regular basis, using it to shape their strategies and stay ahead of changing market conditions. Therefore, as the market evolves successful organizations adapt their strategy and decision-making in response.

In summary, the knowledge-power paradigm is hugely dependent on the accuracy of data and information collected. Consequently, if information accuracy is a function of the knowledge-power paradigm, then it is also a key function in attaining success. Many organizations recognize this direct relationship and place great emphasis on knowledge gathering systems. What methodologies and systems does your organization employ and how much attention is paid to having highly accurate information to help with strategic decision-making?

3
THE RIGHT PEOPLE

All men by nature desire knowledge.
- ARISTOTLE

IT IS OFTEN SAID THAT GREAT LEADERS ARE GREAT delegators. They empower others to execute formulated strategies and communicate salient information pertaining to performance, and allow them to identity obstacles and opportunities. It is a proven system that is employed in successful, progressive organizations and it has been around as long as humans have been around. Nevertheless, leaders often find the theory of delegation easier to accept than the execution itself. The key to effective delegation is mastering the discipline of managing people and processes, and that is often the source of many business problems.

Within the knowledge-power paradigm it is critical that accurate information is communicated not only to the people who make the decisions but also to the people who influence and execute decisions. It is essential that information flows freely within organizations (though sometimes only on a "need to know" basis). Knowledge is only useful in the hands of people who can make use of it and the people who recognize its importance. This chapter will present knowledge- and people-issues that leaders face, common strategies to help overcome common problems (like 'empire building')

THE KNOWLEDGE-POWER PARADIGM

and review pointed examples for greater understanding.

3.1 Who Are The Right People?

It is clear that relevant information must flow seamlessly to certain parties across an organization, and perhaps even beyond, to help attain goals. Remember that knowledge equals power *when it is in the right hands*, otherwise the maxim cannot work. So who are the people that this knowledge needs to flow to and how can that be determined?

It seems logical that the flow of information, which helps influence effective decision-making, must stream to any and all relevant decision-makers. These can be the leaders at the top of the organizational hierarchy and, depending on the size of the organization, information-flow can also include operational and divisional managers. The decision as to who establishes this flow of information should be a 'two-way' arrangement. The workings of this relationship is outlined and illustrated in Figure 3.1.

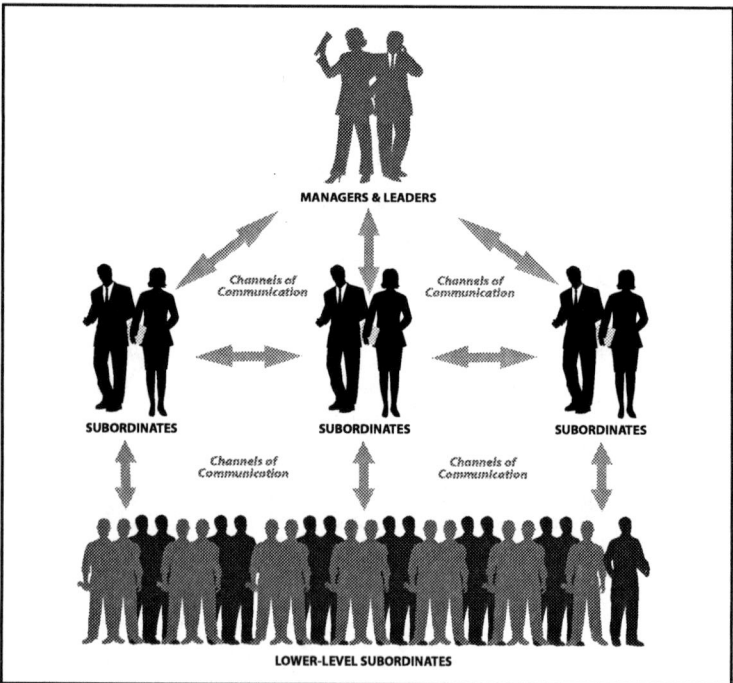

Figure 3.1 - Organizational Flow of Information and Knowledge

First, the leader/manager/supervisor must establish the 'rules' as to the flow of information and knowledge. These 'rules' determine when, how much, what, where, and by whom information reaches the leader/manager/supervisor. Essentially, what is being established are the 'managerial - subordinate' preferences for information-flow. We will discuss the importance and consequences of setting these preferences and attaining success in following sections.

Responsibility, with regards to the flow of knowledge, also lies with subordinates. Subordinates are essentially any individual or group having a direct line of communication or access to the manager or leader. It is up to subordinates to adhere to set preferences, but there should also be leeway that empowers them to have decision-making authority to determine which and how much information is communicated in line with the preferences set by their manager. This is the juncture of communication that lies at the heart of successes and failures associated with effective information-flow. The subordinate must use his judgment when channeling information and knowledge, and the manager should set guidelines for the subordinates, allowing them to channel important and relevant information by using their best judgment.

Just as in standard process management within organizations, it is common to find communication 'bottlenecks' which result in resistance and inefficiencies. The success or failure of channels of communication can be reduced to certain key factors: efficiency, accuracy, openness, management, monitoring and improvement. Therefore, one can argue that the essential part of the process not only lies with the preferences set, as per the channels of communication, but also the managerial effectiveness of these channels of communication.

3.2 Tales of Success and Failure

During the late 1990's, I was working for a division of a Fortune 500 manufacturing organization which was about to embark on a significant research and development project. The project was the potential development and introduction of a revolutionary new product into the market. The company's mid-level managers had the foresight to conduct an extensive market research program to ascertain customer knowledge (perceived and projected needs) for the product family, prior to investing millions of dollars into research and development. The gathered market information was then dissected and structured to help the research and development team successfully design the product. Conceptually the plan was flawless from start to finish. The market research program yielded invaluable information that was shared with product development engineers who were able to use it to develop a product that reflected the needs outlined by customers.

The market research tool that was employed was a hybrid of the Quality Function Deployment (QFD)/quality improvement methodology. This powerful tool dictated the following 10 steps in gathering critical customer buying criteria, with specific respect to product family and service/support factors:

1. Plan and Design Interview Questions. The interview phase was based on two very simple questions. (1) When making a buying decision, with respect to the product in question, what must the product/service have as a minimum to qualify for buying consideration? (2) If you could wish for anything, what do you wish the product/service support had? The interviewees were asked to give short one sentence answers to these two basic questions. Upon completion, as interviewers, we were able to compile long lists of valuable single sentence answers pertaining to specific customer preferences.

2. Identify Customer Base and Decision-Makers for Interviewing Process. Identify a cross-section of decision-makers, representing various markets, who purchase and/or make purchase decisions when acquiring the product/service in question.

3. Execute QFD Interviews. Conduct one-to-one interviews, recording the answers on tape and in notes, and ensuring everything is carefully captured. All answers are given in short single sentences, e.g. "when looking to purchase this type of product, the product must have..."

4. Review and Categorize Collected Interview Data. Take all of the single sentence answers and logically categorize them into two groups; (1) Product criteria and (2) Service/Support criteria.

5. Plan and Design Survey Questionnaire. Assemble all of the varying criteria organized in Step # 4 into a hard-copy survey and send copies of it out to a larger audience to collect input as to importance and priority levels for each identified criteria. That is, in the opinion of the broader audience, which criterion in the survey was the most important and which was the least important when making a buying decision?

6. Send Out Survey Questionnaires to Larger Polling Samples. Execute survey plan and follow up with sample to generate interest and responses. To obtain a respectable response rate a free gift (of significant value) was included with the survey. The result of including a free gift was a 40 percent response rate, which is extremely high for this type of market research program.

7. Review and Categorize Collected Survey Data. Once the surveys were returned each of the answers was captured and responses were aggregated using raw data format to produce structured information, knowledge and understanding about customer buying decisions.

8. Prioritize Buying Decision Criteria with Industry Experts and Stakeholders. Input from industry experts and stakeholders regarding their thoughts on the buying-decision criteria outlined in the previous stage was then taken into consideration.

9. Identify Top 50 Product Design and Buying Criteria to Form Marketing and Development Strategy. The data from #8 was then merged with the customer feedback. This helped to establish a master list of prioritized buying decision criteria. In theory this list can be anything from the top 10, 20, 30, 40 or 50 buying criteria which managers, decision-makers and developers can employ to help formulate an R&D and marketing strategy.

10. Execute Strategy and Review. Once the priority list was created, what management and leadership essentially had in their hands was a quasi-roadmap which gave valuable insight into the customers' mind, i.e. essential information which allowed for effective decisions with regards to product development and service support. The gathered information and knowledge basically highlighted what the managers needed to do and focus on for a successful product launch.

Upon completion of the six-month market research project, the R&D team had a better idea as to what they were going to develop and what functionality the product should possess. Additionally, it gave the managers the 'green light' to move forward and invest millions of dollars into the project with greater confidence, knowing that the project had a far better chance of succeeding.

This project is a good example of how a market research initiative can help to capture meaningful information with the involvement of middle management helping to make correct decisions, which in turn fostered successful product development. However, there is a twist in the tale with this specific example which highlights the importance of having the right people involved at all levels and ensuring an effective flow of communication among all decision-makers and influencers.

You may recall that in Step #4 the information that was collected was broken into two categories, product buying criteria and service/support buying criteria. As it transpired, middle managers only took the information from the product buying criteria and used it to develop a fantastic product that met identified needs. However, middle managers totally ignored vital knowledge gleaned from customers which pertained to service/support from the organization as a whole. Why? It is difficult to state exactly why but it was likely ignored because the information required the organization to change large areas of its existing service/support experience, an alteration that fell beyond the scope and authority of the middle managers. Senior managers were the only people who could effectively use this type of knowledge.

It was clear to me that the organization was missing a huge opportunity in getting the service/support side of their business refocused. That is, some of the gathered information was being ignored and not communicated to the right levels within the organization. Middle managers did not seem interested nor did they have the power to make the required improvements requested by customers through the acquired information. Instead of the middle managers taking charge and communicating critical findings to senior management, they chose to ignore the information altogether. Senior managers didn't even know the company had valuable information related to support in its possession. This information came directly from their own customers and it outlined ways in which the company could significantly improve performance through improved service and support. It seems irrational that an organization would turn a blind eye to something as important as that, but oversights like this occur on a regular basis in many organizations, mainly because communication-flow is impeded or simply not acted upon.

Upon analysis, there are many factors that contribute to such situations, which happen most often in organizations that contain multiple levels of hierarchy, where information flows very slowly or does not flow at all. The greater the number of hierarchal levels, the greater the number of levels through which communication needs to flow to reach the desks of decision-makers to be evaluated and acted upon. Therefore, the crucial question that one must ask is, "why does it happen and how can it be avoided?" The answers can be broken down into categories and for most organizations, regardless of size, varying magnitude of each category may play a part in the diagnosis. The common rationale as to why such communication break downs occur can be categorized as follows:

A. Authority. People at lower levels of hierarchy (and it does not necessarily have to be much lower in the hierarchy) do not feel that they have the sufficient authority to approach the higher level with certain types of information and knowledge. This can be due to a lack of familiarity with the people higher up and it could also be due to a perception that people higher up are unapproachable.

B. Unclear Communication Preferences. As discussed in section 3.1 it is vital that managers, leaders and decision-makers set strong and appropriate communication-flow preferences. This filtering mechanism should effectively and efficiently allow for communication-flow that contains any and all essential information. A break down in communication, due to unclear communication preferences, can often be found in large political bodies and bureaucracies. However, it can also be found in small organizations where the leader (or leaders) has not set any preferences whatsoever, resulting in subordinates not having any guidance on the type of information that should be communicated. Under these circumstances what tends to be communicated is often left to the discretion and common sense of the subordinate.

C. Organization Culture. All organizations create their own culture, which defines how things are done, how people work, how information is communicated. Common stereotypes define 'blue chip' organizations as being rigid and having very defined ways of doing things, with strict chains of command and communication. Whereas, new, 'hip' technology-based companies have the perception of a more relaxed approach in relation to the former, in these organizations communication channels are not as rigid regarding what, when, how, and by whom things are communicated. In these organic business environments open communication-flow is seemingly encouraged across all levels.

D. Subordinate Ambivalence and Negligence. This is the most tragic form of communication break down, and it acts as a barrier in the flow of critical information. It occurs when subordinates become ambivalent to essential aspects of their job and the focus required to successfully perform is missing. This may also happen due to the subordinate not realizing the importance of the information that they possess, stemming from lack of job qualification, experience or even being distracted from the focus required to make such critical judgment calls.

E. Empire Building. This term is attributed to those individuals within organizations who consciously use available methods to get greater control and funding for their areas/divisions to increase their sphere of influence and power. Where knowledge is power they employ the paradigm on a micro scale, which results in highly controlled and purposeful communication-flow of information, which is largely governed by their specific agenda, which is often divergent to the overall goals of the organization.

Communication break down and flow within organizations is a huge area to cover, and while the aforementioned factors are not the only reasons as to why communication break down occurs, they give valuable insight to common reasons with respect to the knowledge-power paradigm. The problem situation, therefore, leads us to potential solutions. In such cases there are numerous solutions available for each of these issue categories. These solutions can be expounded upon at some length but we shall only touch upon a few that specifically relate to the knowledge-power paradigm.

3.2.1 Potential Solutions

Some of the aforementioned communication flow issues can be resolved by leaders clearly establishing communication-flow and content preferences with subordinates, as outlined in Figure 3.1. However, that alone will not necessarily resolve all the issues at hand, as these issues can often be deeply entrenched. Empowerment of employees at all levels of an organization can produce many benefits, including a significant shift in organizational culture. Fostering an environment that encourages and recognizes empowerment, rather than just professing it, helps to instill confidence at all levels of subordinates to proactively make judgment calls, i.e. judging the importance of communication-flow on the merits of each case. Furthermore, such a strategy can help overcome communication 'bottlenecks' and blockages.

Organizations, irrespective of size, have greatly benefited from corporate cultures which actively promote open and honest communication. One of the biggest obstacles which prevents this is the fear that some subordinates have regarding repercussions for being open and honest in a business environment. As a solution, many companies implement initiatives that help keep identities confidential and/or make use of external consultants, as the employees are more likely to be open and honest with individuals who do not represent higher levels of management.

Subordinate ambivalence and negligence is best resolved through progressive recruitment, appraisal and development processes. Strong recruitment processes increase the likelihood of strong candidates and their ability to fulfill a given job role. Effective management of personnel sets the tone for communication channels and expectations. Robust appraisal and development programs allow for individuals to grow in the direction that matches the organization's goals. It can also act as an intervention and measurement tool which helps individuals to progressively develop rather than just relieving them from their job role.

3.3 Six Sigma and Quality Improvement Considerations

> *"The rumblings within GE were unmistakable. In our April 1995 employee survey, quality emerged as a concern of many employees...Getting to a Six Sigma quality level means that you have fewer than 3.4 defects per million operations in a manufacturing or service process. That's 99.99966 percent of perfection."*[1] - Jack Welch

THE KNOWLEDGE-POWER PARADIGM

Continuous quality improvement, irrespective of which methodology is preferred, is dependent on one key component: data and information. Data and information forms the basis upon which quality improvement is built- you cannot improve something if you do not have an initial, quantified benchmark. In the case of Jack Welch and General Electric (GE) he recognized the business and financial ramifications of improving quality of processes and products. Quality improvements in vital processes helps to increase efficiency, reduce cost, and raise organizational performance. As a result GE was able to transform its image, and more importantly its performance. At the core of all of this was having the right knowledge, in the hands of the right people, who had the foresight to use it effectively for improved performance.

Jack Welch described the thinking behind quality improvement with Six Sigma at GE as one of the key programs that helped build his GE legacy. He puts forward a powerful case for Six Sigma but he also cleverly articulates the implications with precise real world examples. Quality improvement must be quantified for it to be useful. It is important to point out that all quality improvement processes, including Six Sigma, are rooted in the knowledge-power paradigm. The standard macro quality improvement process is very similar to that of the knowledge-power paradigm as both advocate accurate measurement, data evaluation, planning, execution, re-measurement and reevaluation. Both schools of thought also heavily depend on the quality improvement of processes and systems for superior business performance.

3.3.1 Six Sigma

Six Sigma is a set methodological framework which monitors and manages process variations that lead to an unacceptable level of defects or sub optimal results. When the Six Sigma methodology is applied to an identified process, the goal is to reduce or completely eliminate sub optimal variations. The benefits of Six Sigma, and for that matter any quality improvement process, can be obvious but quite often those organizational benefits overshadow the benefits that are passed onto the customer. And it is safe to say that if the benefits of quality improvement are not important to the customer, the organization is unlikely to identify the related problems, assuming that there are no other financial ramifications.

Six Sigma was pioneered at Motorola in the mid 1980s but is best known

THE RIGHT PEOPLE

for the impact on GE under the stewardship of Jack Welch. It is reported that Six Sigma saved over $300 million during the first year of implementation alone. Six Sigma can be applied to virtually any situation that constitutes a measurable process. As previously mentioned, its methodology is based on process improvement for existing processes (DMAIC) and new processes (DMADV). These two acronyms stand for the five stages of process improvement in each case:

> **DMAIC** (for existing processes) - Define, Measure, Analyze, Improve, Control
>
> **DMADV** (for new processes) - Define, Measure, Analyze, Design, Verify

If you are familiar with quality improvement methodologies you can see that both DMAIC and DMADV methodologies are not a million miles away from other standard quality improvement process stages. These standard stages can be summarized into four basic categories, as outlined in Figure 3.2.

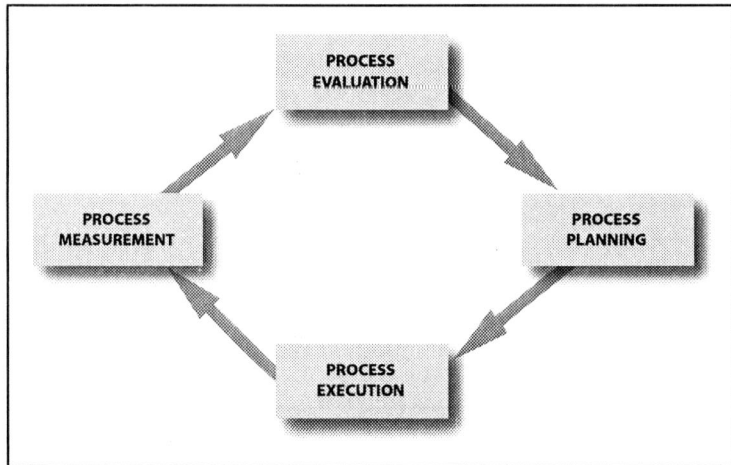

Figure 3.2 - Standard Quality Improvement Process Stages

Figure 3.2 is a classical feedback loop model, and Six Sigma does not significantly deviate away from it in principle. However, where Six Sigma does come into its own, which allows it to succeed, is the role played by different levels of the hierarchy within the organization. Essentially, the process tackles the very issues brought up in section 3.2, barriers to communication-flow and the requirement of complete buy-in at all relevant levels within the organization. This part of the methodology outlines "the right people," i.e. decision-makers, influencers and stakeholders within the company. They are critical to the methodology because they have buy-in to its success. The five defined roles required by the Six Sigma methodology are summarized as follows:

A. Executive Leadership. The role of executives is one of giving approval or disapproval to a project and the various agents within the project. Executive leadership normally sits at the very top of the organization, predominantly as influencers and decision-makers. Without buy-in at this level the whole program can result in failure to launch.

B. Champions. These are identified individuals from within the Executive Leadership strata whose role is to successfully implement Six Sigma within the organization.

C. Master Black Belts. The Champions identify the Master Black Belts as the internal full-time experts on Six Sigma from within the organization. They are the crucial link between the Champions, the Black Belts and Green Belts. They assist the Champions in meeting desired objectives, and they in turn guide the Black and Green Belts.

D. Black Belts. Black Belts are similar to the Master Black Belts in that they devote their full time and attention to Six Sigma. However, they are tasked with executing the Six Sigma quality improvement process. Whereas Master Black Belts are tasked with identifying processes which require improvement.

E. Green Belts. Green Belts are part-time agents within the Six Sigma process and they assist the Black Belts in completing process improvement programs while also focusing on their daily job roles. Green Belts work under the tutelage and guidance of Black Belts.

THE RIGHT PEOPLE

These five layers of the hierarchy form an efficient chain of command with well defined roles, and they also allow for the knowledge-power paradigm to take effect. How? By allowing for defined and expected flows of communication, which carry vital information for evaluation and action through the approval of the decision-makers across all levels of the organization. It is the ultimate form of employee empowerment for organizational problem identification and resolution, with support from a top-down hierarchal approach. Figure 3.3 illustrates how the hierarchy is organized and outlines the channels of communication between levels.

The final factor that is worth mentioning is expectations from the various roles and the processes that govern what is communicated. This is not only essential to a quality improvement process, but it is also critical to the workings of the knowledge-power paradigm. The focus is firmly set on increasing knowledge of identified processes, planning improvements (based on accurate information), executing improvements, re-measuring variables and evaluating results. When executed properly it leads to improved performance and greater success (power). And this is largely

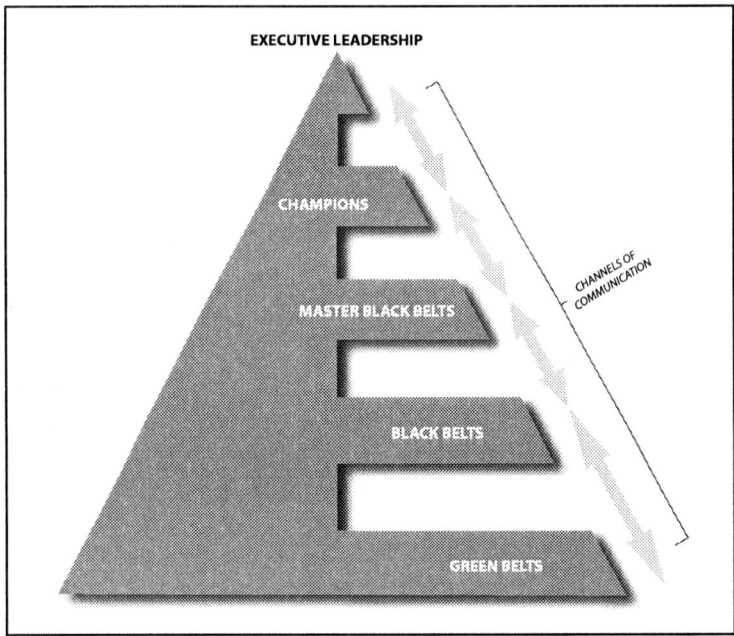

Figure 3.3 - Six Sigma Roles & Communication-Flow Hierarchy

THE KNOWLEDGE-POWER PARADIGM

achieved through buy-in at all the necessary levels of the organization, and clear communication-flow processes governed by the Six Sigma methodology.

In summary, the knowledge-power paradigm only works when certain requirements are satisfied. One requirement is accurate information getting in the hands of the right people who can use it for quality improvement. However, the key factor that prevents this from happening is ineffective and inefficient flow of communication. Therefore, it is critical that leaders pay close attention to what and how information is communicated. Bottlenecks and impediments within the channel often create avoidable inefficiencies that hamper organizational performance. In the next chapter we will discuss the importance of timing as a key requirement of the knowledge-power paradigm.

4

TIMING IS EVERYTHING

The great French Marshall Lyautey once asked his gardener to plant a tree. The gardener objected that the tree was slow growing and would not reach maturity for 100 years. The Marshall replied, 'In that case, there is no time to lose; plant it this afternoon!'
- JOHN F. KENNEDY

IN BUSINESS, TIMING IS OFTEN mistaken for luck, and "luck" is frequently defined as "opportunity meeting preparedness." Nevertheless, knowledge cannot result in power if the knowledge is not presented in a timely manner. Thus, organizations and individuals cannot benefit when information and knowledge is untimely or out-dated. A common example of such an occurrence is when a salesperson finds out, after a proposal has been submitted, that she was unsuccessful because the client's problems and needs were not known until after the buying decision was made. This is a daily occurrence which plays out across all industries. But who is to blame in such scenarios? Did the clients not effectively communicate their requirements, or did the salespeople ask incorrect questions in an attempt to uncover those needs? The answers possibly lie somewhere in between the two but, nevertheless, knowing crucial strategic information like this can be

THE KNOWLEDGE-POWER PARADIGM

financially costly. Therefore, one essential part of the mission of acquiring accurate information is to acquire it in a timely manner.

In this chapter we will explore the importance of timing as it relates to the knowledge-power paradigm. What factors govern the timing of acquiring and communicating knowledge? We shall address this question by looking at specific examples where timely information results in success.

4.1 Right Time vs. Wrong Time

It is often said that history is written by the victors because they ultimately decide what will be known of success and failure. If an organization had known "this," or if a general had known "that," things could have been very different. Fundamentally the "if" scenarios often refer to one essential factor—timing—because acquiring and communicating accurate information to the right people is not always enough.

In Chapter 2, we discussed the importance of having accurate knowledge. One place where accurate knowledge is revered like nowhere else is within the stock markets; because having accurate information and knowledge sheds light on investment strategies. Timely information reduces the chance factor in a game where the stakes are high. Investment strategists will also concede that timing is just as important as having accurate information itself. Markets can be volatile, and therefore timing the point of entry and exit often determines levels of success and failure.

The first chapter in most 'investment' books usually asserts that "you should aim to buy low and sell high!" That is, you get in at a low price and get out at a high price—a truism if there ever was one. Today there are hundreds of stock market software programs in the industry that promise the investor improved timing tools to help with investment and growth strategies. Most, if not all, stock market software programs boast 'real-time' trading results. Why? Because it's critical to stay ahead of the game, and the quicker you can get information, the quicker you can get in or out of stocks. Furthermore, timing is also measured by speed, how quickly information can be transferred, i.e. the speed of communication. Speed has become a crucial marketing differentiator and the weapon of choice for many businesses. Furthermore, customers have become more discerning buyers through increased speed and accuracy of information.

As discussed in Chapter 2, the U.S. stock markets experienced a sensational boom period in the late 1990s, on the back of emerging technologies and technology-based companies. This period was the stuff of legend from an investor's perspective. Not only could investors easily buy and sell stocks themselves but they could do it from the comfort of their homes at nominal trading costs via the Internet. As the Nasdaq and Dow Jones surged, it seemed like garden variety investors could not fail, because practically all technology stock prices were rocketing. CNN ran countless reports of middle managers, teachers, accountants quitting their jobs to become full-time "day-traders." People were investing their savings and retirement money into the market and watching from the outside as their investments swelled.

In all honesty, I was one of these possessed investors at the time, too. I was in my late 20s and it was my first dalliance with the stock market. I really did not have a clue what I was doing but whatever it was, it seemed to be working. "I must have a natural talent for this," I often thought to myself. Instead of choosing fantasy football picks, my buddies and I were trying to out perform each other in the stock market. I even sold property to pull money out of bricks and mortar and put it into the stock market. Ah, to be young and stupid again!

As the old proverb goes, "what goes up must come down," and when the bubble burst it resulted in misfortune for the masses who were still in the market, including myself. I lost tens of thousands of dollars that I never saw again, and it was a very hard lesson but a good lesson nonetheless. The smart investors who knew what they were doing had pulled out before the market started plunging downward towards price-adjustment. They knew when to get in and when to get out. They had gotten their timing right because they had timely information, and they were now just waiting for the market to bottom out before taking their profits and running. Guess what? They bought low and sold high.

Upon reflection, it seems a tough way to learn about having knowledge and understanding timing with regards to attaining goals and success. So let's take a closer look at the impact of timing and how it affects the knowledge-power paradigm. Figure 4.1 illustrates the technology stock boom of the late 1990s. The surge in the technology-laden Nasdaq began in quarter four of 1998 and reached its peak just before the end of quarter one in 2000. During that time, the Nasdaq rose from less than 1,500 points all the way to over 5,000 in nearly eighteen months-an average gain of almost 200 points every month! That growth rate was simply staggering. The market

THE KNOWLEDGE-POWER PARADIGM

timing for area 'A' represents investors who got in and out within an optimal timeframe, while areas 'B' and 'C' represent sub-optimal timing for investors who got in and out of the market. However, can market timing be planned based on a probability of knowing what future stock prices may or may not be? And is timing really a fallacy when it comes to the stock market?

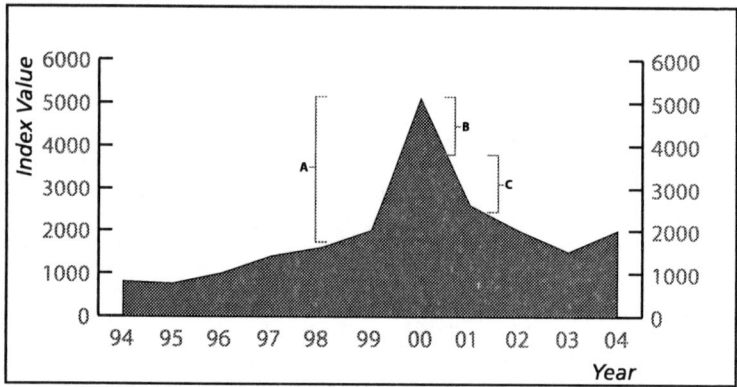

Figure 4.1 - The Nasdaq Boom of the Late 1990s

There is a school of thought that does not believe it is possible to accurately predict future prices, and that the markets are nothing more than gambling. Alternatively there are schools of thought that do believe that it is possible to time the market, and evidence exists that shows how individuals have used mathematical models over a sustained period to time successful entry and exit from the market.

But what of other business examples not related to timing markets? What other aspects of timing exist in the knowledge-power paradigm? How does this affect small and large organizations? How can leaders be more effective with timing the acquisition of information? To help us answer these questions let us take a closer look at specific information-gathering practices of a particularly market-sensitive business sector: car dealerships.

4.2 Knowledge-Timing Implications for Car Dealerships and Vehicle Manufacturers

I recently purchased a car from a local dealership in Florida. It was an interesting experience as the approach employed by the salesman, Stephen, was not exactly what I had hoped. He was short, heavy set, and well groomed. When I initially approached him, he was well-mannered. But, fairly early in the transaction, he began employing sales tactics that were very much in line with the car salesman stereotype–pushy, hard-selling and aggressive. It was not until I had made the decision to buy that Stephen's attitude really changed. He went from being the pushy, aggressive salesman to a softer, gentler Stephen. So my experience with the dealership and the sales process was inconsistent, to say the least. When I picked up my vehicle, Stephen informed me that I would receive a customer survey directly from the vehicle manufacturer in the next few weeks, and if I had any issues or if I was dissatisfied with anything, I should contact him directly. Sounds like a good customer satisfaction strategy, one that takes charge and accountability. In the ensuing weeks I received one letter from the dealership and two more from Stephen reminding me that I would be receiving the aforementioned customer survey, and if I were dissatisfied with *absolutely anything* I was to contact him at the dealership.

It is common knowledge that customer responses to manufacturer surveys are linked to a bonus system that financially impacts dealerships and salespeople. The financial rewards vary, but based on my research these bonuses can be significant. For the salesperson and the dealership to send numerous written and verbal reminders between the time I picked up the car to the time I received the survey, clearly indicated that it was critical to them that I not only complete the survey but that I also provided positive feedback. With so much encouragement by the salesperson and the dealership, I'm sure many other people followed suit in doing what I did, giving a favorable rating, even though not everything was favorable.

Let's explore this whole process from a couple of different perspectives. The vehicle manufacturer is sending out the surveys to poll the customer satisfaction with the dealership and the vehicle. It is important to the manufacturer because (1) it gives feedback data on various performance factors regarding the vehicle, and (2) the manufacturer can poll the customer to find out whether the dealership is operating within the quality levels the manufacturer expects. From the vehicle dealership's perspective, the survey offers (A) feedback on sales performance, and (B) it is a tool that measures the level of bonus the dealership receives from the manufacturer. Therefore, both parties have motivation for collecting and analyzing information.

Acquiring accurate information in a timely manner is a vital requirement which must be satisfied within the workings of the knowledge-power

THE KNOWLEDGE-POWER PARADIGM

paradigm. But you can't help but wonder why such a slow information gathering process is being employed by the vehicle manufacturer, because surveys are sent out in the mail weeks after the sale. Let's take a closer look at the objectives and the timeline of events to get a better understanding. Figure 4.2 illustrates the whole survey and measurement process from the time the buying decision is made to the time the manufacturer receives the data, evaluates it, and then passes it to the dealership.

The starting point is 'Week 0' when the vehicle is purchased and the end point is 'Week 8-10' when the dealership receives survey results back from the manufacturer. We can see that survey data supplied by the customer does not get back to the dealership until a whole two months after the purchase was made! And that is also assuming that the customers complete the survey and return it to the manufacturer promptly. If the customer takes their own sweet time the information timeline gets shifted out even further, due to the added delay. Furthermore, the longer the period between the survey event and the survey being received by the customer, the less likely the survey gets completed, if at all. Thus, the protracted time lag can adversely affect the response rate of the survey. So what are the business implications of acquiring information regarding business performance long after the actual event? Is this regarded as timely information? How can this be an issue for organizations when identifying problems and making decisions?

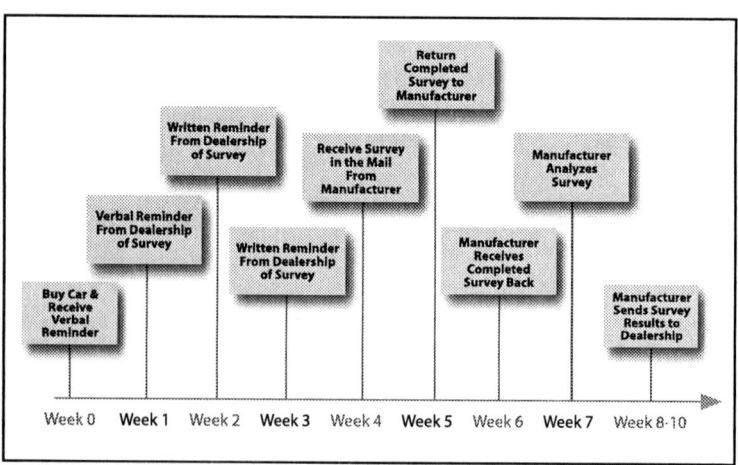

Figure 4.2 - Dealership Survey & Knowledge Acquisition Timeline

If this is the standard process employed by most dealerships in gathering customer feedback data regarding event experience, then the time it takes to gather and evaluate data is absolutely critical. Additionally, if a dealership is performing below expected quality levels shouldn't the manufacturer want to know the results as soon as possible so they can analyze and react? On the flip side, shouldn't the dealership want to know if it's under-performing in certain areas of business? However, if it takes between 8-10 weeks to receive information, how much business has potentially been lost because issues took so long to identify? 'Word of mouth,' both negative and positive, can spread faster than any other form of marketing. According to TARP, based in Washington D.C., an average dissatisfied customer will tell 11 to 20 people of a bad experience. Furthermore, only 4 percent of all dissatisfied customers ever tell the vendor of a bad experience. Therefore, on average, 96 percent of dissatisfied customers do not tell the vendor of a bad experience! Problems that are not identified for prolonged periods (i.e. weeks and months) have the potential to adversely affect performance and result in lost business. However, sometimes information pertaining to lost business is not even known by the dealership or the manufacturer.

Moreover, the information that is being collected is only collected from customers who have gone on to purchase vehicles from the dealer. For every sale a dealer makes there are many more customers who have come in and not purchased a vehicle. The sales ratio can be as high as one in ten depending on the dealership, the talent of the salesperson and the vehicle being marketed. There are also an abundant number of reasons why potential customers do not go on to make a purchase. It can be argued that this information is just as important from a strategic and decision-making point of view to dealerships and manufacturers as it represents the customers that got away. Knowing why a customer did not decide to make a purchase is priceless information because it allows leaders to review their strategy and make changes so that they stand a better chance of capturing more business in the future. If such information were available, and it transpired that potential customers were put off from buying a vehicle from that dealer, then it's invaluable knowledge in the hands of leaders. They would then have the opportunity to rectify problems and the ability to positively influence future business results and performance. Conversely, the dealership and the manufacturer should also want to know what they got right according to prospective customers—this information would be of great help with strategic and operational decision-making, too.

Within the current system, car dealerships receive a hefty bonus based on the results from manufacturers' surveys. However, if a dealership does not receive the results of its performance until two months after each event, then the protracted time lag severely impacts bonuses from every customer transaction within that period. This occurs because they cannot effectively react with an improved strategy until after the results are in. Therefore, they are being penalized due to process inefficiencies and design constraints, i.e. time delays in collecting and evaluating critical information.

So what are the possible solutions to the aforementioned time/speed related issues? The obvious answer would be to reduce the sizable time-lag between the event itself and the gathering of the data from the customer. Two months is too long; indeed, even one month is too long a time lag. 'Real-time' is a term that is often used in the business world with regards to information and communication. Ideally the dealership and the manufacturer need to employ a 'real-time' system that can capture pertinent information from customers who buy and customers who do not end up making a purchase. A reduction in time-lag offers up-to-date information to support effective decision-making and help give rise to timely intervention of business practices which require quality improvement.

Technology has progressed at a staggering rate, dealerships can now capture this type of information at the point of sale. Additionally, such technology is user-friendly and very cost-effective. Even if the manufacturer decided that it wanted to continue sending out its survey to the customer it is still in the dealership's interest to employ its own information gathering system. The rationale for this is quite simple. A point of sale system gives the dealership advance knowledge, highlighting aspects of the customer's experience that are both positive and negative. Such systems yield timely information and also acts as an early warning system. Furthermore, if the system polled clients who did not go on to make a purchase it would provide 'real-time' information, allowing for adjustments to be made at a far quicker rate than just depending on the information supplied by the manufacturer weeks after the event. Dealerships can therefore be more responsive and independent from the information provided by the manufacturer's polling process. The bottom-line is, if the dealership was underperforming in certain areas it would be able to make improvements quickly and efficiently such that the bonus derived from the manufacturer's survey would be protected and possibly enhanced in the medium and long-term.

Most, if not all, major car dealerships also have service departments that see more customers daily than the sales department. Service departments are a major source of revenue for car dealerships; therefore, all of the aforementioned also applies to service departments within dealerships, too. Customers have a broad choice of where they can get their vehicle serviced, and having information regarding their experience and whether a customer is likely to return is also important information to collect. Customers always have a choice and ensuring that they are receiving the best customer service increases the probability of repeat and referral business. Furthermore, such data-gathering tools can also become lead-generation tools if the dealership can successfully identify service customers who are likely to be making a buying-decision in the coming weeks or months.

The car dealership example clearly highlights the importance of timely information-gathering, analysis and communication within the knowledge-power paradigm. But we can take a step back and apply the same principles to any industry where customer service is paramount. Whether it is the medical, legal, accounting, commercial, educational, advertising or not-for-profit industries, the principle of timely knowledge applies equally. Therefore, how can you benefit from capturing information in a timely and speedy manner? Does having knowledge at a quicker rate make you more efficient? How can it help you with your decision-making process?

4.3 The Impact of Timely Communications on Knowledge and Power

So far we have examined the meaning behind 'real-time' information from a purely business perspective. We can positively argue that timely and accurate information can significantly impact the knowledge-power paradigm. The exploration of the importance of timing and speed of knowledge within the world of mass communication is another good example for us to explore. We will first discuss this position from a macro level in the context of global mass communication, and then we will discuss its impact on a micro level, i.e. what it means to individual businesses and people.

Many of us rely on 24-hour news networks like CNN, MSNBC and Fox News to provide us with news whenever we tune in. However, 16 years ago we did not have the type of coverage that we now take for granted.

CNN was a pioneer in this field, first introducing itself to the American public in 1980. By 2005 CNN alone was available to 88.2 million American households and over 1.5 billion people worldwide in over 212 countries. What CNN and other 24-hour news networks bring to the world is knowledge and information about what is happening around the world. Not only do these news stations supply information but they supply it faster than ever before. There have been numerous instances when the American people have received news of world events before their own governments have gotten the news. U.S. military officials have even admitted to receiving information of successful military operations from the 24-hour news networks before their own intelligence service channeled it back to them! A classic example of this is when the first air raids hit Baghdad during Operation Desert Storm. Military generals knew real-time that the first raid was successful because their initial target, the main communications tower in downtown Baghdad, went down. But how was this possible? Because the main feed from the CNN reporters was being broadcast through that particular tower. So when the feed from CNN in Baghdad went down at a predetermined time they knew the air raid had been successful.

The supply and speed of information puts a tremendous amount of power in the hands of the producers and owners of the 24-hour news networks. How? By having the ability to communicate and filter information to a mass audience faster than ever before. Another classic example often cited is the CNN coverage during the First Gulf War in 1990. CNN had reporters posted in various parts within the theater of war–Iraq, Kuwait and Israel. Satellite technology allowed for live reports to be beamed around the world and into the living rooms of a global audience. For the very first time, audiences were able to watch the war *in real-time*– something that had not been possible in Vietnam, for example–and key events unfold from the comfort of their living rooms and offices. This continuous information flow helped mass global audiences to form opinions on such events as they happened. From that moment, global news media and broadcasting of information changed. The communication of timely information to the masses had a huge impact on corporate and governmental decision-making. People no longer had to wait until the evening news to hear reports or wait for the newspaper the following day. All they had to do was tune in and watch it happen right then and there.

The impact of such speedy mass communication on corporate and governmental powers was profound and opinions were quickly formed, based not only on information flow, but also on the political slant of the coverage. Governments, by their very nature, in most nations keep a close eye on public opinion which encompasses all kinds of issues. While it is not being suggested that governments exclusively base their policies on public opinion, there is a significant element of influence exerted by public opinion, ultimately the public determines whether politicians are performing via the ballot box. And with the increased speed of communication the public can make quick judgments, which in some cases has led to overthrow of governments, from the Eastern Bloc uprisings and the subsequent fall of the Soviet Union to changes in policy making, like the war in Kosovo.

There is also a theory that was proposed during the First Gulf War called the *CNN Effect*. The theory implied that the mass gathering of Americans around their television sets had a negative impact on U.S. consumer spending. U.S. citizens decided to spend their time during this period watching the Gulf War on TV instead of partaking in their regular daily activities, one of which was going to the mall and spending money through shopping. Nielsen Media reported that on the first night of the Gulf War over 54 percent of all U.S. homes with TVs tuned in to watch. That was over 85.6 million viewers nationwide. This level of viewership made that first night of the Gulf War one of the most watched events in U.S. TV history. Figure 4.3 illustrates the growth in TV viewership throughout the First Gulf War and its effect on U.S. consumer spending. It was estimated that the impact of this new, speedy news coverage had a massive negative impact on spending in the economy. The theory suggests estimated losses in the billions (of dollars) over a span of twelve months! Truly stunning numbers, if the theory is true.

Incidentally that viewership volume also beat the total number of people who tuned into the networks during prime time on September 11th, 2001, which was estimated to be at 79.5 million viewers. While the viewership is less than the measurements taken during the First Gulf War, it was still significantly higher compared to the average norm. It was also sparked speculation that the *CNN Effect* had an impact immediately after the events of September 11th, 2001 but not to the same extent as the First Gulf War.

If the theory is correct, the *CNN Effect* showed that the speed and content of information provided by news networks can significantly affect people's behavior for a given period of time. Not only were people able to

THE KNOWLEDGE-POWER PARADIGM

access information quicker than ever before but it actually affected their opinions and spending patterns. In comparison to the stock market boom of the late 1990s, as discussed in section 4.1, similarities can be drawn from individual behavior, en masse, due to the increased speed and nature of information that was being communicated. In both cases, large groups changed their spending behavior due to easier access and frequency of information which profoundly impacted the economy.

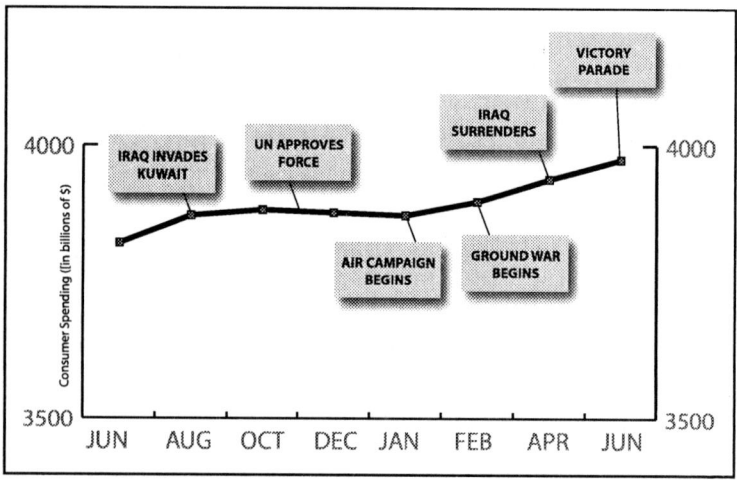

Figure 4.3 - The CNN Effect

But how has this change in knowledge accessibility affected smaller businesses and organizations? The proposed CNN *Effect* may have had a significant impact on small and large businesses in the consumer industry. But to help fully answer the question we are going to explore the broad impact of the internet on small businesses. The World Wide Web has been around since the mid 1980s, and its growth started in the mid to late 1990s, which coincided with improvements in PC technology and PC ownership in homes and businesses. According to figures published by the Internet Software Consortium (www.isc.org) in July 1995 there were approximately 10 million registered internet domain names. Ten years later there were well in excess of over 350 million registered internet domain names. The change in this area reflects signs of exponential growth with little sign of it easing up in the future.

The internet is another media outlet that allows incredibly speedy communication of information to a massive audience, often quicker than that the news networks can muster up. However, the key difference between television and the internet is the social manner in which each technology is used. The TV set is habitually a gathering media source that is shared by two or more people. Families will often watch programs together. In contrast, the internet is quite the opposite, it is an individualistic experience that is not often shared. The internet, therefore, is a one-to-one communication tool which allows easy access of information to a mass audience on an individual basis. It is possibly the single greatest technological influence on social behavioral in the last 10 years. The internet was initially a tool that purely communicated information to users. As internet and software technology rapidly developed it became a new frontier for businesses. It also gave rise to small businesses, some of which became large businesses in a relatively short period of time. Examples like Amazon.com and eBay.com are commonly cited.

In 2004 over $70 billion of retail sales in the U.S. took place online, over $22 billion during the holiday period in quarter four alone. This quarter four rise was a growth of 29 percent compared to 2003. This is significant, not only based on the sheer growth, but also because of a significant slow down in spending across the whole economy. What it reflected was a greater willingness of consumers to purchase items online using search engines, thus, changing their buying habits from going to the mall to shopping from the comfort of their homes and offices.

The internet has also had a profound effect on the growth of small firms who conduct 100 percent of their business online. A good example of this is the thousands of small businesses that have flourished on eBay over the past five years. A report published by AC Nielson in July 2005 states that eBay has had a "significant impact" on America's small businesses. "By enabling entrepreneurs to start a business online and immediately reach a market of 157.3 million registered users worldwide, eBay has become the best place to start, grow and operate a small business." The report also states that over two million people rely on the income they make from their small eBay business as their primary, secondary or supplementary source of income. What eBay has provided is a marketing channel and access to end-user consumers—the eBay community. Reports also outline other benefits of shopping online, which include the ability to compare product information, pricing and of course the speed at which transactions occur. The growth trend of online shopping suggests that there is going to be no let up, and the increase will continue into the foreseeable future.

Within the knowledge-power paradigm the internet provides a portal to billions of people worldwide, not only for media communication but also as a platform to conduct business to the tune of billions of dollars. The growth can largely be attributed to the speed of information communication, having the ability to get the right information to the right people at the right time. Studies also suggest that first-time online shoppers are more likely to shop online in the future and increase their frequency. This single fact has not gone unnoticed by online businesses as they offer significant discounts to consumers for shopping online. Many online businesses also offer discounts due to having lower operating overheads, compared to organizations that operate though traditional shopping outlets.

Closing the loop with the news network discussion at the outset of this section, we are now seeing another shift in the communication of news to a mass audience. The emergence of 'blogging' has given rise to a new generation of news reporting via the internet. 'Blogging' or 'blogs,' as it is often referred to, is nothing more than an online diary, i.e. a web log. These blogs often contain articles and commentary which appeal to various disparate communities. There are thousands of news and political blogs, with tens of thousands of bloggers worldwide who often have up-to-date news out to the public domain faster than the traditional news networks. In fact news networks and politicians openly admit to monitoring certain 'reliable' news blogs for stories they can use and jump on. Blogging essentially takes freelance reporting to a completely new level. Small independent commentators can now voice their opinions to millions of people, and their popularity can have a significant impact on people forming judgments, including large news agencies who sometimes pick up their stories. Timely communication of news, therefore, applies to both small and large companies as well as individuals on a truly global scale.

In summary, the importance of communication and channeling the flow of information and knowledge cannot be understated. Businesses and governments have both been impacted by the speed at which information can now be communicated, not only by making the world a smaller place but also changing the way people react and behave in response to communicated information. The timeliness of knowledge has a profound impact on the knowledge-power paradigm, because power can be attained by large and small entities, especially if they can effectively leverage channels of informational flow. It does not matter what business you are in, when you are dealing with people, internally and externally, the life blood of the organization is the accuracy and speed of information between people. Being able to seize knowledge quicker than your competitors gives you a critical edge; therefore, it is imperative that serious thought is put into 'real-time' knowledge gathering systems and communication strategies, because if you don't, your competitors will.

5

INDIVIDUAL & COLLECTIVE ACTION

Strong reasons make strong actions.
- WILLIAM SHAKESPEARE

THE FOURTH AND FINAL REQUIREMENT within the knowledge-power paradigm is action. That is, once you have acquired information and knowledge, will it be acted upon in the right manner? It has to be pointed out that the term "action," in reference to the knowledge-power paradigm, implies *right* action, which oddly enough may include "inaction," as the acquired information and knowledge may dictate the right course of action is inaction.

In this chapter we will discuss the importance of action and how action dictates success and failure in various aspects of professional and organizational situations. We will also dissect common processes that help to dictate action selection, and use well known examples from current events and business issues to highlight key learning points.

5.1 Moved to Action

Action by its very nature is an aggregate of things we do hundreds of times a day, and for many of us the majority of actions we take are repetitive and often inconsequential. These actions are therefore referred to as "inconsequential actions," and examples include anything from making a cup of coffee to sending out a fax. In terms of the knowledge-power paradigm, inconsequential actions have little or no impact on the grand scheme of things.

What remains is a smaller group of "consequential actions." These are the acts that influence and affect specific situations in a conscious and subconscious manner. We consciously and subconsciously act to situations and events which result in reactions and outcomes. Newton's Third Law of Motion states:

> "To every action (force applied) there is an equal but opposite reaction (equal force applied in the opposite direction)."[1]
> - Newton's Third Law of Motion

The relationship that Newton established was one between initial force applied and equal force applied in the opposite direction. In effect, an action leads to the occurrence of a reaction, i.e. a consequence. A similar principle comes into play when we dissect the process behind human actions. Therefore, we can paraphrase Newton's Third Law roughly as this:

> "To every human action there is a reaction."

Essentially, all "consequential actions" will result in a reaction. When most of us were young our parents warned us not to put our hands near the hot stove because if we did we would get our hands burned. Obviously in this simple example, where the action was putting our hands near the heat of a stove, the reaction was a burnt hand or a quick retraction of pulling the hand away from the heat. As children we learn quickly, often from experience, that there are things we should not do as there are consequences to such actions. From a young age, we build up a databank of knowledge which helps us steer clear of trouble. From this simple principle we can build a knowledge-action process for success, and the illustration in Figure 5.1 helps to model this process.

To initially build a knowledge base, an event has to take place which establishes understanding: for example being told by parents why an act

INDIVIDUAL & COLLECTIVE ACTION

should or should not be performed. In other cases, learning and understanding comes from a negative or positive action itself. We carry this simple model with us subconsciously throughout our lives, learning as we move along. The model breaks down in cases where we refer to individuals who "do not learn from their mistakes." For example, I know that eating cake everyday is bad for me, but I choose to ignore this understanding and carry on eating cake, eventually this action is likely to result in poor health.

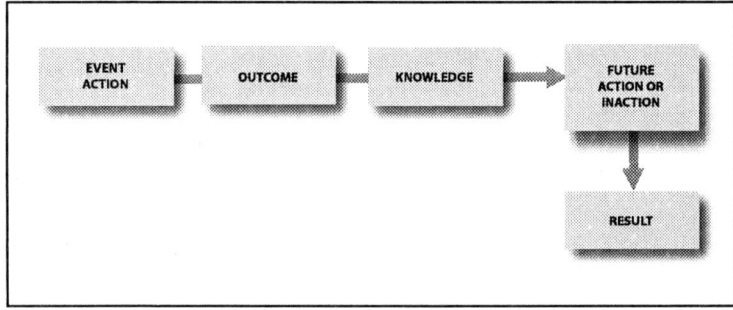

Figure 5.1 - Simple Knowledge-Action Process

In the business world the principles of this model are often used to gain experience, so that we learn from our successes and failures. Our future actions frequently depend on our past actions and the results of those past actions. However, there is one single factor that renders the model in Figure 5.1 inoperable—an *inconsistent* event or outcome. That is, I know that if I put my hand to a flame 10 times that I will burn my hand each and every time. The event and outcome is predetermined and governed by scientific law which is consistent 100 percent of the time. However, outside the laws of science, events and outcomes constantly vary. For example, a business that operates in a volatile environment, like the fashion industry, is likely to experience a different outcome within relatively short periods of time. Items that were fashionable last year, or even last season, soon become less desirable or completely undesirable. Another example is the medical industry where drugs and methods employed can often change due to technological innovations and knowledge advancement, where events and breakthroughs affect actions and results. Today patients who suffer from cancer may need chemotherapy, but with future breakthroughs in research, "events" and "outcomes" will change through new procedures offering better outcomes. Many experts believe that advancements in nanotechnology science will make chemotherapy procedures a thing of the past in the treatment of cancer. Therefore, the "knowledge", "action" and "result" stages within this key process are likely to change dramatically.

The tenet of inconsistent events and outcomes apply to every type of business because external factors result in a constantly changing business environment. Examine any industry over the last 10, 20 or even 30 years, and change is instantly recognizable and evident. Some industries operate in more volatile environments, whereas, others are more stable. The factors that often affect such changes include:

- **Competition.** Actions taken by rivals can force changes to the business environment, through strategies, innovation and decisions.

- **Legislation.** Changes in legislation can create or reduce opportunities, forcing organizations to make changes in the way they do business.

- **Technological Advancements.** As technology advances it often impacts the way people and organizations work.

- **Economic Fluctuations.** Changes in the economy often lead to events and outcomes that differ over time.

- **Political Climate.** As national and international political climates change, organizations operating in them have to adapt in response.

A complete list of the aforementioned factors can be endless, but it gives us a basic understanding of the factors that influence events and outcomes where inconsistency is often the norm. Referring back to Figure 5.1, we can see that "knowledge" follows the event and outcome stages respectively. It is critical that we fully understand this relationship as it is vital to the key message in this chapter–appropriate action, based on accurate information and knowledge. Therefore, when the event and outcome is constant, knowledge can be derived from it:

$$Event\ (e) + Outcome\ (o) = Knowledge\ (k)$$

This simple and predictable equation will work every time. However, we know that both "e" and "o" in the 'real world,' outside of science, can change over time. Therefore, we can logically infer that knowledge itself is likely to change, too. **In other words, if events and outcomes change then knowledge is also likely to change; what I knew yesterday may not be applicable today as it is subject to change.**

This one equation explains why we experience business cycle fluctuations, why organizations, economies, states and the world as a whole are constantly changing. Accordingly, progressive organizations constantly search out new information, knowledge, and understanding, essentially working the equation in reverse. If they can acquire new information, they can analyze how events and outcomes can change, which helps to determine best course of action (strategy) to employ in attaining goals. In business these defined goals are growth and profitability.

To illustrate this point, let's look at the example of a museum currently considering the potential construction of a new exhibit that will cost over $5 million to complete. The museum is operating in a city where it faces stiff competition from other attractions like the local zoo, theme park and aquarium. While the museum benefits from some grants and donations, it is largely dependent on the business it attracts from the local community through ticket sales and the purchase of annual passes by patrons. Dr. Hubble is the president of the museum, and he sees the proposed new exhibit as an investment, a cost burden he must initially cover in the hope of turning it into profit in the next five years. In effect, Dr. Hubble has a couple of options when deciding on whether to proceed and approve the building of the proposed new exhibit:

1. Trust his own judgment and that of his team, and proceed with the plan to commission the new exhibit. The few people that he has spoken to have indicated that people from the local community seem interested with the theme of the new exhibit.

...Or...

2. Collect meaningful information and knowledge which will help reduce the risk of making an incorrect and risky decision (action), solely based on the personal judgment and beliefs of his team and the little knowledge that they have from the local community, i.e. the customer. That is, really test the market to gain insight and understanding as to the customers'

desire for the proposed new exhibit, and garner knowledge as to the likelihood of the community making the trip to the museum to view the exhibit.

Reason dictates that Dr. Hubble should collect as much knowledge from his customer base as he can to help him choose the correct course of action- basically, is the investment going to be worthwhile? Is it likely to provide him with an increase in business that will help turn a profit and establish a successful exhibition? Is the reaction to the proposed exhibit positive? If he chooses option (1) he is literally basing his decision on the results attained by having limited knowledge and the actions may or may not produce a favorable result, because the outcome is still largely unknown. By choosing option (2) he is significantly reducing the probability of making the wrong decision and putting the wrong actions into motion, as the information gathered offers illumination to what the right course of action should be. This leads us to two basic questions: (1) what information and knowledge can Dr. Hubble collect, and (2) how can he collect it to help him figure out what course of action is required?

It is important to point out that Dr. Hubble is in a similar situation to that of many decision-makers within organizations today, trying to determine an effective and reasonable course of action. It is clear that making an incorrect decision can lead to the failure of attainment of goals and an unsuccessful, or misguided, appropriation of resources. Therefore, the decision-making process, prior to action, is highly dependent on quality, accuracy, and timeliness of collected information.

5.2 The Decision-Making Process Vis-à-vis Knowledge

We have established basic decision-making principles and the importance of having sound knowledge prior to executing actions. We will now explore more complex and expanded decision-making models, with specific regards to businesses and organizations. The model in Figure 5.1 helped us to understand the basic relationships and dynamics that highlight the role played by knowledge in relation to events and actions. Figure 5.2 illustrates a more intricate strategic management process. This type of knowledge not only attempts to expand on the decision-making side, but it also mirrors the model in Figure 5.1, including the basic concepts of Six Sigma.

INDIVIDUAL & COLLECTIVE ACTION

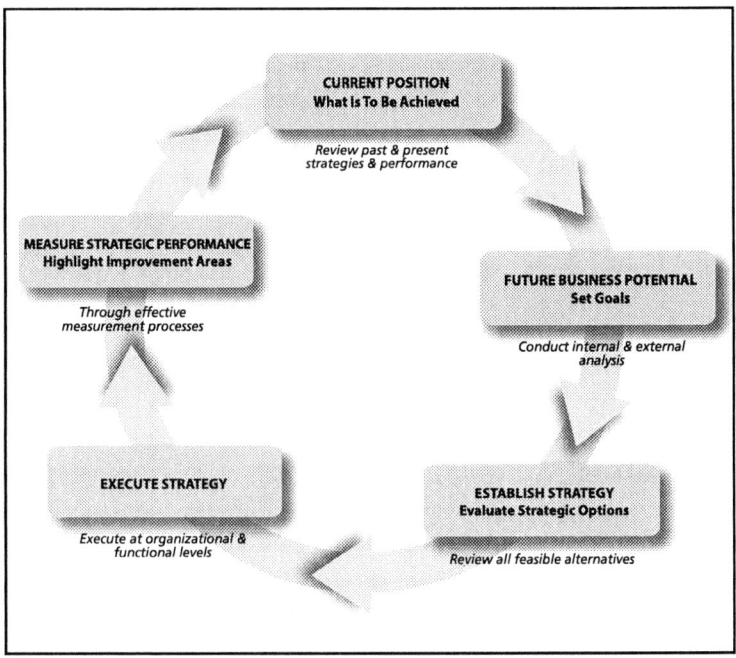

Figure 5.2 - A Typical Strategic Management Process

The strategic management process contains five stages and numerous sub-stages which support and govern successful strategic management and decision-making. The stages are briefly discussed below:

1. Current Position. Outline past and present strategies, and their outcomes. Acquiring this information helps to ascertain and establish your mission.

2. Future Business Potential. This involves the gathering of information of internal and external forces which influence the organization. This information will help in setting long-range objectives.

3. Establish Strategy. This is the planning stage. Once information has been collected, plans can be drawn up that relate to derived knowledge and understanding.

4. Execute Strategy. This stage refers to the execution of the plans drawn up in the previous stage.

5. Measure Strategic Performance. This stage encompasses the monitoring, controlling, and measurement stage of the process. This stage helps to establish whether the execution and implementation of the plans are going according to schedule, and helps to quantify deviations. Evaluation and control is crucial because the feedback loop provides critical information that acts as an input into stage (1), where the process begins a new cycle.

This model is an excellent and simple way of looking at and analyzing strategic management processes. As previously mentioned, it holds many similarities to the Six Sigma processes because it is essentially a quality improvement process. There are a couple of points that need to be made with respect to the knowledge-power paradigm and the importance of correct action. First, over 50 percent of the stages and sub-stages require the gathering, processing and evaluation of information and knowledge. This number is quite incredible. In fact, no decision with respect to even planning a course of action can be reached until 40 percent of the model is successfully completed.

Second, once the planning and execution stage is completed, the model advocates a return to monitoring, measuring, and evaluating performance. This in turn feeds back to the starting point to reassess the management process. This step is absolutely crucial within any decision-making and quality process improvement model. It assumes that there is no "finish line" when it comes to goals and targets—you can always improve. Therefore, having a system in place which can supply accurate, timely and meaningful information, which pertains specifically to performance indicators, is priceless in the hands of effective leaders.

5.3 Common Issues and Prejudice Within the Decision-Making Process
Decision-making models and management models, like the ones previously discussed, work in theory. However, in the world of business and organizational behavior, rational theories are often forgotten or completely ignored. The fact remains that people are the agents who execute all decision-making and management models, consciously and sub-

consciously, and when dealing with people you are dealing with varying personality types, prejudice, and bias. Hundreds of studies and models have been proposed that help us to understand human psychology. Theories suggest that we are all different in the way we work and interact. The work of Jung, Briggs-Myers and Friedman are among the best known in this field. While we are not going to explore psychological human states in this book, it has to be noted that this area does influence individual and collective action to some degree. What we are going to explore in this section are broader issues that come into play within the decision-making and action taking process. These are the states that often cause breakdown in decision-making, plan execution, and goal performance.

Information-seeking is critical in deciding what, if any, actions to take to reach specific goals. We often see individuals being selective when evaluating information that supports a person or group's belief, thus, selectively influencing decisions and actions. The ramifications of using partial information includes incorrect decision-making, and in turn, incorrect action. Many argue that the second Gulf War shows clear signs of this very issue, where the underlying desire was to oust Saddam Hussein from power and the intelligence gathering was selective in trying to establish enough rationale to achieve a means to an end. Many countries opposed the invasion and requested more time to collect concrete intelligence to confirm the existence of Weapons of Mass Destruction (WMDs). Several reports in the U.S.[2] and the U.K.,[3] after the invasion, came to the conclusion that WMDs were never located in Iraq and there is little or no evidence that they even existed in the first place. Was this a case of certain information being ignored, with information which helped support a desired course of action being highlighted? That conclusion will be left to the best discretion of the reader; nevertheless, for the sake of analysis let us assume that is exactly what happened. According to many reports in 2005 and 2006, the situation in Iraq was desperate, and initial goals had to be reevaluated.

Similarly, this principle of selective information and action can, and often does, harm organizations. How many organizations have suffered from poor investment, recruitment, and strategic decision-making, where the knowledge that supported certain decisions was partially due to prejudice and bias?

Resistance to change and lack of persistence are other individual traits that negatively influence information and knowledge gathering. Some people often make decisions based on personal experience and "gut feel." They can find it hard to change this type of "decision-making" habit when they consider moving to a different information-gathering model to improve performance. However, as previously discussed, the business environment is in constant flux, where change is the only thing that remains constant. In turn, information that helped attain successful results in the past may not necessarily work now or in the future. Therefore, individuals who are resistant to change in this aspect are likely to suffer from progressively poor performance over time. These types of people are commonly referred to as "corporate dinosaurs," not being able to keep up with change, which allows them to attain a certain level of performance. This lack of change can be attributed to a fear of change itself, where the individual is unfamiliar with a new method or process, and this triggers something that results in the dismissal of the process or information itself. Furthermore, the individual may also be too attached to previously gathered information, refusing to believe that anything has changed beyond his initial understanding.

Related to individuals who do not readily embrace change are individuals who are not persistent in seeking out new information and knowledge. While these type of individuals recognize the importance of seeking information in determining the correct courses of action, they invariably pay "lip service" to the rule by not digging deep enough to acquire true knowledge, which may greatly benefit them. There are many reasons why this may occur. One common reason is not knowing how to acquire the right information and also not knowing when they have the right knowledge to proceed in formulating positive action plans.

The "glass half empty / half full" syndrome is a metaphor that reflects an individual's perception of the same situation. A person who is negative by nature will see a glass half empty, while a positive by nature person will see the glass half full. When collecting information and basing actions on gathered information, it is critical to keep an objective and impartial view on things. A negative or optimistic perception can adversely affect decision-making and performance.

Initial information can often influence the understanding and perception of subsequently acquired information. That is, information that is initially gathered can influence the way in which any succeeding information is perceived. Such situations can be dangerous, especially if the initial information is inaccurate or even outdated. The problem situation is compounded by the individual's belief that the information they have is correct, when in reality it is not, and wrong actions and strategies can be based on wrong conclusions.

Influence and hidden agendas are the cornerstones of political undertones within organizations. They definitely play a major role in the knowledge-action process in a positive and negative way. Individuals and groups can positively influence positive processes and corporate ethos, where the knowledge-action and knowledge-power paradigms propel teams to success. Conversely, influence and hidden agendas operate in a negative way, where individuals and groups can take the organization in a different direction. Therefore, hampering effective planning, decision-making and action planning. Associated with these hindering factors are agents who discard credible knowledge sources and processes because of inherent bias, perhaps due to past events. Leaders may not revisit previous methods and processes as they may not have produced desired outcomes. Remember, if the environment is constantly changing it is conceivable that what we thought was wrong or inaccurate yesterday may ring true today. This principle relates closely with that developed by Nicolaus Copernicus in his sun-centric theory[4] (heliocentrism) of our solar system. It was blasphemous in the 16th century to even suggest that his knowledge-based theory was accurate. While he was a credible knowledge source, key people did not want to even consider it due to their bias, influence, and agendas, which resulted in Copernicus being widely ridiculed for his beliefs. Does this happen within your organization? Are knowledge agents and sources (internal and external) often ignored because they are not deemed credible?

No matter what, it is impossible to completely avoid prejudice and bias from the decision-making and knowledge-action process. Intra-organizational politics and individual behavior will always be a big factor when it comes to making right decisions based on sound knowledge. But as a leader it is critical that you know how to avoid such mistakes so that you can use accurate and relevant information to form your strategies (actions). This paradigm cannot and does not work in a vacuum. The role played by leaders within this process is critical. It is clear that prescribed actions, rooted in sound knowledge, can provide a good basis for goal attainment and success—but it does not guarantee it. Leaders that set the tone and expectation often determine the adherence to this principle, regardless of the size of the organization or industry. That is why the popular and adaptable Six Sigma quality improvement process works well, it sets out the roles and expectations at all levels and is initiated from the very top.

The actions that individuals, groups and organizations implement originate from structured and unstructured decision-making. We have examined the importance of realizing that correct action often originates from sound knowledge and decision-making. That is, acquiring good information forms a strong knowledge-base, which is a critical precursor to setting the table for quality decisions and actions. However, there are many obstacles that stand in the way between the former and the latter, and these obstacles often determine whether sound decisions can be made and whether action plans help to achieve desired goals.

PART II:
COMMON ORGANIZATIONAL FAILURES & MISSED OPPORTUNITIES

6

THE KNOWLEDGE-POWER SUCCESS MODEL

You can know the name of a bird in all the languages of the world, but when you're finished, you'll know absolutely nothing whatever about the bird... So let's look at the bird and see what it's doing–that's what counts. I learned very early the difference between knowing the name of something and knowing something.
- RICHARD FEYNMAN

IN THE LAST SECTION WE INTRODUCED the key principles behind the knowledge-power paradigm, discussed its importance in the role of modern organizational leadership, and outlined how it is being used effectively in various organizations to establish long-term competitive advantages and market leadership. We also reviewed examples of unbalanced knowledge-power paradigms from business, medicine, political and militaristic standpoints, where suboptimal results accrue if the four major knowledge-power paradigm requirements are not met. These four requirements are the cornerstones of the paradigm, and benefits are very difficult to attain without them.

In this section of the book, we will focus on the workings of the organization, as well as on common mistakes and failings that hinder successful implementation of the paradigm. In this chapter we will

THE KNOWLEDGE-POWER PARADIGM

introduce and explain the *'Knowledge-Power Success Model,'* a holistic way of looking at how the paradigm can successfully work for you. We will thoroughly investigate each segment of the success model to gain a complete understanding.

6.1 The Knowledge-Power-Success Model

Knowledge alone does not result in power; it is what one does with knowledge that determines power (success). Very few organizations place a premium on acquiring accurate information or employ systems that help to acquire relevant knowledge. Even if a company does have the talent to use acquired knowledge to its advantage, it falls short when it does not share the right knowledge, with the right person, at the right time. This basic principle of the knowledge-power paradigm is illustrated in Figure 6.1 as follows:

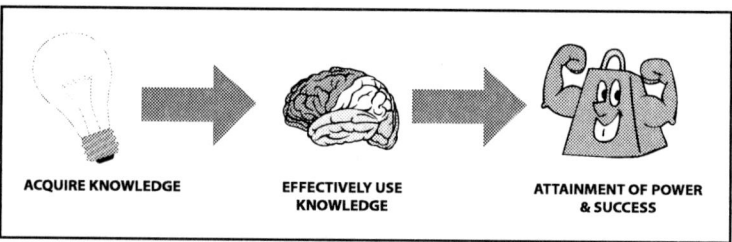

Figure 6.1 - The Basic Principle of the Knowledge-Power Paradigm

The first step within the paradigm is the acquisition of knowledge. What effective methodologies and systems are used to ensure that valuable data, information and knowledge is being captured in your organization? Once data is gathered, evaluated, and communicated, is it being used in an appropriate and effective manner? In Chapter 5 we explored a strategic management process. The model outlined a process where strategic management can work effectively given certain sets of events, including the accrual and evaluation of information and knowledge. In this chapter we are going to propose a simplified management process model that effectively helps foster and grow a knowledge-power environment. This Knowledge-Power Success Model, illustrated in Figure 6.2, is similar to most quality-improvement models as it places great emphasis on process measurement, evaluation and feedback.

THE KNOWLEDGE-POWER SUCCESS MODEL

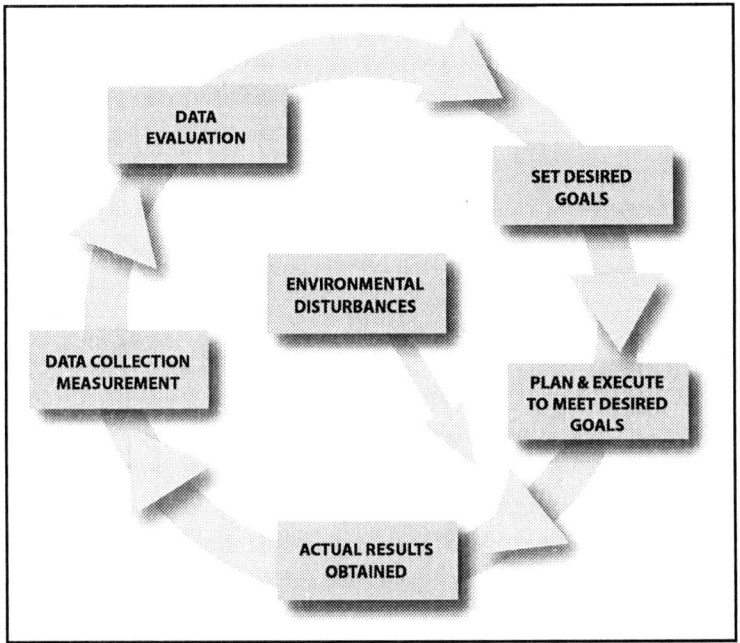

Figure 6.2 - The Knowledge-Power-Success Model

The most noticeable aspect of the Knowledge-Power Success Model is the absence of a defined starting point, which has deliberately been left out. The absence of a starting point does not assume that the model can be initiated at any one of the five stages. Instead, the model is most often initiated by decision-makers, managers and leaders at either the 'Set Desired Goals' or 'Data Collection Measurement' stage. This distinction can be made depending on the type of goal that is being set; i.e., is the goal a macro or micro goal?

A macro-level goal is broad, and its achievement depends on the successful accomplishment of micro-level goals. A good example of a macro-level goal is the following declaration by John F. Kennedy in 1962:

> "...no nation which expects to be the leader of other nations can expect to stay behind in this race for space...we choose to go to the moon in this decade and do the other things, not because they are easy, but because they are hard.[2]"
> — John F. Kennedy

THE KNOWLEDGE-POWER PARADIGM

"We choose to go to the moon" is a macro-level goal that could only have been achieved with the successful completion of thousands of micro-level goals. An example of a micro-level goal in this particular case is a successful lunar orbit prior to the final descent onto the lunar surface. So how does this relate to which stage should begin the Knowledge-Power Success Model? Essentially, this book highlights the importance of data-collection measurement and data evaluation as a precursor to goal-setting, planning and execution. It is essential to have knowledge about your business environment prior to setting any goals, as the 'lay of the land' often dictates what goals should be set. For example, a CEO of an organization cannot declare that she wants to increase customer satisfaction by 20% unless she has some indication as to what the current customer-satisfaction levels happen to be. Otherwise, how is she to know whether the goal is under- or over-stated?

There is an exception to this rule, however, and that is the macro-level goal itself. Because macro-level goals are broad in nature, it is possible to set them without requiring in-depth data collection, measurement, and evaluation. They are, in essence, short mission statements of intent, even though they bear all the characteristics of goals, per se. Therefore, decision-makers and leaders should decipher whether their intended goal is a macro-level (broad) goal or a micro-level (specific) goal before establishing a starting point on the Knowledge-Power-Success Model. Now that we can determine where to begin within the model, let's take a closer look at each of the various stages.

6.2 Data Collection Measurement

For simplicity's sake, we will assume that goal setting, as described in this section, is micro level as opposed to macro level. As previously mentioned, the data collection measurement stage is highly recommended as the starting point for micro-level goals, as it can often dictate what the goal(s) is going to be. Consequently, the two questions that need to be answered are (1) what is to be measured? and (2) how is it going to be measured?

What is measured is determined at the discretion of the decision-maker, manager or process owner. He or she must be clear regarding which aspects of the process are measurable and what questions should be asked. Essentially, the goal is to establish a base of data/information/knowledge that will dictate what the goal is going to be.

To illustrate this point, we will use a specific example. Penny Hardcastle is a new sales manager for an insurance company, and she has a team of ten salespeople that report into her. She has been hired to reverse a downward trend in sales results, and her goal is to make the right decisions to turn the ship around. As a new manager she may want to speak to each member of her team, other managers and employees to get a feel for what is going on. Eventually she will have to look at raw numbers from past performance to try and deduce what is going wrong and how things can be turned around. So rather than merely setting arbitrary goals for growth—in effect, a wish list—it would be wise for Penny to get a good 'lay of the land.' One way to do this is by figuring out what to measure beyond just raw sales numbers. While sales numbers reflect the performances of individuals on her team, there may be other, deep-rooted issues causing the overall downward trend. Therefore, Penny also may want to measure customer-satisfaction levels, employee-satisfaction levels, compensation packages, development programs, and other relevant factors. The more accurate the information she gathers and evaluates, the more corporate intelligence she possesses. Based on this knowledge, she will be in a far better position to set accurate and achievable goals.

The second step relates to how the measurement process will take place. If Penny needs more information, how can she establish measurable variables within that process? Are systems in place that measure process performance? If so, are they accurate and do they give a full picture, or are they biased in some way? Often measurements are taken by doing straw polls or through informal conversations prior to strategic decision-making. This can lead to problems; as it's not a very scientific approach, and bias can creep in as the information is based on opinion rather than fact.

Information Technology (IT) in the last twenty years has advanced rapidly, transcending every industry and revolutionizing the way we work. Very few jobs and organizations remain untouched by this revolution, and even though IT was not initially embraced by all industries, uptake was inevitable. As a result, today we see an overabundance of data. In fact, we may have more data available than the time to meaningfully analyze it. Data-gathering technology that dovetails with existing processes is the key to success within this stage of the Knowledge-Power Success Model.

'Change' is often met with resistance, and technology that dictates change is less likely to succeed than technology which effectively integrates with existing processes. Thus, in order to get a better understanding of what is going on within her sales team, Penny should investigate and employ systems that provide quantifiable data.

But what of other industries? How does this initial stage affect them? Effective data-collection measurement, ensuring the data provided specifically addresses the needs of the leader, is crucial. Data can be collected, but it has to be of significant value to the process owner. Another common characteristic of this data-gathering stage is the information organizations collect from their clients. For many organizations, this is prime data worth its weight in gold. Many organizations allocate vast resources to collect this type of information, in the hope of attaining a crucial competitive edge. But a competitive edge is highly dependent on the quality and quantity of data collected, the standard error, and the organization's ability to analyze it. Information and knowledge allows an opportunity to satisfy specific client-based needs through better understanding and appropriate responses. Furthermore, technology has significantly evolved, reducing the financial burden of collecting and evaluating mass data, and affording even small firms the opportunity to gather critical data. Therefore, small organizations have no excuse for not making the knowledge-power paradigm work for them. We will discuss the nature, type and availability of such technology in greater detail in Chapter 11, with specific focus on how small- and medium-sized organizations can leverage the latest technology to build a significant competitive advantage.

6.3 Data Evaluation

While the data-collection and -evaluation stages are separate, they are complementary. Data collected can be useless if it's not evaluated, and it cannot be evaluated unless it is collected. The main reasons why these two stages are separated are outlined as follows:

1. Data becomes meaningful information once it's evaluated. Data has no structured meaning, whereas information has structured meaning, affording better comprehension of what is being measured.

2. The systems employed in collecting data often differ from those systems involved in evaluating data.

3. Organizations often collect data and, for one reason or another, never get around to evaluating it. This emphatically underlines the importance of the data-evaluation stage within the Knowledge-Power Success Model.

Let's take a closer look at point (3). Why would organizations collect data and not evaluate it? Clearly this is self-defeating—almost like buying a winning lottery ticket but not bothering to show up to collect the winnings! One issue, something we touched upon earlier, is that there is so much data available and often not enough time to evaluate it all. The obvious solution to this problem seems to be (a) reduce data collection, or (b) employ automated systems that assist in the data-evaluation process. Reducing data collection is not the ideal answer, as it can result in losing vital information critical to corporate intelligence. Furthermore, reducing data collection increases the standard error, which directly ties into reduced information accuracy. Additionally, the solution would be a means to an end and would not address the root cause of the problem.

The root cause of the problem is that often there is not enough time to evaluate all the data. In that case, option (b) is a better solution: Employ systems that aid in the evaluation of collected data, thus reducing the time it takes to derive and draw meaningful information.

To help illustrate this issue, let us use an example of a family-practice physician, Dr. Adam Stewart, who asks his patients to complete a satisfaction form upon exiting his clinic. Adam is interested in meaningful information about his patients' experiences for two main reasons: to maintain quality levels, and to employ an early-warning system on potential law suits brought by dissatisfied patients. Upon exiting the clinic, patients are respectfully asked by the receptionist to complete a hard-copy survey and drop it into a collection box. During an average week, more than 150 patients will complete the survey—in excess of 600 per month. Adam's data-collection process is very efficient, potentially providing valuable insight, directly from his patients, regarding the well-being of his practice.

Conversely, Adam works long hours, like most physicians, and he cannot find the time to evaluate effectively all the data that is being captured. His staff also face the same predicament—a of lack of time—as they are barely keeping up with the daily requirements of the practice. Adam therefore browses through a handful of the surveys every couple of weeks, just to get a feel for what his patients are saying. This is not even close to an ideal evaluation solution, but time is the enemy and Adam has few options. As observers, we can see that Adam is doing a great job collecting data, but it is of little use to him; he is severely hampered by the inability to convert that data into meaningful information through evaluation. Adam's problem is common to many small organizations: Even when data is available, there are serious obstacles that prevent leaders from leveraging the fruits of their labor. But what can be done?

In the Knowledge-Power Success Model, the easy part is figuring out the data-collection stage. I frequently see organizations paying insufficient attention to the data- evaluation stage which allows them to convert the data into meaningful information–the critical base upon which business goals and strategies are planned and executed. The intent is admirable, but the practice and results leave much to be desired. Consequently, many organizations eventually abandon the process, as it is difficult to gain any benefit from unstructured data alone. The key to the success of this model often lies in the completion of this core stage, employing a process and a system that allows for easy evaluation where the time constraint is effectively eliminated from the equation.

Before implementing a data-collection process, Adam should answer three main questions to help him along his way:

1. What data should be collected? He must have some idea what he wants to know and therefore what he needs to collect.

2. What methodology should he employ, and how will he evaluate the data that his system has captured?

3. Once he has evaluated the collected data how will he use it to improve his strategies, decision-making, and performance?

Currently, Adam is stuck with question number two; after persevering with data collection for a while, he cannot reap the benefits of finding solutions to the remaining two questions.

To solve the data-evaluation problem, Adam must investigate and implement technologies that can assist him. He must find processes that are financially viable and allow him to gather and evaluate data in a fraction of the time it currently takes. By automating this process, he truly reaps the benefits of the knowledge-power paradigm, as he effectively completes the first part of the equation: acquiring relevant knowledge! Armed with the knowledge, he must then use his strategic and management acumen to leverage success for business performance.

In summary, the data-evaluation stage is just as important–perhaps moreso–than the data-collection stage. It essentially sets the stage for understanding the knowledge that drives goal setting and execution. Leaders often do not pay enough attention to this stage, and therefore the Knowledge-Power Success Model breaks down before it even gets through its first loop.

6.4 Setting Desired Goals

Acquiring accurate and meaningful information paves the way for setting desired micro level goals. Knowledge is the base upon which goals should be set. Not only does information make goal-setting more meaningful, as it's based based on pertinent data, but it also makes it credible. If a leader sets a goal based on a 'wish'–i.e., the goal represents something she wishes she can attain or accomplish–then there is no rational thinking behind the likelihood of the goal being achieved. However, if she bases goals related to pertinent knowledge, then there is evidence and information that helps support the likelihood of reaching that goal.

The other assumption within the Knowledge-Power Success Model is that leaders, decision-makers and managers have the necessary skills set to employ knowledge to set desired goals. It is possible to have knowledge but completely ignore it and progress directly to the goal-setting stage. This may happen due to numerous biases, or perhaps because the leader does not completely understand the information she possesses. What is the point of acquiring information and knowledge if you do not, and cannot, put it to good use?

Besides being attainable, desired goals should also be measurable and quantifiable. It seems like an obvious point to make, but it needs to be stressed nonetheless. A loosely defined goal could be something such as: "We aim to increase sales revenue!" In fact, you could argue that this is a macro level goal, something that is broad and needs to be supported by micro level goals. Measuring desired goals, however, is critical, as it gives us a scale to measure against: Did we exceed our target or did we fall short? The most common measurements are based on productivity, i.e., financial, percentage, and time. Instead of stating that the goal is to "increase sales revenue," the goal should be specific: revenue will be increased by how much, by whom and by when. Specifically, that goal could be restated as "marketing to increase sales revenue by 15% by the end of this calendar year." The John F. Kennedy macro goal about landing a man on the moon clearly states a couple of those macro measurements:

> "*We choose to go to the moon in this decade and do the other things, not because they are easy, but because they are hard.*"
> \- John F. Kennedy

The U.S. will set a goal of going to the moon by the end of the decade—the 1960s—clearly outlining the who and the when. This was not accidental; all good leaders, whether the President or the owner of a small organization, should make the goal(s) explicitly clear and definitive.

6.5 Planning and Executing for Desired Goals

By this stage we should have captured accurate data, evaluated it to decipher information, and from that information set clear, measurable goals. By successfully getting to this stage we are in a great position to plan and execute strategies to meet desired goals. This stage of the Knowledge-Power Success Model is the most variable and least scientific, as there are many ways to attain set goals and an even greater number of strategies which may help/hinder the attainment of these goals.

Successful leaders possess the ability to attain information, set goals, and plan and execute strategies. While strategic theory can lead to success, a changing environment can often impair those plans. We have discussed essential leadership characteristics of some well-known leaders. The likes of Napoleon, Churchill, Gandhi, Martin Luther King Jr., and Mother Teresa were all were extremely knowledgeable and skillful visionaries who attained their goals by consciously and sub-consciously adhering to some forms of Knowledge-Power Success Model principles. All were adept at finding ways, often in extraordinary circumstances, to meet their goals. While they possessed excellent leadership talent to plan and execute, they were also supported with knowledge, which clearly influenced their strategies.

A leader who is skillful in planning and execution can easily make mistakes and fail without accurate information. Conversely, with the right knowledge, a leader who is less adept can succeed at planning and execution because he has made a good start within the process. The power of information cannot be understated; it is often the key ingredient to the evolution of good leaders. Accurate information in the hands of someone who applies simple common sense in the planning and strategic process is enough to affect a positive result. If I know my sales numbers are down because customers prefer a significantly cheaper rival product, then I have information that can help me form a positive strategy in response. My options can range from reducing my price to improving the communication of my product value. Essentially, information becomes the trigger not only for goal setting but also for successful strategic planning and execution for leaders.

The most important factor, with respect to the knowledge-power paradigm and the strategic planning process, is staying with the process. It is critical that information and drawn conclusions are not abandoned; they should form the central part of this process. A common mistake is to ignore what has preceded—a veering off the path, if you will. Do not ignore collected information in relation to set goals.

The Knowledge-Power Success Model is a tried and tested model, employed for centuries in one form or another. Modern leaders can consciously benefit from it, even if the central focus is only to successfully complete this stage alone.

6.6 Environmental Disturbances

We already have discussed environmental disturbances, but in this section we will address them in the context of the Knowledge-Power Success Model. Environmental disturbances are those aspects from the external environment that impact the achievement of goals and performance. For example, a change in legislation can negatively or positively affect the attainment of goals. When a state makes it mandatory for motorcyclists to wear helmets, it is a positive boon for motorcycle helmet manufacturing companies, with a knock-on effect of improving business performance. Other common examples of environmental disturbances include the behavior and strategy of rivals, technological advancements, economical fluctuations, and a change to the national and international geopolitical climate.

A common characteristic of an environmental disturbance is organizations' lack of control regarding when they occur. Leaders should be aware that disturbances do occur; in response, leaders should try to predict and prepare for them, but also realize that there is probably little that can be done. The weather is a good metaphor to illustrate this concept. We all have daily, weekly and monthly plans within our busy lifestyles, and those plans are often at the mercy of the weather. Playing a round of golf is dependent on the weather. Going to work or school can be dependent on the weather, during hurricane season for some coastal regions and during the winter months for northern states.

Organizations can suffer and benefit from business environmental climate changes (i.e. disturbances). There are, of course, exceptions to this rule. Organizations in certain industries form strong lobbies and cartels influencing and initiating environmental disturbances. Examples include lobbying for changes in legislation, controlling supply, and winning contract bids. Such control mechanisms, however, are pretty much exclusive to large, well-connected organizations, which often impacts medium- and small-sized organizations who have little or no influence.

With regards to the Knowledge-Power Success Model, it is clear that environmental disturbances impact the attainment of goals. Therefore, the goal(s) originally set can fall short or even exceed expectations. In fact, the need for effective data-gathering and -evaluation is further amplified, as it acts as an early-warning system to highlight environmental disturbances that should be reviewed before becoming problematic. The sharp rise in oil prices between 2004-2005 had a domino effect on industries that critically depend upon it. The price hike was largely passed on to the customer, while organizations absorbed the rest. This particular type of environmental disturbance hit hard on the travel industry, the courier industry, and the energy industry, just to name a few. Many organizations in those types industries recognize that price fluctuations can be detrimental to their business goals and have developed early-warning systems as a protection mechanism.

By chance, six months before oil prices began to rise, I happened to bump into an executive from the oil industry who shared information with me regarding the upcoming price hike (i.e., a market disturbance). How could this information be in the hands of key people within the industry months before it even occurred? Organizations that are sensitive to such fluctuations depend on and use this acquired knowledge to adjust and set goals and strategies. In effect, acquired knowledge keeps them ahead of the game and softens the blow of environmental disturbances.

As part of the knowledge-gathering process, leaders must pay close attention to information sources that can potentially predict changes to the environment. This forms a crucial part of the Knowledge-Power Success Model, comprising probably the most volatile and unpredictable aspect of organizational and system performance. Therefore, the organizations which have the most accurate and timely knowledge system have the better capability to counteract market disturbances.

6.7 Actual Obtained Results

Results obtained represent the fruits of the preceding stages within the model. Were set goals met? What were the reasons as to why goals were exceeded or not attained? How can things be done differently next time? This stage represents a data-measurement and information-gathering process; it's difficult to determine whether goals have been achieved unless a measurement process is in place. We know that the best-laid plans may not come to fruition due to many reasons—environmental disturbances, unattainable goals, wrong strategy, poor data, and deficient data evaluation, to name but a few. This stage is not the end of the line as far as the Knowledge-Power Success Model is concerned; it represents performance that feeds data back to initiate the second cycle.

Quality gurus of the twentieth century, such as Deming, Juran and Crosby, openly advocated feedback-measurement cycles in their methodologies. They knew that the attainment of quality within organizational processes has "no finish line"; rather, the pursuit of excellence was always constant. The cycle is iterative. Only through measurement, improvement, and repetition does the organization progress in the right direction. This is the mantra of quality improvement (knowledge-power) that Japanese organizations use. It allowed them to become leaders in key industries, from motor vehicles to electronics, offering high-quality products at significantly lower prices. Quality improvement is far more developed today because of technological advancement, which also allows small organizations to employ the Knowledge-Power Success Model effectively and reap the same rewards large organizations have enjoyed for decades.

The Knowledge-Power Success Model is a powerful tool

THE KNOWLEDGE-POWER PARADIGM

that helps to conceptualize the key stages of organizational strategic goal setting, planning, and execution. The central force that binds the model is effective data-gathering and evaluation. Leaders who effectively complete these key stages can plan for and succeed in meeting set goals. In the next chapter, we will focus on the importance of the feedback loop within the Knowledge-Power Success Model: What is the feedback loop? Why is it important? How does it work? And how can you benefit from it?

7

DATA COLLECTION & EVALUATION FEEDBACK LOOP

The beginning of knowledge is the discovery of something we do not understand.
- FRANK HERBERT

THE KNOWLEDGE-POWER SUCCESS MODEL, as discussed in Chapter 6, is a process successfully used by leaders to help achieve goals in the for-profit and not-for-profit arenas. There is nothing ground breaking about its various stages, particularly the goal-setting, planning, executing and results stages; they are well-known and acknowledged. Likewise, the data collection measurement and data evaluation stages are nothing new or even ground breaking. Yet very few leaders exercise discipline within the process, which often yields enormous dividends. We have explored the various stages in some detail, and explained their inner workings and importance. In this chapter we will "peel the onion" even further and explore the model in greater detail.

The secret in accomplishing the Knowledge-Power Success model lies not only within the attributes of each stage, but also within the data collection

THE KNOWLEDGE-POWER PARADIGM

and feedback loop. The data collection and feedback loop allows the system process to be iterative, setting the table for constant improvement and progression, and it also addresses the problem of of environmental disturbances. In this chapter we will explore the feedback loop mechanism in greater detail, highlighting its importance and giving real-world examples of how this fits into critical processes.

7.1 The Feedback Loop and Knowledge Management

A feedback loop occurs when specific outputs/results within a system become the inputs into the same system, thus resulting in changes to the desired state. A simple example of a feedback loop is how a thermostat works within a heating and cooling system. Figure 7.1 takes the stages of the Knowledge-Power Success model and illustrates how they can be applied to this basic principle. The desired temperature is set to 75 degrees. The job of the thermostat is to recognize that the desired goal governs the necessary variables (heating and cooling system) to ensure that the temperature is maintained at 75 degrees. Feedback occurs through measurement via a thermometer, which constantly checks the temperature and looks out for deviations from the desired goal. Any deviation is communicated to the thermostat, which once again controls the heating and cooling system to get back to equilibrium. The system is therefore iterative and self-managed via the feedback loop.

For the heating and cooling system to operate successfully, it relies on the smooth operation of the feedback loop portion of the process—via the thermometer readings and the thermostat control mechanisms. With the ability to effectively measure the deviation from the goal, the thermometer evaluates data to control the heating and cooling system to affect the actual temperature.

This same iterative system is applied to cruise-control systems found in motor vehicles. Cruise-control systems also work with a feedback loop system that constantly monitors the actual speed of the vehicle relative to the desired "set" speed, all the while controlling the power output from the engine. Less than a few decades ago, advanced thermostat systems and cruise control functions were unheard of, but today they are simply taken for granted. Why is this the case? The answer lies, once again, with technology. Advances in microchip and computer technology allows complex systems to be effective managed by sensors, and

DATA COLLECTION & EVALUATION FEEDBACK LOOP

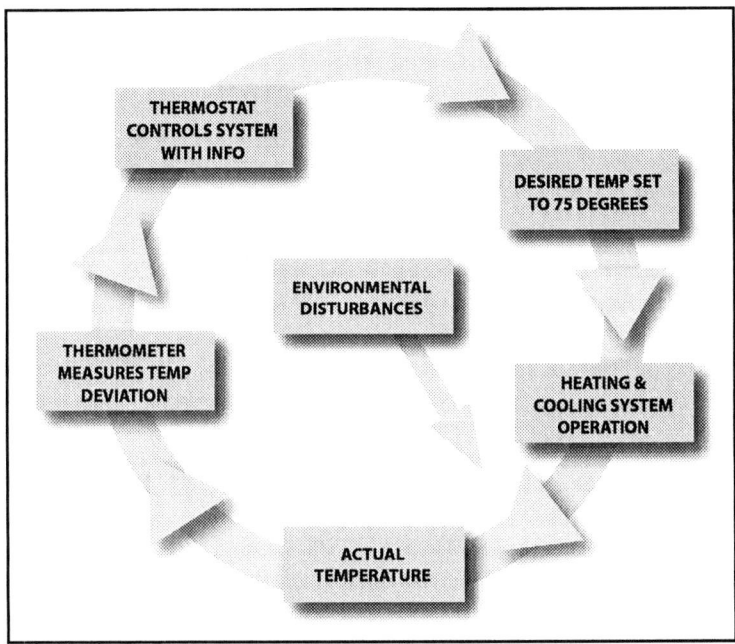

Figure 7.1 - The Knowledge-Power-Success Model Applied

then monitored and controlled by computers. This in turn allows the feedback loop to be completed and controlled, making our lives easier, safer and more comfortable.

Feedback loops occur through a measurement process which confirms deviations from what is expected. A well-known example of a feedback measurement loop occurred when an unknown patent clerk from Germany released his 'General Theory of Relativity' (GTR) in 1915. In his heart, the patent clerk knew that his proposed theory was true. But he did not have absolute proof of theory, via a feedback measurement loop–for which he was much maligned. His theory stated that large masses bend space around them; therefore, light does not travel in a straight line, but instead follows the curve. The curvature of space and time, GTR posited, is caused by the influence of gravity from large objects. The nearest object to earth which allowed GTR to be measured was the sun, but tests could only be conducted during a total solar eclipse. In 1919, a British expedition led by astrophysicist Arthur Eddington traveled to the Tropics to carry out measurements to find out whether GTR was correct. The tests clearly proved that the theory was true and that light did not necessarily travel in a straight line. The patent clerk in question was, of course, Albert Einstein, who overnight went from being a complete unknown to one of the most important physicists in history. The feedback measurement loop, in this case, came four years after Einstein published his GTR; nevertheless, it was a landmark event in the 20th century, but only after being confirmed by a measurement feedback loop.

We observe similar feedback measurement loops when we compare such examples to organizational systems. Technological advancements have allowed organizations to effectively employ measurement systems to create successful feedback loops, thus allowing the Knowledge-Power Success Model to function properly. The model leverages measurement, evaluation, decision and execution processes, essentially adhering to the knowledge-power paradigm. Today's leaders have the opportunity to be creative by employing various technologies to figure out ways to efficiently and economically capture and evaluate data. This evaluation, in turn, forms the basis of knowledge and understanding, which influences goal setting, strategic planning, execution and performance. The only restrictions for organizational leaders are the limits of their own creativity and their willingness to use technology to achieve desired goals and objectives.

For a remarkable example of how technological advancement can create a systematic feedback loop for knowledge-gathering, consider game-preparation by today's professional baseball players. To a purist, aspects of the game can be likened to a chess match: essentially a duel between pitcher and batter. The pitcher is constantly trying to outfox the batter with pitches to strike him out, and conversely, the batter is trying to figure out what the pitcher is likely to pitch, so that he can better handle the ball coming his way at speeds up to 95 miles per hour. Examining the evolution in how each player approaches that match illustrates the benefit of technology. Just ten years ago, the batter would go into bat and carefully note every characteristic of each pitch the pitcher threw at him. Back in the dugout, he would likely continue to watch the pitcher as other players took the plate. The batter could also refer to scouting reports on the pitcher to look for tendencies and patterns in his pitches. This would have helped him better prepare for the next visit to the plate against the same pitcher.

These processes offer a semblance of a feedback loop in which the batter acquires knowledge as he plays, so that he can make adjustments to his strategy and attain a better outcome next time.

With rapid advancements in technology, however, every Major League Baseball (MLB) game is now televised—which equates to thousands of baseball games each season. Furthermore, MLB teams have acquired video and editing equipment which captures live images from the game in progress and stores them in a hard drive that can easily be accessed at any time. Today's batters (when playing at home) have the ability to go into a video room, normally adjacent to their dugout, and review film of the opposing pitcher's performance. Essentially the data capture and evaluation process, as in the Knowledge-Power Success model, has advanced significantly. Instead of depending on mental notes made during the game, the player now has a team of people collecting information and video evidence to refer to during the game! This offers the batter far more information to create a significant advantage, potentially tipping the scale in his favor the next time he goes to bat.

Now, this does not necessarily mean that the batter can go to the next at-bat and 'crush' the ball out of the park. But data from the Major League reflects that in the last ten years the average number of home runs and hits has been significantly higher than it has ever been in the history of the game. Experts and commentators have pointed an accusing finger at performance-enhancing drugs, batter-friendly parks and batter-friendly balls. While these factors probably have contributed in some way, few experts credit the enhancements in data collection and evaluation methods, which may also have affected these numbers.

7.2 System Break Down

A clear case has been made for the feedback loop as a vital part of the Knowledge-Power Success model. Without an effective feedback loop, the model cannot work; it would stop after the first cycle. Figure 7.2 illustrates what the strategic model would look like without a feedback loop.

The system in Figure 7.2 reflects goal-setting based upon little or no knowledge, creating a function where such decisions would be based upon a 'wish list' or, at best, an educated guess. Subsequent planning and execution strategies based on initial goals and obtained results would reflect shortfalls in the process. Essentially, the process places little emphasis on data, information or knowledge, and each stage is influenced by the limitations of the preceding one. The actual results obtained are likely to be less than

THE KNOWLEDGE-POWER PARADIGM

50/50 with regard to success or failure. This concept ties in with the following Sun Tzu maxim:

> "If ignorant both of your enemy and yourself, you are certain in every battle to be in peril."
>
> - Sun Tzu

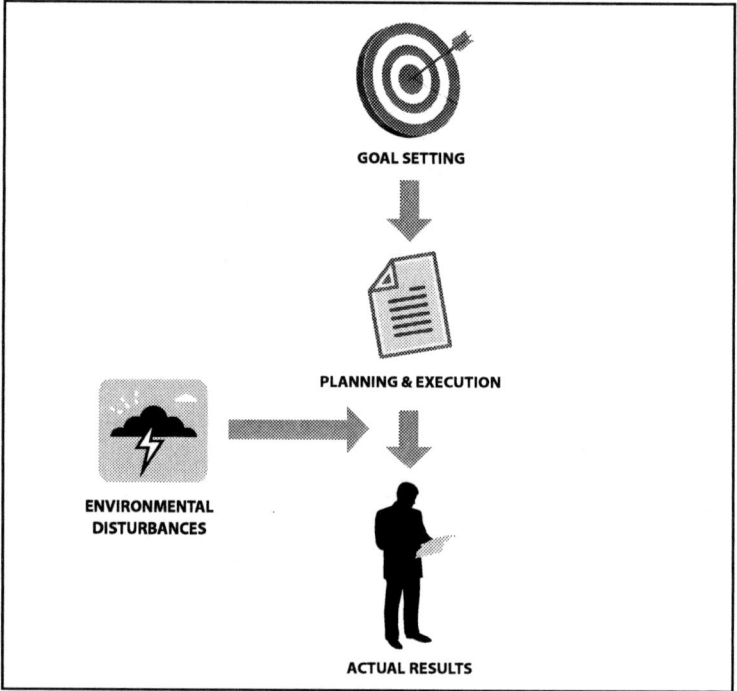

Figure 7.2 - A Non-Feedback Loop Strategic Process

While the argument to seek out and evaluate information is strong and logical, it is hard to imagine leaders not adhering to it. But leaders in all types of companies formulate strategies and makes decisions in the manner described in Figure 7.2. Little consideration is placed upon the knowledge-management function and the feedback loops that are essential to attaining success. The knowledge function is imperative, so why is it so infrequently considered? What do leaders do when they do not achieve desired goals? What options are available to leaders to avoid decision-making mistakes, as outlined by the model in Figure 7.2?

The most common reason for effective knowledge management being omitted or ignored from decision-making is a combination of the resource allocation burden and leadership ignorance. Establishing data collection and evaluation systems has traditionally placed a significant resource burden on organizations. The resources required to establish these protocols were definitely not conducive to small- and medium-sized companies. Large companies, conversely, have resources, and many have excelled in knowledge management and corporate intelligence for goal attainment. GE and Motorola are excellent examples, especially in light of Six Sigma, in which the knowledge-management function is central to success.

While some leaders are aware of the significance of knowledge management in relation to the knowledge-power paradigm, they choose not to incorporate it as an essential part of what they do. Ignorance is still prevalent largely as a function of the resource burden issue: They maintain the mindset that the resource burden still exists. Technology has advanced sufficiently, however, so that the resource burden is now a fraction of what it used to be. But we still see a breakdown in the Knowledge-Power Success model. Leaders who are true visionaries and possess the courage of their convictions tend to embrace new technologies and adopt new ideas. Unfortunately, the leaders who remain stagnant either dwindle away or are forced to adopt these new technologies at a later stage, often at greater cost.

A good example of this type of situation includes organizations who benefit from feedback from existing, previous and potential clients. This seems a given; what organization does not want to know what its clients think? Five to ten years ago, firms would have to commit major resources to undertake programs to adopt knowledge–management processes. In Part I of the book I outlined an example of a market research program that I helped institute, which cost tens of thousands of dollars during a period of six months. Additionally, in order to glean useful knowledge, the data captured through these methods required analysis and input from experts. The resource burden was extremely high, but it was deemed worthwhile, because the value of the information obtained exceeded the cost of the needed resources.

That same process of capturing customer data and evaluation has changed greatly, due to two factors:

THE KNOWLEDGE-POWER PARADIGM

1. Technological Advancements.

2. Significant Reductions in the Resource Burden Required.

Technology has advanced sufficiently to allow smart systems to dovetail with existing processes to capture data and information. These smart systems allow for quick and easy evaluation of data, paving the way for better decision-making and strategy formulation. Additionally, the smart systems in question cost very little to employ and maintain. In the past, a knowledge-management system could easily cost an organization tens of thousands of dollars to implement and operate. That cost has come down to a matter of a few dollars a day! In effect, the knowledge-management barrier to entry, which many large organizations utilized but smaller companies were unable to enjoy, has been broken. Organizations of all sizes can now reap the benefits of knowledge management. Leaders, therefore, need to look deeper into these new technologies to see how they can benefit organizational and strategic needs.

In Chapter 4 we discussed a specific example of a typical customer feedback survey process employed by a vehicle manufacturer and car dealership. The two main issues with the customer feedback process were the following: (1) It took in excess of six to eight weeks to attain feedback, and (2) the knowledge that was gleaned was potentially inaccurate due to the time delay. Ideally, the information could have been captured in a shorter period of time and evaluated instantly by the dealership and manufacturer, unearthing valuable information about customer service and dealership experience.

In this particular example, the knowledge-management system is somewhat breaking down, even though a knowledge-feedback loop is in place. That is, the feedback loop exists but the time factor has rendered it nearly ineffective. If, for example, a significant proportion of customers polled had indicated a less than positive experience, the model is not effectively allowing for the information to get into the right hands as quickly as it should. Therefore, even though a feedback loop is in place, the system can break down. Why? Because the same requirements that govern the knowledge-power paradigm also govern the Knowledge-Power Success model: the right information, to the right person, at the right time, followed up with the right action. In this particular case, the requirement of 'right time' is preventing the process and paradigm from working optimally.

In contrast, the same effect can cause breakdown if the assumptions for 'right knowledge, ' 'right person, ' and 'right action' are not adhered to, even if a feedback loop is in place. The Knowledge-Power Success model can cease to work if the data that is being collected and evaluated happens to be the wrong information that goes into the decision-making process. Such a breakdown is often seen when the content of the methodology, rather than the methodology itself, is out of sync, resulting in the gathering of inaccurate and wrong information. Furthermore, if the knowledge-management and feedback loop is effectively working, it is critical that the information obtained is communicated to the 'right people.' The right people happen to be anyone who directly or indirectly influences or owns a particular process. In terms of the vehicle/dealer customer survey example, the leaders should have the information communicated directly to them. With this information they can monitor non-financial performance from a quality perspective, which directly influences current and future organizational performance. Finally, even when all of the aforementioned assumptions are satisfied through knowledge management, the 'right people' are required to take the 'right actions.' Sometimes negative and positive information is either totally ignored or inappropriately used by leaders. This in itself would constitute wrong action, thus resulting in system breakdown.

Efficiently operating the Knowledge-Power Success model alone does not guarantee success. System breakdowns occur due to numerous reasons and assumptions not being met. These issues can be handled easily if leaders are mindful of them and skillful in handling them.

7.3 Making Sense of Data Evaluation and Data Mining

One of the key aspects of effective knowledge management is the evaluation of data and making sense of what has been collected. We know that the evaluation process should not be time consuming or a burden on organizational resources. These two factors are critical in rendering any evaluation process inefficient and unsuccessful.

One of the key aspects of effective knowledge management is the evaluation of data. We know that the evaluation process should not be time consuming or a burden on organizational resources. These two factors are critical for the sake of efficiency and productivity.

We can strongly argue that the greater the amount of relevant data gathered and evaluated, the greater the accumulated knowledge. The more knowledge that is accumulated, the stronger the potential effects of the knowledge-power paradigm. For example, Rio Tinto[1] is a large multinational organization, a global leader in locating, mining and processing mineral resources. The mineral resources that Rio Tinto primarily mines—aluminum, copper, diamonds, coal, uranium, gold and iron ore—are among the most valuable resources on the planet. Acquiring and evaluating knowledge of these minerals is almost as valuable as the minerals themselves. For decades, Rio Tinto acquired knowledge about mineral deposits around the world; in fact, until recently, the company had only a couple of master copies of priceless maps—so valuable to the organization that very few people have access to them, and they are kept under lock and key at an undisclosed location. The rationale for this was to keep vital knowledge out of the hands of rivals. The secrecy was so complete that, in some cases, even the governments of the various countries designated on the maps were unaware of the information!

Essentially Rio Tinto's performance is not based purely on what it currently produces, but also on the organization's ability to gather and successfully evaluate data for future production. It is vital in the mining industry to be the first to possess accurate information about significant mineral deposits, even if immediate access to the minerals isn't possible. In some instances, Rio Tinto has held knowledge about vast mineral deposits in countries where it cannot obtain immediate access due to the political and social climate. Socio-political climates do change, however, and eventually gathered organizational intelligence will create significant new opportunities.

An efficient and effective data evaluation system that complements the data-gathering process is crucial. There is not much point in gathering data if sifting through the evaluation process takes a significantly long time. Conversely, it can be very damaging if the evaluation process is rapid but gleans inaccurate information. Fundamentally, the data gathering and evaluation process is a fine balancing act that must complement each stage of the knowledge-management process if it is to have a chance at success.

Technological advancements and innovations have allowed for efficient data collection and storage. Today's organizations can capture and store vast amounts of data in databases, broadly defined as any medium that stores records and statistics, but most commonly associated with the ability to electronically store masses of data. In this book we will refer to a database exclusively as an electronic medium for data storage. The advancement of database technology has been breathtaking over the last fifteen years. Indeed, there are very few industries that do not employ some form of electronic database for research, production, marketing, service and support. Databases have become an integral part of the way we work; indeed, organizations often cease to function without them.

In the knowledge-management process, the database is only as useful as the ability to have easy and effective access to data. If leaders cannot easily disseminate data into structured, meaningful information, then the database is limited in its use. Furthermore, the data should allow for easy 'data mining' (also known as 'knowledge discovery'), the process of searching vast volumes of data to reveal meaningful information. If an organization collects tens of thousands of records of customer feedback about a particular product or service, the information would be incredibly useful if it could yield information based on certain parameters. For example, the managers at Blockbuster video would benefit from knowing the percentage of females between the ages of 21 to 30 that enjoy watching thrillers. It would also be useful for Dell Computers to know what proportion of their male clients within a particular age range purchase a certain type of computer. You can see how knowledge of this kind can be very powerful in terms of organizational goal setting, strategy planning, and execution. Decisions can be determined from the knowledge that has been collected and 'mined,' and the probability of making incorrect decisions is greatly reduced as the 'chance' factor has been taken out of the equation.

Some of the best-known exponents of such knowledge-management strategies include companies like Wal-Mart and FedEx. Wal-Mart bases its inventory and distribution strategy purely on a sophisticated data-gathering, evaluation and communications network. The company can monitor and execute anything from inventory management and delivery schedules to customer buying patterns. This knowledge then feeds back to decision-makers, who use it to successfully help formulate future plans.

While this process is beneficial for large companies like Wal-Mart, Blockbuster video and Dell Computers, how does it translate for small- and medium-size companies? As previously mentioned, small- and medium-size companies have not traditionally had the resources required to benefit from traditional knowledge-management systems. That is now changing, however, as technology, and to a greater degree software, is being made available to smaller organizations. Today those companies are able to manage knowledge systems in order to better understand data, to perform and gain a real competitive edge. Small companies across all industries are gathering vast amounts of data to effectively evaluate information and improve processes and decision-making. Software stores the data in a manner that allows for easy evaluation and trend analysis. Marketing and sales, in particular, is one sector within small organizations which is collecting and/or even buying data from third-party sources to better strategize their endeavors. The old adage 'it's a numbers game' is being challenged by a shift from volume to value. Sales teams are strategically using pertinent information about target markets to become more effective and efficient in their daily, weekly and monthly activity. Improvements in data collection and evaluation have facilitated a shift for many sales teams toward being more selective regarding a target audience, rather than marketing to a mass audience. Organizations that have been slow in adopting these new methods are consequently being left behind as they are fighting for scraps.

In another example, small organizations are also using technological advancements to better measure vital processes within their daily routines. These measurements are recorded and then evaluated by managers for various purposes, from process improvement to the reduction of organizational liability. This, in turn, has a positive knock-on impact on business performance and the quality of service offered.

7.4 Resetting Goals and Strategies

Progressive organizations collect more data, glean more information, and communicate it at a quicker rate. This means that they are better-equipped to manage disturbances in the business environment, and they are more sensitive to these changes. As a result, goals and strategies have a greater propensity to change over shorter period of time. Wal-Mart's use of data evaluation and communications systems to determine inventory and distribution strategies is a perfect example. On a micro level, the actual action plan and strategies for inventory and stocking now differ from store to store, depending upon what is purchased and what the 'hot' items are. But just ten or fifteen years ago, typical inventory strategies were based around sharing a common method, regionally and nationally. Now each store continuously updates and changes its goals and strategies. Why? Because they can. Technology serves organizations better and allows them to be far more responsive to changes in the market. Therefore, they are better equipped to serve their customers and to increase their profits.

The data collection and feedback loop section of the Knowledge-Power Success model has seen rapid advancement in the last ten years. This advancement has coincided with advancements in technology, creating improvements in data gathering and storage, as well as massive improvements in data evaluation. Improved data evaluation has resulted in information being more readily available than ever before, and it is allowing leaders to make better decisions, set better strategies, and improve business performance.

In the next chapter we will explore the role of the leader in greater detail. The role of the leader is essential to the knowledge-power paradigm, as the leader is the driver of the car; because no matter how good the car is, it is the capability of the driver that eventually determines whether the car performs or not.

8

THE ESSENTIAL ROLE OF LEADERSHIP

Duty in mind, pipe in hand
That's how Captain Carefree stands
Smiling wide, with eyes ablaze
Nothing can escape his gaze.
He looks out on the ship and sea
His crew obeys him 1-2-3
Calmly Carefree stands in ground
And takes in everything around.[1] "

- ALBERT EINSTEIN

THE KNOWLEDGE-POWER SUCCESS MODEL and the paradigm are largely dependent on the knowledge management function, i.e. the ability to gather and effectively analyze data. The two most essential aspects of knowledge management function are (a) the data collection and measurement processes, and (b) the data evaluation processes. These two macro stages create the foundation for attaining and understanding knowledge for use in successful planning and decision-making processes. Having said that, the people that govern and manage these systems and processes are the agents which influence their effectiveness. Furthermore, the agents who effectively use knowledge are leaders who ultimately determine strategy and allocate resources to attain business results. Essentially, they are leaders of processes, systems and people.

The leadership role is critical because it is a very subjective area. When dealing with individuals, teams and personalities, rationality is often superseded by human behavior and its idiosyncrasies. In this chapter we will explore the various leadership roles, their characteristics, and some examples of knowledge-power leaders, and we will discuss the concept of 'agents of change.'

8.1 Leadership Roles and Characteristics

Numerous studies and models have been proposed in relation to leadership roles and characteristics. The reality of the matter, however, dictates that there is not one style or one group of characteristics that embodies a good, effective or great leader. If the function of a leader is to manage roles and relationships within a group to achieve desired objectives, then differing leadership styles can be successful in meeting these objectives. An effective leader could be a people-person, working closely with her team, engaging each member and facilitating goals, whereas another effective leader could be a hard, goal-oriented autocrat who manages by fear but is equally successful at meeting the same set of goals. There are certain characteristics, though, that can lead to team and role breakdown, in which the effectiveness of the leader and the team eventually diminishes. The fear-based leadership style mentioned above is an example of one such characteristic.

Fast Company magazine published an article in September 2005 that outlined some of the keys to effective leadership, based on a study conducted by two Harvard Business School professors (Mayo and Nohria). *Fast Company* asked, "What are the elements of this alloy we call 'leadership'?"[2] They outlined factors including vision, integrity, perseverance, courage, hunger for innovation, and willingness to take risks. Comparing the likes of Henry Ford, Ray Croc, Estee Lauder and Jack Welch, the authors found that each possessed a characteristic called "contextual intelligence"–a term coined by Mayo and Nohria. According to *Fast Company*, these particular leaders possess "an acute sensitivity to the social, political, technological, and demographic contexts that came to define their eras. And they adapted their enterprises to best respond to those forces." The magazine went on to state that not only did the times influence the leaders, but they also influenced their industries and the markets as a whole.

This particular study is fascinating because of the key words Mayo and Nohria use when defining certain successful leadership characteristics:

"contextual intelligence," "acute sensitivity," "adapting their enterprises to best respond to those forces," and "sensing opportunities."[2] Let us take a closer look at these specific terms. The first one that jumps out at us is "contextual intelligence." What does this mean? "Contextual intelligence" refers to a leader's ability to use his or her intellect and acumen appropriately given the situation and environment within which they operate. Exceptionally successful leaders have the appropriate knowledge (intelligence) and verve to apply attained information successfully to critical processes within their business environment. Interestingly, the authors mention Jack Welch; we have already touched upon his leadership skills and vision with specific regard to the Six Sigma program at GE. We know that he invested heavily in Six Sigma, and we also know the important role of knowledge management within the Six Sigma process. Furthermore, we know the tremendous success Welch and GE experienced with Six Sigma on a financial and performance basis.

The next term Mayo and Nohria used is "acute sensitivity." In relation to leadership, their study described most successful leaders as exhibiting "acute sensitivity to the social, political, technological, and demographic contexts." If sensitivity is another way of saying "understanding,"[2] then these leaders had strong understanding of the social, political, technological, and demographic environments. They understood and had a good grasp of the environment that they operated within. This understanding came from the knowledge they possessed and the talent to bring it all together. Consequently, knowledge led to understanding, to which they applied their talent to produce results.

"Adapting their enterprises to best respond to those forces"[2] refers specifically to leaders realizing that they operate in an organic environment. Industries are constantly changing, so possessing a survival mindset is truly dependent on successfully adapting to change. Additionally, there are forces in the market that impact and influence change, i.e. "environmental disturbances." Estee Lauder is a prime example of a leader who operated in a constantly changing environment: What was fashionable last year is no longer fashionable now. Lauder's supreme knowledge and understanding allowed her to stay ahead of the curve for a sustained period of time and to successfully lead within her industry.

The final term of interest is "sensing opportunities." Some people interpret this as luck, which also can be defined as "opportunity meeting

THE KNOWLEDGE-POWER PARADIGM

preparedness"–the most accurate interpretation in a discussion of great leadership characteristics. Broadly, leaders such as Ford, Kroc, Welch and Lauder sensed opportunities. This sense can partly be ascribed to talent and skill, but also to the ability to connect knowledge, understanding and the realities of their environment. This ability enables them to see clearly the opportunities at hand. In effect, "sensing opportunities" is the culmination of each of the previous terms used wisely to create success.

Let us review these terms, and their definitions, in the context of the knowledge-power paradigm:

- *"Acute Sensitivity"* is a leader's excellent understanding of his environment.

- *"Contextual Intelligence"* is the ability of the leader to successfully apply her knowledge to the environment she operates within.

- *"Adapting Their Enterprises to Best respond to Those Forces"* refers to interpreting feedback from a small sample of customers who may or may not represent a representative cross-section of all customers.

Finally, "sensing opportunity" is the ability to bring all these factors together to carve out significant business opportunities. Comparing that to the Knowledge-Power Success model, we can see a direct correlation on a macro level, where gathering data is followed by evaluating data to attain knowledge and understanding. Once knowledge and understanding are established, the leader uses his skill and talent to plan and execute a specific strategy to realize positive results. These results then become the first stage of the feedback loop, where the cycle begins again.

Mayo and Nohria's findings are concurrent with the knowledge-power paradigm, and highlight the key role leaders play within it. Without strong leadership that fundamentally understands the paradigm, significant gains may not be attained. If the likes of Jack Welch did not realize the huge benefits of Six Sigma, what would his legacy have been? Would he have achieved the iconic status that he has clearly attained? After all, great leaders are judged, first and foremost, on their results; all subsequent characteristics and traits are secondary.

We have explored the broad characteristics of leadership discussed in the Mayo and Nohria study at Harvard Business School. But what are the more specific traits that help define a good leader? And how do these traits relate to the knowledge-power paradigm? The following leadership characteristics were studied by House and Podsakoff[3], in 1994, who outlined valuable styles, as opposed to definite styles. Their "styles" are outlined as follows:

A. Leadership Vision: This is the ability of a leader to outline his vision of desired goals that will help him attain to success. It is often said that some of the best leaders are "visionaries"–individuals who have a clear idea of how to get from where they are to where they want to go. These leaders have the intrinsic ability to effectively communicate a vision that inspires and motivates people to join the cause. This characteristic is almost a prerequisite for great leadership; few extraordinary leaders lack the ability to articulate a clear vision. Spiritual teachings and accounts point to great leaders like Jesus, Mohammed, Moses, Buddha and Krishna as having "vision" that inspires billions of people over millennia. Conversely, in the field of politics and business there have been many great leaders who have led billions, rightly and wrongly, through the ability to inspire through vision.

B. Passion and Self-Sacrifice: Great leaders tend to show passion and strong faith in their vision and strategies. Part of this passion includes self-sacrifice for their cause. A good example of self-sacrifice is that of Jesus, especially in the final forty-eight hours that led to his crucifixion. A modern, and less dramatic, example of this is Howard Hughes, who was just as passionate about film-making as he was about advancing airplane technology. His passion for his business ventures was legendary, almost to a fault. Additionally, he showed tremendous self-sacrifice with his willingness to put everything on the line, from financial stability to physical well-being. Hughes not only helped design and engineer his airplanes, but he also test-piloted them. With his fabulous wealth he could easily have hired a test pilot and avoided the risk of life and limb. But his cavalier approach and leadership instincts almost always came to the fore, inspiring his team and sending a message to rivals trying to out-do him.

C. Confidence, Determination and Persistence: Successful leaders often demonstrate high levels of confidence, especially in times of crisis when, deep inside, their confidence is not high. This confidence is personal propaganda that communicates a message to followers which helps to breed confidence within them. Winston Churchill was the epitome of stoic confidence and strength during World War II, even in the darkest days, such as the Battle of Britain and the German blitz of London. His confidence and strength inspired the people of his nation, translating into a national defiance and determination invaluable to defending Britain during the war.

Confidence also helps breed levels of persistence. Leaders who are determined and persistent can achieve great things, including influencing others into being determined and persistent. During the Cuban Missile Crisis[4], President John F. Kennedy showed plenty of stoic determination and persistence during a very delicate situation with a great deal at stake. Not only did he go toe-to-toe against the Soviet Union regarding the placement of nuclear missiles on Cuban soil, but he also had to fend off strong opposition from within the U.S. that opposed his diplomatic strategy to avoid conflict. This was arguably Kennedy's finest hour during his thousand days in office; there is an abundance of other examples from his legacy that outline determination and persistence.

D. Image: A leader's image of herself, as well as the image perceived by followers, is critical to success. Image is essentially a personal marketing statement, from the way someone looks and speaks to how she works and interacts with others. Successful leaders often perceive themselves as a "brand," and therefore, their image is critical when creating a persona of credibility and ability. Nowhere is that more evident than in politics. In 1960, Richard Nixon appeared to be sweating and pale during the first televised Presidential debate[5] with John F. Kennedy, watched by 70-million Americans. In contrast, Kennedy was the young, handsome candidate, tanned and healthy, who spoke eloquently and with great poise. That Presidential race was one of the closest in history. Many commentators cite the image created by Nixon as one of the key reasons he lost the Presidential race—by 0.2 % of the popular vote.

Image is everything in politics. That's why millions of dollars are spent by politicians on advertising to create a "positive image." In an organizational setting, a leader will create a positive image through the various means of communication at his disposal, e.g. presentations, meetings, projects, emails, sales calls, etc. The most successful leaders are those who create an image based on depth and ability. The problem with creating an image based on "smoke and mirrors" is that the leader invariably gets "found out." A positive image that affirms proven strengths is more likely to yield long-term success.

E. Role-Model: Effective leaders who have built a positive image and gained the trust of followers can become role-models. People who model themselves on a leader identify something positive in that person which resonates inside them. An excellent example from the world of advertising is the 1990s *"Be Like Mike"* campaign produced by Gatorade. While Michael Jordan was already a role-model to many, the Gatorade commercials leveraged his leadership and athletic ability to expose role-model virtues to a wider audience, therefore helping to promote the Gatorade brand–but also strengthening the Michael Jordan brand. In everyday life, role-model types that children look up to include parents and teachers, while professionals in the world of business often look up to coaches, mentors, sports stars and organizational leaders.

F. Representation/Spokesperson: Leaders are sometimes appointed and sometimes assumed. Appointed leaders are figures of authority chosen for a specific role requiring leadership. Assumed leadership is a mantle that a leader assumes due to some of the preceding criteria, hence propelling him into a leadership role that identifies him as a spokesperson for a group or organization. While Mahatma Gandhi neither held office nor was a formally appointed leader, he is recognized in history as the leader of the Indian people during their struggle for independence from the British. His leadership style demonstrated vision, passion, self-sacrifice, confidence, determination, persistence, image, and role-model credentials, which endeared him to millions of people. Gandhi was so effective in his spiritual and non-violent beliefs, rooted in defiance, that his triumph is still the only known example of a victory between nations where the oppressed overcame the oppressor through non-violent means. So great was the strength of his leadership that he continues to be a role-model to millions, decades after his untimely and tragic death.

G. Performance Expectations: We have referred to the ability of strong leaders to perform to their capabilities, but according to House and Podsakoff[3], strong leaders communicate expectations of elevated performance to meet expectations. An example of such a leader is John Wooden, probably the greatest college basketball coach of all time. Wooden coached the UCLA men's basketball team to a record number of national championships. The cornerstone of his philosophy was hard work and teamwork. Wooden did not always have the most talented individuals on his team, but his coaching methods consistently produced the best teams. He emphasized an expectation of high performance and he instilled confidence and trust in his teams to help meet those expectations. Followers can achieve elevated goals because their leader gives them the confidence to help them reach their potential; Wooden was a master at that skill.

H. Selective Motive-Arousal: Leaders use this technique to stimulate in their followers motives that are pertinent to achieving certain goals. This is likened to micro strategy, rather than just broad leadership; the leader makes a connection through specific motives that resonate within the followers he is addressing. Good politicians are specialists in this field, often termed 'playing to the crowd.' This is a very effective strategy if the leader's base is segmented, with different motives representing different priorities within those segments.

I. Frame Alignment: This is the ability of a leader to form a bond by linking her followers' hopes and ideals to her own ideology. It's a method used to create a shared goal: 'What you want is what I want.' Hitler used this methodology effectively to garner a broad following, even though his methods were incredibly inhumane and barbaric. Connecting his misplaced philosophies to form a common bond, he was able to link the German people's deep desire to rise up during a time of great depression. The ultimate results were disastrous, but he used the technique well enough to seize complete power and authority across the whole German legislature, including the support of the people during that time.

J. Inspirational Communication: There are talkers, and then there are great communicators. We all notice and remember the communicators who are inspirational, whose words and passion stir us. They stand out from the rest because they are able to articulate a message. This style is not something that can be taught, but it can be refined in leaders who have the intrinsic ability. John F. Kennedy is a classic example of such a person. Even though his time in office was relatively short, he delivered an extraordinary number of speeches that brought inspiration. He spoke with passion and verve, telling vivid stories, and he showed compassion and strength. Kennedy was able to connect with the people of his generation through the supreme ability to communicate. Bill Clinton modeled himself on Kennedy's example. People from both sides of the political aisle agree that, for all his shortcomings, Bill Clinton shared Kennedy's ability to communicate in an inspirational manner. Few leaders have that ability.

8.2 Knowledge Management and Leadership Failings

We have explored different leadership styles and attributes and their relationship to the knowledge-power paradigm. We also know that the leader's role is absolutely critical if the paradigm is to succeed; we cited several examples in the last section. What we are now going to discuss is the relationship between those factors and knowledge management. Furthermore, we will outline the most common leadership failings that cause breakdowns in the knowledge-power paradigm.

According to House and Podsakoff[3], leadership vision, confidence, determination, and persistence are among the key attributes that successful leaders show. Within the realm of the knowledge-power paradigm and the knowledge-management system, these attributes are critical. The story of Jack Welch at GE and the Six Sigma program is a glowing example of just such a situation. Welch was not against knowledge management and quality improvement, but he "felt that the earlier quality programs were too heavy on slogans and light on results.[6]" To move from that position to implementing one of the largest, and most comprehensive, knowledge-management and quality-improvement programs was a significant adjustment. The results of making this adjustment are well documented, and what Welch showed was true leadership and courage. He alone was capable of making such a program successful within GE, because he bought into it and drove it from the top. Furthermore, Welch's vision for the program was backed up by supreme confidence, steely determination, and relentless persistence in seeing improvements to completion. That is the critical role the leader plays in effective knowledge management and in the knowledge-power paradigm.

The glamour of the leader's success at the helm of one of the largest companies in the world is fine and dandy, but how does this translate to

THE KNOWLEDGE-POWER PARADIGM

everyday leaders at the helm of small- and medium-sized companies? The reality of the Welch example is that the principles he demonstrated can apply to all leaders, regardless of organizational size or industry. Leaders of small organizations have many tough decisions to make, too. They have to set their vision, goals, and strategies, just like CEOs in large Fortune 500 companies. If they want to succeed, leaders at all levels of industry must demonstrate the courage and vision exhibited by Welch.

When I was 6 years old, like many kids of that age I was absolutely petrified of the dark. Images of gruesome monsters waiting for me would come to mind, causing instant fear and panic. My anxiety was so great that I would bully my cousin into accompanying me up the stairs in our home. It was comforting to know that if I had to go into the dark, I wasn't going alone. The fear was eased because it was a shared fear—even though he was probably not as scared as I was! As I grew older the fear subsided as I came to the realization that there were no gruesome monsters. My courage superseded my fear, and at some point the dark no longer struck fear or dread inside me. As we get older, our childhood fears are replaced by other fears, but the common link between these fears is its deep-rootedness in the unknown. Our understanding of the rationality of the situation is clear: Of course there are no monsters! Still, venturing into the unknown requires a leap of faith, and there are no guarantees.

This is where average leaders become great leaders. Great leaders not only understand and see the vision of how things will benefit them, but they inspire their followers to take that leap of faith into the unknown with them. This is where courage is greater than fear. This does not mean that leaders should be encouraged to make decisions with reckless abandon; all decisions should be carefully considered. But when the benefits are clear, let courage and rational thinking rule the implementation or adjustment of business processes, rather than the fear of the unknown.

Once a leader has made an adjustment with knowledge management and the Knowledge-Power Success model, it is critical that he monitors, adjusts (where required), and persists with the quality-improvement principle. Many leaders will buy into the process, and some will attain immediate and short-term benefit from it. Nonetheless, the reality of the principle dictates that the long-term success lies in the number of cycles the Knowledge-Power Success model goes through. That is, the more revolutions the Knowledge-Power Success model cycles through, the more efficient it will become. And if executed correctly, improvements in quality will likely ensue. This is one of the principles that helps Six Sigma, and other similar methodologies, to be effective quality-improvement tools. But if a leader does not persist with the model, or stops monitoring the results from the knowledge feedback loop, the model stops working and the benefits evaporate. Leaders, therefore, play a critical role in the make-up and success of such quality improvement initiatives. If dedication and persistence are one of the mantras of successful leadership, then this is a crucial factor in attaining desired results.

8.3 Knowledge-Power Leaders and Events

We already have mentioned Jack Welch as a true knowledge-power leader; he is an obvious 'poster child' for this type of example. But who are some of the other true knowledge-power leaders, and what types of events help define the knowledge-power paradigm? What did they do to attain such status? What did they achieve? What made them knowledge-power leaders? The following examples of leaders and events offer a brief synopsis of iconic leaders and their methods that truly embody the knowledge-power paradigm, highlighting the critical role of leadership within the paradigm. It also should be mentioned that many such leaders started off small; their grasp of the knowledge-power paradigm resulted in greater accomplishments as they progressed in using it.

Mayer Amschel Rothschild (1744 - 1812)

The Rothschild dynasty is among the most well-known in world history and within finance circles. Rothschild's legacy continues even today, Forbes named him in their "*Twenty Most Influential Businessmen Of All Time*[7]" list in 2005. The Rothschild fortune was initially made during the Napoleonic Wars, from financing to speculating in European stock markets. Rothschild had five sons, each stationed in one of the commercial centers of Europe to give the family crucial access to knowledge in these financial hubs. This was a wise move in a time when communication and flow of information was slow; Rothschild knew that having information was the key to success and power. In fact, Rothschild established a network of messengers and carrier pigeons across Europe, which enabled his family to communicate vital information about events. This, in turn, helped him with decision-making in investments and business strategy.

The information system employed by Rothschild was incredibly sophisticated for the time, creating an infrastructure that essentially was a barrier preventing other people from entering his arena of business. Rothschild was a very smart leader. He knew that others were watching him closely to glean information on what stocks he was investing in. Legend has it that before the outcome of the Battle of Waterloo was common knowledge, Rothschild started to 'dump' stock, indicating that Napoleon was the victor–but he knew that was not the case. His tactic sparked others to sell their stocks, which caused a serious price devaluation. As prices hit rock bottom, Rothschild happily bought up everything he could. He beat the market by basing his strategy on having knowledge before anybody else, and he made a huge amount of money in the process.

Sun Tzu (544 - 496 BC)

We already have touched upon Sun Tzu, and we are going to revisit his philosophy and his most influential book, *The Art of War*. There is limited information about the man himself, save for his books and a biography written about him by Sima Qian in the 2nd century B.C. Sun Tzu lived in the 6th century B.C.E. He was a general and also a revered thinker of his time. *The Art of War* was his masterpiece and also a military discourse that outlined various battle strategies for leaders. Sun Tzu influenced many great militaristic generals, and his thinking has been adopted, metaphorically, for modern day corporate warfare. His discourses are seen as truisms, words of wisdom heeded by the smart and the wise. The underlying principle in much of his work, however, is the leader's ability to garner knowledge and information necessary for critical decision-making. Many Japanese organizations live by these principles–the same Japanese organizations that led the quality revolution in the 1960s and '70s. "Know thyself" and "know thy enemy" are among the key lessons in the book. Sun Tzu argued that as long as leaders have the right information, the outcomes of wars and battles are known. Essentially, if a general chooses to go into battle and has the right information, the battle itself is merely an act to play out, with the knowledge that victory will be the result. The key to success is having the right information, and this principle clearly translates to the battle that business leaders face today.

The Space Race (1946 - 1980s)

While the era of the space race does not represent a single individual but rather the collective will of two nations, it is an extraordinary example of a knowledge-power paradigm. The space race between the U.S. and the Soviet Union began at the conclusion of World War II. Space was seen as the next great frontier for the assertion of global power, and glory would go to the nation that conquered it through the attainment of knowledge. Space exploration, the moon landings, modern satellites, space stations—all are essentially representations of man's ability to uncover scientific, mathematical and engineering knowledge. Therefore, getting to space symbolized the ability to be the first with knowledge and the ability to apply that knowledge to meet program goals. Knowledge boundaries during this time were pushed at an accelerated rate to meet aggressive goals.

The former Soviet Union beat the U.S. into space, but the U.S. was the first—and still the only—nation to make manned missions to the lunar surface. Such adventures and leaps in technology paved the way for modern communication and sociopolitical advances. Much of the power that the U.S. wields today, from nuclear missiles to advancements in communication, can be traced back to the start of the race. The key to acquiring and using knowledge is advancement, because it leads to superior power. Today, countries such as China and India have their own space programs, and they have joined in the race to stake a claim for power through knowledge.

The role of the leader is critical as he is the agent that drives the knowledge-power paradigm. You can liken the leader to a driver and the knowledge-power paradigm to a race car. Neither can operate successfully without the other; they work in tandem as one. Therefore, the qualities and abilities of the leader are crucial to the adoption of knowledge management and a continuous quality-improvement principle. The qualities that make a good leader are the same qualities needed in the leader to recognize the importance of knowledge and information. When necessary, the leader must make the required adjustments to steer the organization onto the right path.

9

DECISION-MAKING & OPPORTUNITY COST

Opportunity is missed by most people because it is dressed in overalls and looks like work.
- THOMAS A. EDISON

WHEN FACED WITH OPTIONS FOR critical business decisions, which way should a leader choose to go and how can the knowledge-power paradigm help? What methodology can a leader employ that will positively affect the outcome of critical processes? And once the decision has been made, how can the results of that decision be evaluated and measured to reflect whether there is an opportunity cost associated with it? In this chapter we will take a close look at decision-making processes and relate them to the knowledge-power paradigm and the Knowledge-Power Success model.

How can the knowledge-power paradigm and knowledge management assist successful decision-making and reduce opportunity cost? We will explore how successful leaders arrive at making the right decisions and how they can leverage information to aid and assist that process. We will also explore the pitfalls and trade-offs leaders often encounter regarding opportunity cost. Finally, we will discuss how successful leaders use strong decision-making methodologies to create non-traditional barriers to entry, making it difficult for others to compete on a level playing field.

9.1 Problem-Solving and Decision-Making

All leaders tackle problem-solving and decision-making on a daily basis. It is a fundamental role they play, and those most efficient and effective at handling these processes are often the most successful. Problem-solving processes and decision-making processes are closely related and complementary. Problems arise all the time in business, often relating to resource allocation, personnel, strategy, marketing, product development, manufacturing—the list is endless. Problems require solutions; otherwise they create more problems, ultimately leading to system breakdown and poor performance. A solution is a specific course of action leaders take through decision-making processes. Therefore, problem-solving is the essential precursor to the decision-making and execution process.

Problems are considered to be negative or sub-optimal situations which relate to a process, person, group or system. For example, a critical manufacturing machine has broken down and the production of 'widgets' has come to a halt, so the manager needs to find a solution and make a decision about the correct course of action. Sometimes, however, leaders face issues that are termed 'a nice problem to have.' These 'nice' problems are often opportunities that require a specific decision: Should I go with opportunity A, B or C?

Both problem-solving and decision-making issues have various methods that help leaders conceptualize how to get from the problem situation to a final decision. The role of a problem-solving process is to identify a problem, collect information about the problem situation, ascertain the root cause of the problem, and suggest solutions. The decision-making process analyzes the various options, weighs the cost-benefit of each option, looks for alternatives, executes a solution, and finally measures the effectiveness of the implemented solution. Figure 9.1 outlines the problem-solving and decision-making process and outlines the relationship between the stages.

According to Joseph E. Champoux in *Essential Tenets of Organizational Behavior*[1], decision strategies have three main characteristics that help to categorize strategy into one of two groups. The three characteristics are the 'routine-nonroutine dimension,' the 'recurring-nonrecurring dimension,' and the 'certainty-noncertainty dimension.'

The 'routine-nonroutine dimension' refers to decisions being either common or uncommon; i.e., is the decision standard or not? The 'recurring-nonrecurring dimension' refers to the frequency of the decision; i.e., does it happen often or is it infrequent? Finally, the 'certainty-uncertainty dimension' expresses the level of consistency of the decision. Once a given problem is described in these terms, it is possible to categorize it in terms of a 'programmed' or 'unprogrammed' decision strategy.

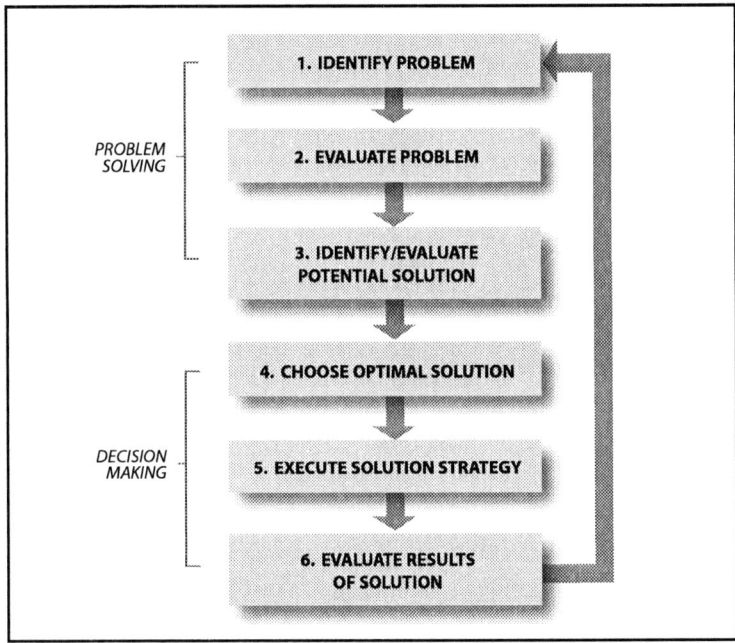

Figure 9.1 - The Problem Solving and Decision-Making Process

A 'programmed' decision strategy is one where the decision is routine, recurring, and certain, whereas an 'unprogrammed' decision strategy is one in which the reverse applies. A 'programmed' decision strategy is one that standard, set procedures handle every time it occurs. For example, when the Xerox machine in the office breaks down, the 'programmed' decision strategy is for the office manager to call a service engineer to come and fix the problem. This type of problem-solving and decision-making is not the kind that often troubles managers and leaders.

Conversely, the 'unprogrammed' decision strategies are the non-standard issues that leaders must tackle. These types of problems and decisions affect business results and an organization's successful functioning. Referring back to the problem-solving and decision-making model in Figure 9.1, we notice similarities to the Knowledge-Power Success model. Both models contain a feedback loop, where the output of results obtained becomes the input of the initial stage at the completion of a cycle. What this entails is measurement and monitoring of performance, and also self-regulating quality improvement—the greater the number of cycles, the better the actual results. This should start to look very familiar to you by now!

That is not the only similarity between the two models. Steps one, two, and six of the problem-solving and decision-making model indicate strong knowledge-management characteristics. Sometimes problems reveal themselves without the requirement of measurement and monitoring, just like the earlier example of the broken Xerox machine. However, many problems encountered by leaders are of the variety that is hard to detect, unless there are systems in place designed to recognize them. For example, the owner of a small business assumes that his customers are relatively satisfied with the service he offers, but believes there is an occasional dissatisfied client. Without formally measuring customer satisfaction levels, what he does not know is the actual level of customer satisfaction—whether it has changed or is fluctuating. Other questions that are related to measuring such variables include: What does the customer like about the service? What do they not like about the service? Who is dissatisfied? What time periods represent the greatest satisfaction and dissatisfaction? Did they like the attitude of the server? Would they recommend the organization to their friends and family?

The list of variables is dependent upon the type of information the leader needs to know. These types of factors are often unknown and tend to be difficult to detect with any level of accuracy when identifying problems. If a leader is unaware that he has a problem, how can he fix it?

Once a problem has been identified by management, it is critical that the problem be thoroughly evaluated. The evaluation stage allows for the problem to be put into perspective. This can be likened to taking your car to a mechanic who tells you that you have a problem with the radiator; essentially, the problem has been identified. But you are likely to ask follow-up questions: How bad is it? How much will it cost me? How long will it take to fix the problem? Follow-up questions allow the problem to be put into perspective through measurement—in this case the cost and the time it will take to fix the problem. Within organizations, the evaluation principle still applies; measurements must be set so that leaders know the severity of the problem(s). In the case of the customer satisfaction example, the measurement is likely to be the percentage of people that indicated they were satisfied or dissatisfied. It is up to the leader to set acceptable standards that reflect whether a problem exists. If satisfaction levels drop below 90%, that should automatically flag a problem. These benchmarks are subjective, and they depend upon the leader's performance expectations. I have personally seen satisfaction levels set as high as 99.9% by some organizations!

Another evaluation tool that successful leaders depend upon when assessing the severity of potential problems is the ability to compare and contrast current problems to those of other similar products and services. For example, I recently went in for a check-up and my physician was worried by what she saw on my EKG chart, which measures whether the heart is functioning properly. The 'inverted T-wave' she saw sometimes can indicate issues related to heart disease. But an 'inverted T-wave' can also be normal, depending on the particular individual.

Because the doctor did not have a previous EKG graph to compare my results, she could not ascertain whether this was a normal condition for me or something more serious. Subsequently, she decided to order more tests until she was satisfied that my heart was functioning properly and that there were no issues. In this example, the severity of an actual problem depends upon the ability of the process manager—the doctor—to evaluate and measure the problem.

The output from Step 6 is the measurement of the actual results, i.e. performance. This is the start of the feedback loop, similar to that of the feedback loop found in the Knowledge-Power Success model. This step is critical, as it assesses the effectiveness and performance of the decisions. Were they correct and effective? Did the chosen course of action execute properly and resolve the identified issues? Can the process be improved? The data gathered from the completion of this step becomes the input back into Step 1, helping to determine whether the problem has been solved to the leader's satisfaction. If the identified problem is a quality issue, then the cycle is iterative: there is no finish line, and the measurement, monitoring, solution identification, assessment, and execution is continuous.

Numerous problem-solving and decision-making models have been

THE KNOWLEDGE-POWER PARADIGM

developed to assist leaders in conceptualizing and understanding such processes. They are similar to the model we have just discussed; the major variations lie within the assumptions that govern their functionality. What remains constant is the knowledge-management part of each model—that is, the importance placed on acquiring key information.

All problem-solving and decision-making processes are fundamentally knowledge-management tools. The ability to gather and evaluate information is the foundation for the performance of all quality-improvement processes. The system cannot function without the ability to gather accurate information and efficiently evaluate problems, solutions, and performance. Therefore, the importance of knowledge management is highlighted as the key driver that allows leaders to attain success in critical aspects of organizational functionality.

9.2 Human Bias

> *"Decision makers use several heuristics or guidelines to simplify the task of processing an often bewildering array of information amassed during decision making. These strategies let them move quickly through the process but also limit the information to which they attend. Although heuristics can lead to accurate decisions, they often introduce biases in human judgment. People are not always aware that they use heuristics."*[1]
>
> - Joseph E. Champoux

Champoux really reaches the core of one of the key problems in managing knowledge-human bias. He correctly points out that in the face of a 'bewildering array of information,' decision makers often move quickly through the decision-making process, which can limit the evaluation of the information at hand. While leaders may make sound decisions, bias often can creep into their judgment. Champoux points to the following human biases which hinder effective problem-solving and decision-making:

Availability Heuristic: This heuristic highlights the human tendency to recollect and apply information stored in our memory that we remember most vividly. The characteristics of such types of information may be related to our emotions, comprise recent information, or have to do with something that is particular to the problem and decision at hand. We have established that the business environment is constantly changing and that this type of bias is often at the root of poor decision-making, mainly because the information in hand is incorrect and/or out-of-date. Broadly, this heuristic is an assumption that the information we recall is accurate and still applicable, but this cannot be known for sure. To overcome this obstacle, there must be a consistent knowledge-management system in place that indicates the validity of known information, thus negating the bias associated with the availability heuristic.

Representativeness Heuristic: This type of bias occurs when a leader associates the current problem with a past problem. For example, if my car breaks down, the reason for the breakdown may not necessarily be the same as when it broke down last time. The bias and assumption I make that the events are related is a representative heuristic.

Anchoring and Adjustment: This bias occurs when a leader bases the result of a desired adjustment to an initial point that may be an inaccurate starting point. For example, a manager assumes that the current overall satisfaction of his company is approximately 80%, and he sets a goal of a 15% increase in overall satisfaction for the coming quarter. In reality, however, the current overall satisfaction is much lower, at 60%, and therefore the 15% increase is not where he would ultimately like to be at the end of the quarter. Again, the decision bias is based on an assumption that may result in a less than desired outcome.

These three heuristics clearly make a case for having the best possible information—unless the heuristic happens to be right. The principle is the same within the legal system. The judge and jury require the most accurate information before they can make a final decision. Basing the verdict for one case on a previous case, however similar, would render the legal system unjust and open to huge inaccuracies. In the same manner, leaders must function as judge and jury, demanding the most up-to-date, accurate information in order to solve problems by making important decisions. Deviating from this process easily results in bias through inaccurate assumptions, which leaves the result of the decision-making process vulnerable.

The final human bias we are going to touch upon is the **Framing Effect** bias. This bias occurs due to the perception of the decision at hand. Studies have shown that people are likely to avoid risky decisions where perceived gains are involved, and people are likely to take greater risks where perceived losses are involved—risk-averse and risk-seeking behaviors. Essentially, what this bias points to is the way a particular problem is presented, whether as an opportunity to gain or an opportunity to lose. Playing the stock market can be viewed in such a manner. For example, a risky investment can be presented as an opportunity to make a sizable return on investment (the up-side). Alternatively, a risky investment can be presented as an opportunity where the down-side is a considerable loss through speculation. The manner in which information is presented is critical in avoiding the Framing Effect bias.

Therefore, the essential question to ask at this point is, "how can leaders become better at problem-solving and decision-making in the context of avoiding human bias?" First, decisions can be made by using specific techniques that involve the judgment and influence of many people, rather than just one individual. A classic case of this would be the way the President makes critical decisions that relate to important national issues. The Joint Chiefs of Staff report, inform and often counsel him on some of the most complex decisions he faces. This process allows him to receive varying points of view and a range of information before he makes his final judgment. The process does not necessarily guarantee success in his decision-making, but it does reduce the chance of any bias he may hold toward the problem at hand.

The second, and possibly the most influential, method is the use of technology in the problem-solving and decision-making process. As previously discussed, technology allows leaders to acquire and evaluate information to gain a better understanding of problems. Not only can technology help to identify problems, but it can facilitate compilation of accurate and up-to-date information that significantly reduces bias and improves the process of making important decisions. Therefore, it is clearly in the leaders' best interests to embrace and seek out technologies which aid performance and increase competitiveness.

9.3 Decision-Making and Opportunity Cost

Opportunity cost is the cost of a foregone opportunity—that is, the benefits that could have been had from that opportunity. For example, I have one hour to spare before I need to get to work. I could either mow the lawn or watch my favorite sports team on TV. I decide to watch TV. The opportunity cost is the benefit I could have accrued by mowing the lawn instead. This concept, in relation to the knowledge-power paradigm and decision-making, is crucial on a couple of different levels. Leaders face tough decisions every day that affect and determine the performance of departments and organizations. These decisions range from resource allocation to strategy formulation to recruitment. Decisions can easily be second guessed, and often are. Therefore, it is critical that leaders employ a strong decision-making process that ensures accurate information.

The first opportunity cost that leaders should consider is employing a formalized knowledge-management system, which allows for the gathering and evaluation of data on a regular basis to assist the leader within the problem solving and decision-making process. Table 9.2 outlines the advantages and disadvantages of employing a knowledge-management system.

Noticeably, the advantages outweigh the disadvantages from the information shown in table 9.2. Just like in any decision-making process, options should be carefully considered; traditionally, disadvantages have been a big factor for leaders who have not implemented knowledge-management systems. For example, we discussed the importance of knowledge management to Mayer Amschel Rothschild in the last chapter. His wealth and success were due largely to the intricate network of information he had gleaned from various sources across Europe. This informational network was his competitive advantage, even though it was costly and extremely labor intensive. In modern business, as recently as ten years ago, only large organizations could afford to employ incredibly sophisticated knowledge-management and communication systems. These organizations benefited from the same principles that Rothschild benefited from and enjoyed. This in effect reduced the effect of opportunity cost.

For small organizations, the cost implications, while greatly reduced, may still be prohibitive, as resources cannot match those of larger organizations. Knowledge-management systems for leaders of small organizations were, until very recently, still out of reach. In the last several years, however, that cost, coupled with advancements in technology, has significantly reduced the disadvantage barrier for small organizations. New technologies now allow small organizations to communicate more efficiently, at a reduced cost, while affording effective knowledge-management practices, without being labor intensive.

ADVANTAGES	DISADVANTAGES
• Steady stream of information and knowledge about processes, performance and business environment • Knowledge feedback loop assists in quality improvement • Accurate decision-making • Problem identification • Building of information and knowledge bank • Ability to monitor trends and patterns in what is being measured • Competitive advantage • Ability to respond quicker to problems • Pinpoint exact issues within process and performance • Fewer mistakes • Improved performance • Potential to increase customer satisfaction • Creates a barrier to entry	• Financial cost involved • Time taken to implement and manage • Inaccurate information

Table 9.2 - Advantages & Disadvantages of Knowledge-Management Systems

When I was young I would watch all of the James Bond movies. I enjoyed the action and adventure, and most of all I loved his cool gadgets. In the early movies he had a car phone and a global tracking device—very science fiction for that time period. Fast forward several decades, and mobile cell phones and GPS navigation devices are commonplace in our everyday lives. Sometimes I wonder how we managed without mobile phones; we are totally dependent upon them. These types of technologies have changed the way organizations operate and the way we work, and in many cases helped businesses to be more productive. In the same manner, things that seemed well out of reach for small organizations ten years ago have become a technological reality from an informational, data gathering, and evaluation perspective. Therefore, many of the disadvantages outlined in the previous table do not necessarily exist or apply to organizations. Leaders who recognize and embrace technology-based systems to assist their knowledge-management needs are thriving. They are enjoying the benefits of having information and knowing exactly when problems arise. They have the comfort of making decisions and solving problems based on accurate information, which reduces the probability of making wrong decisions. Most importantly, technology is positively improving performance from a quality and financial perspective.

The second level of opportunity cost is associated with the actual results of business decisions. It can be argued that the probability of specific opportunity costs is greater than when effective knowledge-management systems are in place. Without good information and knowledge, the leader is limited to the very human biases that cause uncertainty and inaccuracies in decision-making. Furthermore, even when knowledge is available, human bias creeps in to create new opportunity costs. A good example of this is illustrated in the decisions made by leaders during the early days of the automotive industry. Henry Ford was a pioneer of motor vehicles and manufacturing assembly lines. His Ford Model T was produced between 1908 and 1927. The one factor which made Model T successful was its affordability to the masses. The Model T was a rugged and robust vehicle for its time, and it handled remarkably well on indifferent road conditions, many of them being dirt roads. Ford initially enjoyed an economic monopoly within the automobile industry, which he helped to create. But other manufacturers, like Chevrolet, had Ford well in their sights.

As the automobile industry developed, increased traffic spurred the need for better quality roads. Improvements in road quality came about because of a shift in consumer preference. The consumer had become more sophisticated and wanted luxury and performance from their automobiles. This knowledge was known to Ford, but he chose not to act upon what the consumer wanted. A willing and able Chevrolet Corporation did. The Chevrolet Corporation introduced the 'Classic Six,' which helped to erode away the Ford market share by simply listening to customers and developing products that met their needs, solving their problems, and fulfilling their desires. Eventually Ford relented, designing and building the Model A, which superseded the successful Model T. But it was too late. He had allowed Chevy to get a foothold in the market, and the rest was history.

History is littered with examples similar to Ford and Chevy. We can see the impact of having knowledge, making good decisions, and the effects of opportunity cost. If Ford had employed customer knowledge from a position of strength, the opportunity cost of making the decision of not developing a successor to the Model T may not have been so significant. That one decision cost Ford millions of dollars (billions in today's value), and it also opened the door for a rival to enter an industry he created and dominated. Mistakes similar to Ford's are still made today by leaders, resulting in varying degrees of opportunity cost. Some of these miscalculations are due to human error, some to not having enough information, and some to a combination of the two. Modern management thinking, mostly led by the quality improvement gurus, places a premium on knowledge management, thus tipping the scales of success by reducing opportunity cost in their favor. Furthermore, progressive leaders recognize the importance of these lessons and are investing in knowledge-management systems to assist in problem-solving and decision-making.

9.4 Barriers to Entry and Competitive Advantage

Barriers to entry are those factors that prevent others from entering a specific industry or market. While barriers to entry do not promote competition, they are the elements which organizations try to cultivate because of their true competitive advantage. The most common and broad barriers to entry are highlighted in table 9.3.

The list of barriers to entry is by no means comprehensive, but it does highlight the most common and well-known ones. Many, including economies of scale, regulations, investment and price, have existed since the days of the industrial revolution. In some industries these traditional barriers to entry have either eroded or even completely disappeared, due to advancements and changes to the business environment.

The last item on the list in table 9.3, information and knowledge, has come to the forefront during the last several decades. Information and knowledge is now viewed as a precious commodity in most industries: *"what I know, and you don't, makes me stronger and more successful."* While this is not a new barrier to entry, it has become an essential weapon in gaining a competitive advantage.

BARRIERS TO ENTRY
• **Regulations** - specifically governmental regulations and laws which prevent, or exclude, firms easily entering a market.
• **Patents** - a firm may hold a patent and a legal right that prevents other firms from copying a product or service.
• **Price & Economies of Scale** - some firms enjoy a lower cost of production or have greater resources to be able sell products at a significantly lower price, deterring others in entering a market.
• **Cost or Investment** - the sheer cost of entering certain markets prohibits many organizations.
• **Marketing** - according to some business experts this is one of only few long-term barriers to entry which exist today. Companies with effective and large marketing programs can prevent others easily entering their market.
• **R&D** - this is one form of knowledge and its cost often discourages firms from entering markets, a good example of this is the telecommunications industry.
• **Access to a Network or Channel** - firms that depend on selling via a large network or channel have a significant advantage over firms who do not have access to the same channels.
• **Information & Knowledge** - having information and knowledge which pertains to a particular market that others may not.

Table 9.3 - Common Barriers to Entry

The development of information and knowledge as a barrier to entry in American organizations has been parallel to that of significant developments in IT and communications. As technology and communications have advanced, so has the end product of that technology. The ability to acquire pertinent knowledge quickly results in a significant competitive advantage. Where organizations traditionally competed on price and economies, they now compete over knowledge and marketing. Not only are the new knowledge organizations managing their information and knowledge better, they are also placing a premium on recruiting more knowledgeable workers. We have established that possessing accurate information is not sufficient; the information must be in the hands of the people who know how best to use it in order to reap the benefits. Therefore, recruiting knowledgeable workers becomes one of the paramount aspects within knowledge management.

In September 2006, Patricia Dunn, Chairwoman at Hewlett-Packard

(HP)[2], underwent a criminal investigation concerning her alleged approval of wide-ranging physical and electronic surveillance of the company's board members. Dunn allegedly approved of this spying because it had become clear that critical information within HP was being leaked to an external source (CNET)[3], and the type of information being leaked could only have come from a fellow director. While the investigation and the debate into the ethics of corporate spying continue, this particular case underlines the key role information plays in organizational competitive advantage. The situation deteriorated so completely after an internal source leaked critical information, drastic measures were considered necessary. While this high-profile case has caught the eye of the media, occurrences of corporate spying (internal and external) is on the increase. Devices that make electronic spying easier are now widely available on the market, further highlighting the role of knowledge as a key competitive advantage.

Problem-solving and decision-making processes often determine the effectiveness of a leader. Knowledge-management systems play an essential role in aiding effective problem identification and resolution. They shed light on unknown factors that help organizations to understand issues and opportunities. The better a leader is at fully understanding a problem and opportunity, the better equipped he is to choose the right path.

Human bias is one obstacle to a successful knowledge-management system that leaders need to consider. Bias often can lead to inaccurate problem perception and ineffective decision-making. Associated with bias is the opportunity cost from (a) not employing a knowledge-management system, or (b) making decisions without accurate information. When knowledge management systems function effectively, they give organizations a barrier to entry, and thus a competitive advantage. This type of non-traditional barrier to entry has become more prevalent in our modern economy, largely due to advancements in the fields of IT and communications.

10

INDUSTRY STUDY: KNOWLEDGE MANAGEMENT IN HEALTHCARE

Knowledge must come through action; you can have no test which is not fanciful, save by trial.
- SOPHOCLES

So FAR WE HAVE REVIEWED various factors which determine the success of the knowledge-power paradigm. We have also reviewed technological and human elements that significantly impact the paradigm. At this point it's worthwhile for us to consider how a specific industry has developed, the issues it faces, and the extent to which the knowledge-power paradigm can influence it.

In this chapter we will take a closer look at the medical and healthcare industry. This industry is unique in many ways; it's an industry that is in constant flux, where advancements positively affect practices and the way people work. Furthermore, the medical industry in the U.S. has evolved into a highly litigious arena, so the work carried out has to be precise, especially when processing/transferring information. We will also explore some of the most pressing issues that medical offices face, and we will review applicable comparisons in the corporate world.

THE KNOWLEDGE-POWER PARADIGM

10.1 The Times Are A-Changin'

I have never had a time in my life when someone within my family was not a physician. My grandfather was a general practitioner, as are my sister and my brother-in-law. I'm also fortunate to have many friends and clients that are physicians, so my understanding of the industry is based on personal and professional experience. Growing up with a physician in the family was a wonderful luxury—knowing that someone was there to treat you when you were not well. I remember falling off a rusty old swing in our back yard in London and cutting myself. My grandfather was there to quickly administer a tetanus shot. I was also prone to catching colds, and he would always be there with the right medication. What a great comfort he was.

One thing that I always remember was the number of patients that my grandfather would visit at their homes. He would carry his small black medical bag with his instruments inside, and sometimes he would take my sister and me along. When we arrived at the patient's home, they would welcome us like old family friends, and frequently we would sit down and have a meal with them. I have very fond memories of my grandfather, and from what I gather he was an excellent physician with outstanding bedside manners. He was also a spiritual man who had a huge heart and genuinely cared for the well-being of people.

Memories of my grandfather as a physician stretch back more than 25 years; today when I look at relatives and friends who are physicians, I can see a major difference in the way things are done in healthcare. I'm not the only one to recall a doctor visiting patients' homes or even patients visiting the doctor's home. In reality, the healthcare industry has moved on, and the role of physicians and their staff has greatly changed. The healthcare industry has experienced a period of unprecedented technological advancement, during which breakthroughs in patient care have occurred in a relatively very short period of time. At the same time, healthcare has entered the realm of being business-focused, rather than just offering a service. Many physicians now recognize that not only do they need to perform well in their profession, but they also need to be smart entrepreneurs and leaders in the business sense. Finally, the impact of healthcare malpractice is something that all physicians have hanging over their heads at all times. Any mistake can prove costly—professionally and financially. Physicians put it all on the line each and every day of their careers.

Let's take a closer look at each of the three major factors that have impacted healthcare and explore the role that the knowledge-power paradigm plays within each of these areas:

Technological Advancements: This category is by far the largest contributor to change in healthcare over the last 50 years. Centuries ago, progress in healthcare came from advancements in our own knowledge of the human body and medicine, and while this continues to be true, today that progress is catapulted by huge advancements in technology. Technological advancements have not been limited to any specific branch of healthcare; they have affected every field in varying degrees. For example, MRI machines offer physicians diagnostic imaging for practically any part of the body, allowing for accurate patient diagnosis and treatment. While basic MRI technology has been around since the 1960s and '70s, its widespread use did not take effect until the '90s. Now MRI technology is an everyday occurrence benefiting hundreds of thousands of patients every year. Additional advancements in the imaging arena are breaking ground with the latest wave of PET/CT machines and software that offers breathtaking imagery, enabling physicians to better diagnose and treat medical problems.

Along with advancements in medical technology, we now see progress in the fields of software, IT, and communications. These advances have widespread implications for all types of businesses, and also for the business of healthcare. Walking into a regular physician's office five or ten years ago, you would likely see huge secure filing cabinets containing folder after folder of patient medical records—time-consuming and bureaucratic to keep updated. Indeed, this is still the case for many hospitals and physicians' offices. But thousands of healthcare facilities are now moving to electronic medical records (EMR). This technology allows for easy access and storage of files including patient data, clinical notes, prescriptions, and electronic scheduling, to name but a few. Additionally, computerized scheduling and billing streamlines these functions. Healthcare facilities also are benefiting from improvements in telecommunications, as physicians and support staff are communicating vital information more efficiently and with far greater accuracy.

Insurance: Medical insurance companies exert a huge influence over the healthcare industry because they make the payments on behalf of their

THE KNOWLEDGE-POWER PARADIGM

members, i.e. the patients. Going back 10 or 20 years, the medical insurance industry had just a handful of players offering basic insurance plans. Today, insurance companies provide coverage to millions of people, offering them a broad suite of products to meet varying needs and incomes. Furthermore, there are a multitude of medical insurance companies that fit into three tiers in relation to size: small, medium and large. While the large providers such as BlueCross BlueShield, United, and Aetna dominate the industry, there are many small providers that serve regional areas in the U.S.

Therefore, for the physician, both patients and medical insurance companies end up being clients. The reality of free-market economics dictates that insurance providers are 'for-profit' organizations, and because they control some very large purse strings, they tend to wield a lot of power regarding how things get done in the industry. Each medical insurance provider sets the ground rules for procedure payout, billing requirements, authorization, and payment terms. Additionally, they dictate which physicians are 'in-network' and 'out-of-network,' thus influencing where their members go and what the physicians are paid. Many physicians believe that, on average, they see more patients now than ever before. Average insurance payouts per patient have fallen over the years, and physicians are increasing their number of consultations per day and working longer hours, while attempting to keep quality levels high. It's a natural response from physicians in order to maintain a level of income to which they are accustomed. According to the *Medical Malpractice Briefing Book*, published by Public Citizen, Congress Watch (2004):

"*Doctors across the country have seen their fees slashed in recent years as managed care companies tried to increase profits, and government programs, such as Medicare and Medicaid, tried to cut costs. Medicare reimbursement rates no longer come close to keeping pace with increases in doctor's practice expenses. The American Medical Association (AMA) estimates, that since 1991 physician practice costs have risen by 35 percent, but Medicare payments have risen only 10 percent...practice costs have risen two-and-a-half times the rate of Medicare payments.*[1]"

As a result, the many physicians with whom I have spoken admit to being far more time-conscious; they can run significantly behind schedule if they aren't. Furthermore, business principles dictate that the greater the output, the greater the number of errors. This clearly stands to reason, as the probability of errors increases with volume. Some argue that this same principle is applicable to healthcare, and that there are consequences to this growing trend.

Physicians must set very high standards for themselves; they do not have much of a choice, because mistakes can lead to serious consequences. If physicians are seeing more patients in order to maintain income levels, then they also have to maintain high quality levels while 'processing' an increased volume of patients. Speaking to physicians is one thing, but I also have spent extensive time in various doctor's offices, and I can confirm that many are often crammed with people waiting to see the physician. A patient's wait time can range from 15 to 45 minutes, even with an appointment. Thus 'time' has become a precious commodity for doctors and their support staff. Practices are often overloaded with patients and administrative tasks, creating a work environment that is intense and highly pressured—while still having to maintain accuracy.

Tort: Physicians pay millions of dollars in medical malpractice insurance every year. The average annual malpractice premium for physicians over the last 30 years has risen[2] steadily—a direct correlation to the number of malpractice suits filed during that time, though malpractice payouts have dropped in recent years. We live in highly litigious times, and the thought of a lawsuit is the kind of worry that can keep a physician awake at night. Warranted lawsuits for physician negligence, however, are in place to protect patients.

This is the reality of modern healthcare, and there are a couple of by-products. First, there is a perceived rise in 'defensive medicine,'[3] i.e. medical diagnosis and procedures conducted to protect the physician from malpractice liability. An example of 'defensive medicine' is a physician who makes and stores copious notes on each patient, detailing everything carefully. She will inform her patients, verbally and in writing, when specific instructions have not been followed. Although this does not reduce the quality of care given to the patient, it does change the way the physician naturally approaches their patient.

Secondly, physicians have fought vigorously for changes in tort law, pushing for 'tort reform.' A contentious subject, socially and politically, tort reform advocates regulation on a state and federal level to protect

THE KNOWLEDGE-POWER PARADIGM

physicians against frivolous lawsuits. Reform opponents argue that tort reform takes away claimants' rights to have their day in court. In a medical malpractice case, the plaintiff must prove each of the following: (1) a duty was owed by the defendant, (2) the duty owed was violated, (3) the violation of duty resulted in an injury, and (4) substantiated damages as a result. While the judicial system is clearly not broken with regards to medical malpractice, each side of the reform debate disagrees on how to regulate what gets to court and what does not. Physicians also claim that if a lawsuit is brought against them, and they successfully defend it, the fact that a lawsuit is on their record is unsatisfactory. Additionally, there are often cases in which the malpractice insurance company will settle the lawsuit against the wishes of the physician. This is often purely a business decision on the malpractice insurance company's part, as the legal cost may exceed that of the settlement being paid out. On a business level it's a rational course of action, but for a physician it's an issue of integrity and reputation—and definitely not something one would want on his or her record.

The aforementioned examples outline three major influences that have had an impact on the healthcare industry over the last couple of decades. We will revisit each of these influences later in the chapter. We will also discuss how the knowledge-power paradigm and knowledge management systems help physicians and healthcare facilities improve efficiency, performance, and reduce liability—regardless of healthcare facility size.

10.2 Lessons From Corporate America

The one constant that is applicable to organizations across all industries is change. There are few industries that have not experienced radical change over time; some have experienced great change, while for others it has been moderate. In healthcare the rate has been medium to high, depending on the field in question. And if a glimpse of the future, through the promise of nanotechnology, is anything to go by, then the rate of change is unlikely to ease. We discussed the major influences on the healthcare industry and the effects of these influences in the last section. From 30,000 feet, what we see in the last 20 to 30 years is a shift in the way we view healthcare, from primarily a service industry to a service-oriented, highly specialized business. Fundamentally, the factors stated in the previous section have resulted in physicians being required to perform as medical experts, and also as leaders and entrepreneurs. Some physicians have consciously recognized this and have made the leap from being solely a physician to developing their business skills and acumen, understanding business principles, and being good leaders of people. Conversely, there are many who have yet to fully make that required shift, with the aim of attaining full potential as modern physician/business leader.

This point is highlighted by a sharp increase in the number of doctors who are going on to complete their MBAs after medical school. According to a *USA Today* article in July 2002, more and more doctors are recognizing that healthcare is a business, and "that the bean counters are taking over, physicians are embracing the enemy: They're becoming MBAs."[4] The exact reasons why they are completing MBAs is varied, but the overriding rationale seems to be that they are "hoping to change what they say is a health system spiraling out of control."

Studies conducted by the *American Medical Association* (AMA) highlight this opinion; since 1997, the number of medical schools offering joint MD/MBA programs has increased from 28 to more than 36 schools. Furthermore, schools such as *Johns Hopkins, Tulane, Carnegie Mellon* and the *University of California* offer other specialized MBA and business courses tailored specifically for doctors and healthcare professionals.

These business courses contain syllabuses often found in regular MBA courses including finance, accounting, economics, and management theory. But MD/MBA courses also focus on the application of business theory, i.e. the ability to put essential business tenets into practice in healthcare.

On the flip side, according to *USA Today*, "the number of physician-executives with MBA degrees is still small, but it's rising. Since 1999, those reporting they have MBAs has risen 23%, according to an annual survey of 12,000 physician-executives by *Cejka & Company* in St. Louis, a healthcare recruiting firm."[4] Studies by *Cejka & Company*[4] show 16% of the physicians surveyed had an MBA, but since then (2002) the figures have increased as more MDs have acquired MBAs after completing medical school.

Doctors are starting to adjust and assume this new role, recognizing that being a good physician is not enough. They know that they need to understand business, leadership, finance and management, because changes in healthcare dictate which doctors advance and which doctors stagnate. Whether they want to understand and speak the same language as medical administrators and be part of the healthcare decision-making process, or

THE KNOWLEDGE-POWER PARADIGM

they just want to be more competitive in the healthcare business, it's the classic scenario of survival of the fittest: The ones who best adapt to a changing environment are more likely to succeed.

So, what are the lessons that can be learned from the world of corporate business? And how can they be applied to the world of medicine and healthcare? In reality there are too many lessons to cover in this book alone, but we can outline several categories that tie in with the knowledge-power paradigm.

So far we have discussed the paramount importance of time, cost, quality of service, communication and decision-making in the field of modern healthcare. Let's take a step back and reflect on modern businesses, per se. What we notice is a similarity between factors that are important to traditional businesses and factors that are important to the business of healthcare. Once healthcare organizations started seeing themselves as businesses, the convergence of factors that dominate the business landscape was largely inevitable. As a result, strategic thinking and business operation practices have become applicable to the healthcare industry.

To help us break down and grasp how the knowledge-power paradigm can help physicians, we will explore three distinct and specific categories: business process reengineering, quality improvement and decision-making, and communication. These categories were explored earlier in the book, but we will discuss them within the context of healthcare and how physicians can greatly benefit from the knowledge-power paradigm.

10.2.1 Business Process Reengineering (BPR)

BPR is the practice of reviewing business processes, identifying inefficiencies, and 'reengineering' them to attain improved results through better efficiencies. BPR has been attributed largely to Frederick Taylor's 'time and motion' studies from the early 20th century. Another well-known example of BPR is the assembly-line process employed by Henry Ford for the production of the Model T. BPR reengineered existing industrial assembly processes and set up a platform that allowed for the Model T to be produced, en masse, for the developing automobile market. Since the Ford assembly line, BPR has developed as a discipline across many industries, solving inefficiencies, improving quality, and saving time and money.

Healthcare practices consist of hundreds of thousands of processes, many of which have started to embrace BPR to reap the benefits attained by organizations in other industries. Inefficient business processes often result in a loss in productivity and business performance. This also holds true in healthcare, where there is a more worrisome outcome: reduced patient care and safety. A physician's primary concern is the well-being of the patient, and the business must come second.

For physicians, who are also leaders, it's critical to review some of the most important business processes within the workplace. What is the objective of each process? How can the process be improved? Can technology help? Will reengineering the process improve the quality of service, save time, and reduce overhead costs? These are all valid questions to ask when embarking on a BPR study. The study itself does not necessarily have to take up much time, especially if the physician has a good handle on how the process is functioning.

Let us take a close look at a common process that is found in all general practitioners' offices and many medical facilities: the process of ordering a diagnostic image for a patient. There are several ways doctor's offices can handle this process; the most common method is illustrated in figure 10.1. The process is not complex, but it contains inefficiencies, the potential for huge liability, low quality service, excessive time consumption, and limited information and knowledge on the physician's part. Let us cycle though the process and see what conclusions we can draw. After a doctor determines that her patient requires a diagnostic imaging test (e.g. an MRI, CT scan, x-ray, etc.), she will likely fill out a basic script for the patient and sign it off. This script is often given to back-office staff who will complete the paperwork with the patient. The back-office staff will give the patient instructions, identify appropriate imaging centers, perhaps give an imaging center a call to set an appointment for the patient (even though this is not always the case), give the script to the patient, and fax the script to the imaging center. Whether or not the physician's office schedules a test, the onus is on the patient to get the test completed. The imaging center will then send the test report and the film to the physician's office. The physician is required to review the report, sign it off, and notify the patient of the results. The report forms part of the diagnostic process that helps the physician to determine the next course of action, which may include a request for further tests.

The process in figure 10.1 is typically completed in hard-copy format, with little or no use of technology. Highlighted below are some of the

THE KNOWLEDGE-POWER PARADIGM

issues involved with the process, along with some questions physicians should ask themselves:

- What records are kept regarding the number of scripts written within certain time periods, e.g. weekly, monthly, quarterly and annually?
- Does the office keep track of which imaging centers receive scripts?
- Of the scripts written, how many require authorization?
- Are the scripts easy to read, and are all the fields correctly filled out?
- How much time does it take to process and place orders and authorize requests?
- Is the physician's office doing all it can to offer quality service by placing the order for the patient and giving all the necessary preparation information?

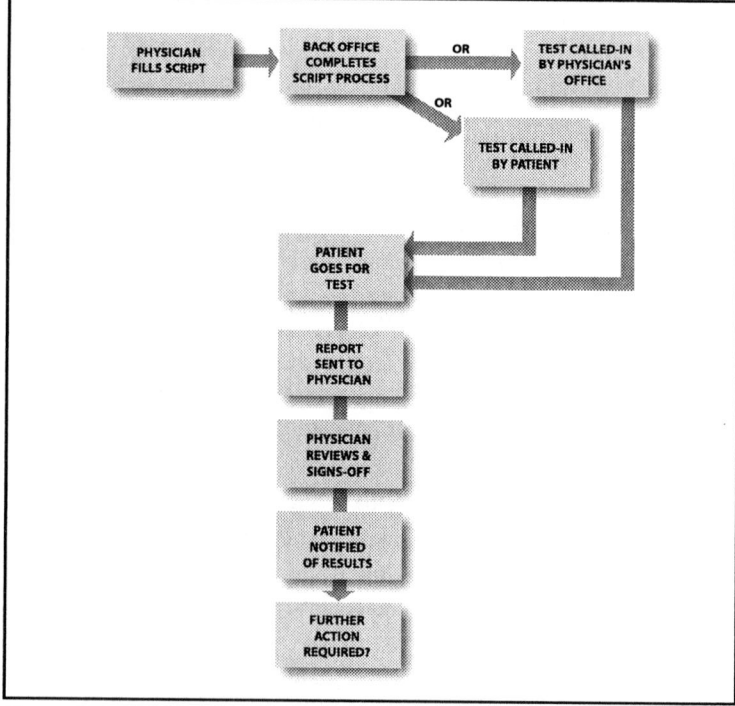

Figure 10.1 - A Common Diagnostic Imaging Ordering Process

- *Have all reports for requested patient scans been received? How many are outstanding?*

- *Does the patient know what to do next and what prep is required?*

- *Has the imaging center been notified of the order?*

- *Has the physician reviewed and signed-off all the reports which have been returned?*

- *How much time does the back-office staff spend identifying ICD-9 & CPT codes?*

- *Is basic scripting information easy to retrieve? For example, where have patients been sent and how many scripts have been referred?*

- *What early warning system alerts the physician of an incomplete stage within this critical process?*

When reviewing this process, one must ask: Can the process be improved and streamlined? Which inefficiencies can be reduced? What are the liability points? How can we improve the quality of service offered to patients and imaging centers? What can we do to reduce the time it takes to cycle the process? How can information flow to the physician and the back-office staff be improved for measuring and monitoring purposes?

The process can definitely be streamlined with the aid of technology, and without making any radical changes to the process itself. Software can act as the main hub, automating the ordering and information/knowledge bank. Here are the ways the physician can benefit from a semi-automated, software-driven process:

1. Time Savings: Automated software can save the back-office staff in processing diagnostic imaging orders, as well as in processing authorization requests. Software also can save the patient time, as the electronic processing will automatically place the imaging order, thus leaving the onus on the radiology group to call the patient and set an appointment. The process in figure 10.1 highlights potentially huge time lags when the order is not placed by the physician's office, and the responsibility is left on the patient to call in the order and set an appointment. Putting this obligation in the patient's hands can lead to a protracted period between when the script is written and when the test is completed. If the order is placed immediately, the time lag is reduced. This allows physicians to diagnose ailments and complete their billing quickly and efficiently. Medical facilities and physician's offices spend considerable time finding ICD-9 and CPT codes for tests. With an automated system, the search time can be reduced or even erased, giving back-office staff more time to dedicate to other pressing matters.

2. Improved Communication: Essential information can be communicated to various parties involved within the process. Software can collect and communicate a patient's preferred appointment date and time, allowing the imaging center to reference its schedule to check for availability prior to calling the patient to set an appointment. By electronically placing the order by fax and e-mail, the physician's office immediately notifies the imaging center of the very information it needs to handle and process the test efficiently.

3. Knowledge & Information: Further into the process, the physician can query the software to find out how many tests have been ordered (by modality and physician), how many have resulted in returned reports, how many reports have been reviewed and signed-off, and how many patients have been notified of the test results. With only a few mouse clicks, the software system can produce information on any variable being collected. Such information in the right hands can lead to improved problem-detection and decision-making.

4. Reduce Liability: The inherent liability within this process can be significant for the physician. For example, if the physician requests that a patient complete a diagnostic imaging test but fails to act in 'good faith and with due regard,' he can be held liable. This can easily occur if the report for an ordered test is not received or goes unchecked, and the patient happens to have a positive diagnosis. Cases involving this exact scenario have been brought against physicians and healthcare facilities. Many lawsuits do not even reach the courtroom, as the physician and healthcare facility settle out of court for significant sums. If physicians and healthcare facilities do not keep track of how many tests have been ordered, how do they know whether the reports have been received, reviewed, and communicated to the patient? A software system that tracks each and every order would help to significantly reduce such liable risks. As an aside, all states have their own statutes and constitutions for this very issue; Florida's states the following:

"Chapter 766 - Medical Malpractice And Related Matters (766.102 Medical Negligence; standards of recovery; expert witness)
(4) The legislature is cognizant of the changing trends and techniques for the delivery of health care in this state and the discretion that is inherent in the diagnosis, care, and treatment of patients by different health care providers. The failure of a health care provider to order, perform, or administer supplemental diagnostic tests shall not be actionable if the health care provider acted in good faith and with due regard for the prevailing professional standard of care."[5]

While I am not a lawyer, the aforementioned statute seems pretty open to debate when it comes to acting properly in 'good faith and with due regard.' It can easily leave the door open to lawsuits. But with the correct use of software technology, plaintiffs will have a far more difficult time proving that the physician or medical facility has been negligent.

5. Quality Improvement: Through process reengineering and with the use of software technology, quality improvement can be viewed in internal and external terms. Internally, physicians save significant time in the completion of the process, improving communication with imaging centers and making vital information available to the process owner. Externally, physicians offer a better service to their patients by placing orders for them, getting them tested quicker, and successfully tracking each vital test from the very start to the finish.

10.2.2 Decision-Making and Quality Improvement

In Chapter 6, we discussed the knowledge-power success model, and concluded that knowledge management is a critical factor within the decision-making and quality-improvement aspect of business. Information and knowledge forms the basis upon which good decision-making and quality improvement is built. In the last example, the use of technology highlighted how improvements in process can lead to all-around quality improvement within certain areas of healthcare practice. The Six Sigma process is similar, in that it advocates iterative cycles for continuous improvement within a defined process, built on measuring, monitoring, and

THE KNOWLEDGE-POWER PARADIGM

using information.

Many businesses place a premium on collecting customer experience data; it is the ultimate acid test when measuring product and service performance. Knowing what your customers think about their experience of your product and service is priceless, as it opens the door to understanding how they see things and allows for adjustments to improve and develop. Many businesses in corporate America recognize the power of this type of competitive advantage and therefore put a premium on gathering and analyzing such data.

If principles from corporate business and the business of medicine are convergent, then this logically should be important to physicians. Many physicians collect data through surveys for patient experience. But if a practice sees hundreds of patients a week, it may be impractical to collate the surveys in a form that can easily be evaluated. I have interviewed many doctors regarding this topic, and those who did conduct surveys admitted either to ignoring the data collected after a while or just skimming through a small sample every so often. If knowledge-management processes are dependent on successfully collecting and evaluating data, then there is significant breakdown in this effort. Essentially, physicians who collect data have good intentions, but their execution virtually puts them in the same boat as the physicians who do not bother to poll their patients.

Healthcare facilities also collect data on patient experiences to identify certain areas that potentially lead to lawsuits. Examples of such questions relate to physician demeanor or the amount of time the physician spent with the patient. This type of data relates to targets that need to be met in the hope of monitoring liability and reducing risk.

Many healthcare facilities survey patient experience via questionnaires sent in the mail or by phone. These are traditional methods used by large hospitals, but there are specific drawbacks associated with these methods. Firstly, statisticians will tell you that the larger the survey poll, the less the standard error, i.e. improved accuracy of results. Surveys conducted by mail and phone tend to have very low response rates; hence, the validity and accuracy of the data is questioned. Secondly, both these methods are relatively expensive processes that cost tens of thousands of dollars a year. Finally, the information gathered has a significant time-lag between event, data collection, and evaluation. By the time the patient fills out the survey, returns it, and the healthcare facility has an opportunity to evaluate the data, the time-lag totals weeks and months. Therefore, a healthcare facility could have a serious problem that it's not aware of, because of the process it employs. Furthermore, if data is not collected continuously but is sampled at intervals, it can offer only snapshots of reality. This is not an ideal scenario, as it gives rise to inaccuracies that negatively impact the ability to make good decisions.

How can physicians and healthcare facilities develop their decision-making and quality improvement through such methods? Follow the rules of the knowledge-power paradigm: the right information, at the right time, to the right person who can use it to make necessary adjustments. Progressive organizations have advanced from basic survey techniques, abandoning traditional survey and information-gathering methods such as mail and phone. They employ technology that meets the basic requirements of the knowledge-power paradigm and gives them incredibly accurate, real-time information, with access for managers to make informed decisions and improve quality. Physicians who are serious about quality improvement and advanced decision-making capabilities should investigate these technological options and follow the lead of corporate businesses from other industries.

10.2.3 Communication

In Section I of the book, we paid special attention to the importance of effective, efficient, and meaningful communication within the knowledge-power paradigm. Communication of data and information is the oil in the engine of the paradigm; without it the paradigm becomes inefficient. Communication in the field of medicine has improved dramatically in the last 15 years, as it has in all industries. The two examples typify how technology helps to communicate vital information to parties that require it. It allows for time savings, quality improvements and decision-making, and superior performance.

The three specific, and most recent, communication mediums which have had the greatest impact are e-mail, the worldwide web (WWW), and mobile telecommunications. Never before has information been communicated and transferred as quickly as it is today. The healthcare field is littered with processes in which information constantly needs to be communicated from place to place.

Hardware technology, such as computers, servers, and telephone systems, are critical to this process. But the creativity in the software is what drives the hardware. The design of software is critical in the field of communication, because while software helps us to automate menial and inefficient tasks, it does not necessarily help to improve productivity. Productivity is measured through the ratio between input and output: the higher the output (in relation to input), the greater the productivity. When the first word-processing software became commonplace in corporate America in the early 1990s, many people predicted a significant increase in productivity—because the software was more efficient, easier to use, and more versatile than the traditional typewriter and plain old hand-writing. Productivity results did not reflect any significant upturn for years, however. Why? It is widely assumed that even though word-processing packages had the potential to improve productivity, the people using them spent the time they saved 'jazzing up' their documents! Earned productivity was redirected into tasks that never previously existed. Fundamentally, if software is the key to improved communication, knowledge attainment, and productivity, then software reduces input and significantly increases output, thus increasing efficiencies and performance.

In summary, the healthcare industry has experienced some very significant changes in the last three decades, and that rate of change is unlikely to let up anytime soon. The most dramatic change, besides improvements in medical technology and knowledge, is the shift toward adopting business principles and thinking. It's not enough for physicians to perform well in their area of expertise; today they are required to be savvy business leaders, decision-makers, and entrepreneurs. This shift is largely attributed to insurance companies, tort, and changes in technological advancement. In response, physicians and healthcare organizations should thoroughly embrace business principles and lessons from the corporate world. The knowledge-power paradigm works in the corporate world and is essential to the healthcare industry. But physicians and administrators must have the vision, understanding, and courage to make the necessary shift.

PART III:
THE KNOWLEDGE-POWER PARADIGM IN PRACTICE

11

THE CHANGING ROLE OF TECHNOLOGY IN KNOWLEDGE MANAGEMENT

Who the hell wants to hear actors talk?
- H.M. WARNER

I think there is a world market for maybe five computers.
- THOMAS WATSON (IBM, 1943)

TECHNOLOGY, WITHOUT A DOUBT, is the single biggest catalyst in helping organizations benefit from the knowledge-power paradigm. In the last several decades it has been nothing short of staggering how adept we've become at gathering and evaluating large quantities of data to glean information. Technology has changed the fundamental way organizations work and function on virtually every level and in every industry. Advancement and progress isn't going to let up, and organizations who embrace the benefits are the ones who will continually rise to the top, regardless of organization size.

In this chapter we are going to explore the development of modern technology, the essential role it plays in the knowledge-power paradigm, and the human impact of technology. We will outline how organizations, by understanding technology, realizing its full potential, and effectively leveraging benefits, go from being good to being great. But technology itself cannot operate in a vacuum. For it to be fully effective requires open-minded leadership that is understanding of its value. We will also discuss other human-technology considerations, and outline various types of leadership mindset barriers that need to be overcome for technology to be beneficial.

11.1 Technology, Knowledge, and Power

You could easily put forward a strong case that "technology is power." Throughout history, this has been the case. Prehistoric humans who had effective implements for hunting, farming, and survival techniques were the ones that survived and thrived. The Roman Empire was built largely on the ability to leverage technology to conquer and occupy. In that era, technology was based upon superior knowledge of machines, roads, aqueducts, sanitation, military skills, and science. Technology helped the Romans to advance building projects, further their militaristic ambitions, improve farming techniques, expand shipping trade, and develop printed communication.

The old saying, "*All roads lead to Rome,*" is tribute to their ability to build roads from within their epicenter for militaristic and commercial deployments. The road network was the technology that allowed speedy transportation to various corners of the empire; today, speed of deployment remains a major factor in all modern military endeavors. Aqueducts provided water vital for Roman industry, and sanitation kept the spread of diseases in check. The Roman army was the most technologically superior army of its time. Their machines and apparatus were the tools that helped to conquer many nations and allowed the empire to thrive from the resources of those nations. Finally, scientific, engineering, and mathematical knowledge helped to advance all of the aforementioned technologies.

Looking back, we can trace a technological pattern from century to century, proving that the most technologically superior society/nation wielded a significant sphere of influence. During the Cold War, the superpowers, the U.S. and the former Soviet Union, influenced world events with their ability to wage war through having a technological edge over other nations. This position was attained through development and accumulation of militaristic, industrial, and economic technology. The sphere of influence encompassed the entire world, rather than being limited to reachable nations. In the case of the U.S. and the former Soviet Union, the push for technology was influenced by ideological differences, i.e. communism vs. democracy. The fall of the Soviet Union in the late 1980s and early '90s left the U.S. as the only recognized superpower. The absence of that rivalry has created a vacuum, in which other nations now aspire to become superpowers.

Today, countries like China and India are tipped to be the nations likely to step into the role of superpower. Both countries have all the necessary ingredients: militaristic power, a strong economy and labor force, a broad industrial base, and a thriving technological base. Large and small U.S.-based companies have invested significantly in operations in both these countries. In India alone you will find the likes of Microsoft, IBM, Citigroup, Intel, General Electric, and Motorola, to name but a few, all of which employ hundreds of thousand of skilled workers. The economic boom within these nations was based on the premise of low-cost labor. India, as the largest English-speaking nation in the world, was an attractive off-shore solution for American companies. But after dipping their toes into the water, these large companies found an untapped labor force with significant 'brain power' to innovate and accelerate technological development. In fact, since the opening-up of India's economy, there have been many domestic Indian companies that have recruited talent from within the U.S. labor pool as transfers to India—a reverse 'brain drain.' Therefore, superpower ambition is essentially rooted in the potential of knowledge and its ability to advance technology. These countries possess the essential raw ingredients, as did post-war America and Russia, and those ingredients are fueling the technological revolution, pushing them higher on the global stage.

If "knowledge is power" is true, then "technology is power" is also true in macro terms. But how do technology and knowledge relate to each other, and can the same concept apply in micro terms? Knowledge is a function of technology; all technological breakthroughs are entrenched in the ability to know, i.e. knowledge leading to technology. For example, the modern personal computer is a breakthrough in scientific, mathematical, and electronic engineering knowledge. Without these different fields coming together, the modern computer could not have been developed. The same principle can be applied to space rockets, in which mathematical, scientific, and engineering knowledge came together to achieve space flight. Therefore, if knowledge leads to technology, and "technology is power," then "knowledge is power"! This brings us back, full circle, to the knowledge-power paradigm.

We have discussed the knowledge-power paradigm on a macro level from the Roman Empire to modern superpower nations, but does the paradigm apply on a micro level within modern organizations? If an organization is technologically superior, is it necessarily more likely to be more successful and powerful? There are plenty of technological innovations out there, and while most have amazing functionality, it does not necessarily follow that an organization will gain a competitive edge. Technology can give organizations a significant edge (power) if, and only if, it's applied properly. By the term "*apply properly,*" we mean that technology must give organizations a basis for improvement in specific ways, i.e. productivity, quality, reduced costs, increased revenue, and the ability to improve marketing efforts or save process time. Essentially, productivity is a function of output as a result of input. As we cited in the last chapter, it was widely anticipated that the initial application of PC software would herald a significant increase in white-collar productivity. But that increase did not initially materialize, because the assumption did not take into consideration gains being used up with new processes associated with the technology.

Average U.S. productivity growth between 1974 and 1994 was essentially a flat line[1]. Since 1994, productivity growth has seen two major shifts upward. These shifts have predominantly been attributed to technological advancements, through hardware and software improvements. While there was no productivity gain during the first wave of the modern technological boom of the late 1980s and early 1990s, there was a significant shift after that era. Why did this happen? The productivity growth was a result of improved understanding of how to use new technology, along with improvements in technology design which dovetailed with processes within organizations. Leaders, over a short period of time, were able to get a better understanding of how technology could be applied to improve organizational performance, and they made the necessary adjustments.

When technology is applied correctly, it gives rise to improved performance on a micro organizational level. Organizations who are adept at understanding processes and technology potential can marry the two to significantly impact performance, i.e. productivity. But the process requires a proficient understanding of skillful leadership and management. Leaders who recognize opportunities and have the vision and desire to improve performance through technology can succeed.

11.2 Technology's Impact on Information and Communication, and What it Means for Private and Governmental Organizations

Knowledge management is a double-sided coin. For it to be valuable, organizations must be adept at managing both sides of the coin. The first side is data-gathering, and the flip side is data-evaluation. With the emergence of information technology, our ability to collect data has increased exponentially. For years, organizations have been buying and collecting data to help gain an edge and increase effectiveness in attaining goals.

Since the events of September 11, 2001, the government has established counter-terrorism as the nation's top priority. As early as September 15, 2001, President Bush proclaimed, "Victory against terrorism will not take place in a single battle, but in a series of decisive actions against terrorist organizations and those who harbor and support them."[2] One of the "decisive actions" is greater understanding through intelligence (knowledge) about terrorist operatives. It's commonly understood that terrorists have intricate, international networks which use the Internet to communicate. This new war, just like previous wars, has resulted in the advancement of innovation. One of the most controversial government policies to emerge in this era is the surveillance of e-mail and telephone communications of U.S. citizens. For our purposes, we will not debate the constitutional ethics of the policy; instead, we will touch upon the ethos behind the policy.

The government has developed software that can data-mine millions upon millions of e-mails, Internet actions, and telephone calls.[3] The platform upon which each of these technologies is built is digital, thus allowing for monitoring through sophisticated software. Essentially, the software collects and monitors a large volume of data to produce potential leads.

While the effectiveness of such technology in tracking down terror suspects is classified, what is known is how would-be terrorists in 2006 were intercepted by British intelligence before they carried out the probable bombing of commercial airliners with liquid explosives. British intelligence monitored the suspects for weeks, using tactics that included tapping their Internet and e-mail communications; law enforcement initiated arrests when the terror suspects started to browse airline tickets online. Therefore, one of the battlegrounds in this new century is capturing and analyzing digital information. This particular case highlights its importance to the intelligence community.

Another such area that has benefited by knowledge-management is the ground war employed by the Republicans and Democrats. It is sometimes said that "politics is business," and since the general election of 2000 the Republican party has been credited with a 'ground game' strategy superior to their compatriots', the Democrats. The ethos of a good 'ground game' policy is to reach out to as many individuals on a local level as possible, to connect with them, and to establish commonality in the hope that they will turn out and vote their support at election time. The 'ground game' employed by the Republican party is incredibly strategic and complex, employing sophisticated knowledge-management systems. The strategy is no different than that employed by organizations in private industry: Know your customer, develop products that match their requirements, and then effectively communicate these attributes to generate business. Part of Republican 'ground game' strategy is the ability to have maximum information about individual citizens living in key states around the country.

What kind of information are they looking for and what do they do with it? To help us understand how this works, we need to take a step back and understand how the data is acquired. There are organizations in the private sector that keep tabs on individual transactions, from what we buy, to what we read, where we go, and what our preferences happen to be. This is achieved through technologies that monitor electronic paper trails and surveys—for example, to qualify for special offers and services, we fill out forms containing questions about our hobbies, lifestyles, food preferences, drinking habits, etc. Once this data is collected, it's made available to external organizations for purchase. Data is also available directly through purchases we make, from consumables to household goods. Essentially, the data industry's product is information, and the industry is knowledge.

After acquiring the information, organizations (like political parties) apply it to sophisticated databases, running software programs which evaluate millions of bits of data to map individual profiles by geography. These profiles are sorted into categories within which individuals are segmented. Based upon the type of goods you buy, the things you read, the places you go and the television programs you watch, the information can infer your political inclination. Such profile categories are often accurate, and organizations frequently base decisions and strategies upon this type of information. This method of data collection and evaluation is known as *"micro-targeting."*[4]

Micro-targeting databases can indicate the percentage of a population within a geographic region that happens to place the tax agenda high on their priority list. Having such knowledge allows the political party to target this group directly with communication related to the topic. What is communicated and how it is communicated must then be decided. Multiply this knowledge machine by key districts, and you have a very powerful strategic tool.

The knowledge-management system employed by political parties is hardly breaking new ground; organizations in private-sector industries have been using similar methods to gather and process information for years. What is important to point out, however, is that billions of dollars would not be spent annually on such systems unless they yielded success. For leaders in small organizations, this essentially means two things:

1. Technology which assists in knowledge-management processes already exists.

2. The methods that have been employed reflect a road map for success.

Leaders not currently employing knowledge-management tools must make a shift in their strategic thinking, so that they can understand these methods in greater detail.

The final aspect we will cover in this section is the impact of technology on communication and its role within the knowledge-power paradigm. As we discussed in Part I of the book, if knowledge is the engine then communication is the oil that runs through the engine. Communication of accurate information, at the right time and to the right person, is the key to the knowledge-power paradigm. While technology has greatly impacted the processes of data collection and evaluation, it has also been an enabler of effective communication of information.

The example of how the Rothschild family attained success points to the importance they placed on acquiring and efficiently communicating information. A couple of centuries ago, an extensive network of messengers and carrier pigeons was cutting-edge communication. Obviously things have moved on considerably since then. The development of telegraphy, in the form of telegrams and telephones, changed things tremendously. Rather than taking weeks for news to reach different parts of the nation and the world, it only took a matter of hours. This was a huge step in improving the transfer of information, thus changing the way business was done. In the last fifteen years we have seen massive developments in digital communications, with inventions such as the fax machine, e-mail, the Internet, and wireless communication. The effect of these mediums has been profound: Large bits of information can now be sent anywhere in the world within a matter of seconds.

While these communication mediums have allowed for efficient transfer of information, they also have given rise to information overload. With so much information coming into communications points, the problem seems to be deciphering what is important and what is not. For this, we can refer back to the two critical knowledge-management processes: data collection and data evaluation. Communication advancements have allowed for great gains in the data-collection part of the knowledge-management process, but the evaluation part of it requires more work. While communication technology has greatly improved, the time and effort required to evaluate information and to determine its importance has greatly increased, too. Therefore, in productivity terms, the net gain of efficient communications is somewhat limited by the time it takes to evaluate these forms of communication.

To overcome these issues, technology is getting better at making the evaluation of information a more efficient process. Organizations are training employees to better understand communication platforms and to utilize them more effectively. And technology developers are getting better at giving the user more tools to evaluate quickly which items of communication are useful and which are unnecessary, thus helping to increase productivity.

Communication technology is still developing at a rapid rate. The next generation of devices will allow organizations to communicate more effectively with development in wireless technology. People in all the major cities in the U.S. can virtually go anywhere and make use of 'air cards' which give them constant wireless access to the Internet and e-mail via their laptops. Add the expansion of Internet phones to the mix, and it is not difficult to see that the Internet will be the major platform that will allow access for all forms of communication, at all times, from virtually anywhere. Furthermore, these devices are getting smaller; before long, the field of nanotechnology will allow mini-computers to have greater functionality and power than we currently enjoy from our desktops and laptops. Organizations that embrace these new technologies have improved their ability to perform, and the ones which continue to embrace future developments will remain in leadership positions. The one major difference, however, compared to five or 10 years ago, is the ability of smaller organizations to afford such technological advances. The price of such technology has greatly reduced, due largely to intense competition in technology markets and a significant decrease in the time-to-market for these products.

11.3 Internet and Browser-Based Software Technology

The development of software applications across all industries has helped organizations to improve productivity appreciably. Software enables hardware (computers) to function, and often offers a graphical user interface (GUI) which allows for easy interface operation. Before the development of the Worldwide Web (WWW), software applications primarily resided on individual computers and local shared networks. With the advent and development of the WWW, software programs have been given a new platform upon which they can operate, detached from the limitations of residing on individual computers. This type of technological advancement is also known as browser-based software, viewed and operated through Web browsers such as Microsoft's Internet Explorer.

Browser-based software has many distinct advantages over regular software applications that reside on individual computers. This area is becoming a preferred route for many software developers, including those in the knowledge-management arena. The most obvious advantage is the accessibility it offers to a wide audience. A good example of this is the free browser-based software applications offered by *Google*, such as 'Calendar,' 'Documents,' and 'Spreadsheet.'[5] These software packages have many of the same functionalities offered by applications like *Microsoft Office*, which traditionally reside on individual computers. Such online software application solutions mean that the user does not need to set up the application on the local hard drive; additionally, the user does not need to use up PC memory to save information. Organizations such as Google also have developed browser-based software technology to mimic local software technology residing on PCs; the software has the feel of a local software program. Another advantage of browser-based software is the ability to access it from any computer with Internet access. This technology entails the storage of information on a remote server(s), which provides a two-fold benefit: security and back-up. Large companies like Google spend millions of dollars to secure information on their servers from hackers, and they also back up the data daily. This is beneficial to the user because it means that the likelihood of losing the data or it being stolen is remote.

Software developers, like most product manufacturers, are constantly updating their programs to make them better. Updates to regular software require the user to install the updated version manually or semi-manually. With browser-based software the updates can be 'pushed out' to every user instantaneously, without requiring users to do anything. This is a major benefit from a user's standpoint and also from a developer's standpoint. For example, when an update is made available for a piece of software used by 10 million people worldwide, how would that update occur on a browser-based system as opposed to an application that resides locally on a PC? In the case of an application that resides locally on a PC, the developer would need to formulate a system that could make the upgrade available for installation on each individual PC. This can get complex and very time-consuming, especially if the upgrade applies to many users. Conversely, upgrades to browser-based software can easily be made by the developer through his servers, without the need to trouble each individual user; the upgrade occurs simultaneously and seamlessly.

From a communication standpoint, Web-browser servers offer a major advantage as they are Internet-based, allowing for mass dispersion to many people. And with the continued development of Internet-related technology as a viable platform for software application, we are likely to see a greater migration of people and organizations employing these types of tools as opposed to the traditional software applications that reside on individual PCs. This migration is happening mainly due to several specific factors: (1) the increase in broadband Internet access, (2) advancements in software used via web-browsers, and (3) the user's openness to using this platform for applications. From a knowledge-management standpoint, the development of this platform will help in the three critical areas of data gathering, data evaluation, and communication. There may come a time in the near future when the majority of the most commonly used software will be based on browser platforms.

11.4 Human Interface and Technology

Earlier, we briefly touched upon the important role played by the user within the field of technology. The fact is, no matter how good any technological innovation happens to be, if the user does not adapt to it, it's unlikely to succeed. When the modern computer and software revolution began in the late 1980s and early 1990s, there were many people who did not adopt or adapt to the new technology–even though there were many benefits. What transpired was a period in which the up-take in computer and software technology was slow, but eventually, as the benefits greatly outweighed fear and resistance to change, everybody jumped on the bandwagon. Organizations with the vision and foresight to recognize the potential benefits of technological advancement can take up a leadership role. From a business standpoint, this is a classic example of how organizations that are more adept to change in a dynamic environment are more likely to thrive and survive. Therefore, is it prudent for leaders to be open-minded about new technologies, especially if they stand to benefit from improved performance and superior business results?

Studies and research projects have cited mitigating circumstances as to why technological advances initially result in resistance.[6] In pop culture, groups that are resistant to such technological change are loosely referred to as 'technophobes.' While the strict definition does not fit these individuals well, it's a term that reflects a group that is slow in the up-take of technology. The main factors that contribute to this mindset include:

Change: Personality type often dictates whether an individual is open to change or even welcomes it. For a manager or a leader, it's not a good trait to resist or be closed to change. If the business environment is constantly changing, organizations are required to adapt to succeed. Therefore, it's critical that leaders keep an open mind. A changing environment also offers new opportunities; leaders should welcome this as a platform to succeed. By being open-minded and accepting change, leaders remove the blindfold that obscures true vision. When Henry Ford refused to embrace the changing needs of his customers, he allowed the door to be opened for

Chrysler to take significant market share from his Model T market. In the same manner, leaders who are likely to resist technological change are offering their rivals the opportunity to step up. This mindset potentially creates lower efficiency and the loss of a competitive edge.

Trust: One of the biggest arguments against adopting new technology is a lack of trust. How do leaders know that a new piece of technology is going to provide better results? This is a rational fear, but like many other fears it can be overcome by education. When the first motor car was offered to the public, many people were distrustful; they preferred the horse-drawn carriage. But at some point even the 'technophobes' decided to take a leap of faith, overcoming their fear and embracing the new technology.

Economy: The adoption of new technology can sometimes involve cost, creating a financial burden for the company and also, perhaps, a cost associated with the time taken to adjust to it.

Lack of Technological Understanding: Leaders cannot see the real benefits of technology when they don't understand how it works; this can result in an opportunity cost. When the fax machine was invented, very few organizations initially took to it, some confessing they did not fully understand the technology and others asserting they could not see the benefits. Today there are very few organizations, if any, that do not have faxing capabilities.

Not Fully Understanding Benefits: A leader may understand the way new technology works, but he may not be able to understand the full benefits. Take the quote at the top of this chapter by H.M. Warner: "Who the hell wants to hear actors talk?"[7] At the advent of 'talkies,' Warner, like many industry executives, understood the new technology that ushered out the silent-movie age. But he could not see the benefit for his organization or the paying audience. Perhaps an element of resistance to change influenced his decision. Whatever the reason, his inaction resulted in his rivals getting a jump on him. Other studios were open to adopting the new technology because they clearly saw the benefits. Countless, less glaring, examples like this happen every day, more a testament to leadership shortcomings than the fault of ambiguous technology.

"If It Ain't Broke, Don't Fix It" Mentality: This is another leadership mindset that's closely related to a fear of change. Leaders often do not want to upset the apple cart if a process is yielding good results. To some degree, there is a basis for a good philosophical argument here. But disciples of the quality-improvement continuum will happily point out that there are very few organizational processes that cannot yield better results, regardless of current performance. Furthermore, in the memoirs of successful leaders, the one common thread is the passion and relentlessness to strive for better results. Leaders who reflect this mentality are not synonymous with leaders who exude the "if it ain't broke, don't fix it" mentality. It's not about working harder; it's about finding ways to work smarter.

Vision: In an ideal world, all leaders possess great vision, and that vision translates to performance. The depth of vision that leaders possess varies from organization to organization. Some organizations perform extraordinarily well because of their leadership vision; some perform with acceptable results in spite of their leader's limited vision; and some do not perform anywhere near their potential. As leaders develop so do their skills sets. Those who develop most quickly and most effectively are the leaders who learn from successes and failures. Leadership vision forms part of the skills set fundamental to seeing opportunities and problems before others and the ability to act upon them. This is a crucial trait that separates good leaders from great ones.

The role of technology and its effect in knowledge management has been around for millennia, in one form or another. Technology is a result and function of better knowledge, and the modern IT boom has created an environment of rapid change. Technology has shown, time and again, to be a critical ingredient in attaining success and improving performance (power). Taking the aforementioned into consideration, it is critical for organizations, and leaders, to stay ahead of the curve and remain open-minded about technological advances. New technology opens the door for new organizational opportunities, which in turn offer a platform for improvement. Leaders who are serious about new opportunities and the quality improvement continuum embrace new technologies and thoroughly investigate attainable benefits in relation to the knowledge-power paradigm.

12

1ST DOWN & GOAL: KNOWLEDGE-POWER IN THE WORLD OF SPORT

Sports serve society by providing vivid examples of excellence.
- GEORGE F. WILL

IN THE WORLD OF PROFESSIONAL SPORTS, winning and losing is an everyday occurrence. Without winners and losers, a large part of sporting endeavor is removed, as is the charm. There are many similarities between sporting endeavors and modern organizational endeavors. Terms like success, performance, achievement, glory, leadership, excellence, failure, hard work and preparation are synonymous between the two arenas. In this chapter we will compare the fields, explore how professional sports has moved to the cutting edge of the knowledge-power paradigm, and discuss tactics that can positively impact and teach business leaders about goal-setting, preparation, knowledge management, strategic planning and, ultimately success.

12.1 For the Love of the Game or Business?

It is an old cliché, but how often do you see an old-timer on TV who happened to be a professional football or baseball player, saying, "It was different back in my day"? In many ways these guys are absolutely right, because things were very different in professional sports 20 or 30 years ago. Twenty-five years ago, tennis players used wooden racquets at Wimbledon, the prize money for some of the well-known sporting events was considerably lower than it is today, and technology that offered performance-related knowledge did not even exist. Go back even further, to the golden age of baseball and basketball, and you can make a good case that athletes literally competed for the love of the game. It could not have been for the money, as only the very top athletes were well compensated. The remaining majority made a modest income. Modern professional sports, on the other hand, is unrecognizable in comparison to sports from previous eras. Professional sports is a lucrative business, where franchises and athletes are the brands being marketed. Commercial brand success depends largely on-field performance, but there are a few exceptions. The likes of Tiger Woods, Lance Armstrong, the New York Yankees, LA Lakers, Dallas Cowboys, and Michael Jordan typify the modern era of sports. The move from pure sports to sporting business has resulted in the creation of an industry worth billions of dollars, which in turn has resulted in a greater emphasis on winning, performance, style, and image.

To help illustrate this point, let's look back at the top three money earners on the PGA tour in 1980: Tom Watson, Lee Travino, and Curtis Strange. In 1995 the top three earners were Greg Norman, Billy Mayfair, and Lee Janzen. And finally, in 2007, the top three earners were Tiger Woods, Phil Mickelson, and Vijay Singh. It is not remarkable to see different names on the top of each list; every generation sees a handful of top golfers come and go. What is remarkable is the total prize money earned by each of these golfers over a 26-year period. The total earnings for these players in each of those years is summarized as follows[1]:

1980:

1. Tom Watson $530,808
2. Lee Travino $385,814
3. Curtis Strange $271,888

1995:

1. Greg Norman $1,654,959
2. Billy Mayfair $1,543,192
3. Lee Janzen $1,378,966

2007:

1. Tiger Woods $10,867,052
2. Phil Mickelson $5,819,988
3. Vijay Singh $4,728,377

The percentage increase between the top earner in 1980 to the top earner in 2007 is a massive 2,047%. Furthermore, the 142nd top earner on the 2007 PGA tour money list (Jason Bohn) earned nearly as much as Tom Watson, the top money earner in 1980! How and why did this money come into pro sports, and where did it come from? The rationalization of a sudden increase in money in the PGA has been accredited to the "*Tiger Effect.*"[2] Tiger Woods' performance and appeal over the last 10 years has opened the game up to a much wider audience, creating a swell in the market for an interest in golf, which is now considered a large industry with millions of people playing and watching. The increase in popularity has translated into opportunity for organizations that want to market and reach out to this new audience.

The same effect can be ascribed to other sports, including football, baseball, basketball, Nascar, Formula 1 racing and soccer. Each of these sports is an established multi-billion dollar industry, and its participants are organizations within those industries. Marketing for sports is almost automatic, as it receives constant 24-hour, worldwide media coverage with the help of media giants like Disney (ESPN) and Rupert Murdoch (Sky Sports). While sporting organizations seem glamorous, their goals, objectives and methods do not differ much from other organizations. They have the same growth goals, profitability targets, market-penetration expectations, customer service demands, quality concerns, and performance-related issues.

So what does this have to do with the knowledge-power paradigm? If we have established that professional sports is a business and each sport represents its own industry, then the teams, the stars, and the related companies represent brands which make up that industry. Therefore, the principles of the knowledge-power paradigm must equally apply to sports as to other industries and organizations that we have highlighted. In the following sections we shall explore specific sporting industries and how players in these markets are positioning themselves to be on the leading edge of knowledge management, and how they apply knowledge to continuously improve performance in the relentless pursuit of success.

12.2 Tour de Lance

The compelling story of Lance Armstrong is well documented. Armstrong set a record seven consecutive Tour de France victories between 1999 and

THE KNOWLEDGE-POWER PARADIGM

2005, making him the most successful cyclist in tour history. The Tour de France is recognized as one of the most grueling races on the professional cycling calendar; indeed, it is among the most physically taxing events on any sports calendar. The tour takes place every July for three hellish weeks, with 200 cyclists covering more than 3,600 kilometers amid some of the tallest mountains in Europe. Participants can burn as many as 10,000 calories a day! Notwithstanding these staggering numbers, the difference in the final times between the yellow jersey and the chasing pack is often less than one percent. After nearly one month of constant cycling, the race often comes down to a difference of a few seconds. Those are the margins which differentiate winners and losers in this sport. That one percent difference at the very top can also be found in most other modern professional sports—incredible margins considering the hard work that goes into preparation and execution by each participant or team.

Armstrong's story is compelling largely due to his impressive victory over cancer, and then his subsequent seven Tour de France victories. His dominance in the event compares to greats such as Michael Jordan, Muhammad Ali, Jack Nicklaus, Tiger Woods, and Roger Federer. The money at stake for Armstrong, his team, the sponsors, equipment suppliers, and the cycling industry as a whole depended solely upon whether he achieved success. Without those incredible performances, his business brand could not have attained the kind of success that it has. And what is his brand? Himself.

As previously mentioned, success on the field of play is critical to professional sports, and often that is all that matters in this highly competitive industry. Armstrong's personal ambition was always high; his personality traits are similar to those of other great leaders in fields where success is of paramount importance. In that relentless pursuit, nothing is left to chance. Armstrong is a prime example of a leader who put a premium on the principles of the knowledge-power paradigm. He recognized that the margin between success and failure is slim and that certain factors would tip the scales in his favor. But what were these factors and what could he do to influence and manage them? In Armstrong's case, having superior knowledge about equipment, preparation, and conditioning (married with his superior physical talent) could make all the difference—notably with the aid of knowledge-management technology. "Today, the race is a marvel of technology," Armstrong said in an interview. " The bikes are so light you can lift them overhead with one hand, and the riders are equipped with computers, heart monitors, and even two-way radios."[3] In the process of establishing various knowledge-management processes himself, Armstrong forced his rivals to change their own preparation and racing methods by adopting similar knowledge-management techniques just to keep up with him. But he was astute enough to stay one step ahead by acquiring better and more advanced information.

The knowledge-management process is a critical component within the knowledge-management success model. The knowledge-management process advocates the gathering and evaluation of data, which then forms part of the planning and decision-making process. This process is iterative, and when applied properly it yields performance and quality improvements. Armstrong recognized this fact early on and faced the challenge to get a better understanding behind the science of cycling. He admitted, "I geeked out. I tackled the problem of the Tour as if I were in math class, science class, chemistry class, and nutrition class, all rolled into one. I did computer calculations that balanced my body weight and my equipment weight with the potential velocity of the bike in various stages, trying to find the equation that would get me to the finish line faster than anybody else. I kept careful computer graphs of my training rides, calibrating the distances, wattages, and thresholds."[3] He dedicated himself to better understanding how the following variable factors affected his performance and how, through conscious and rigorous data gathering and evaluation, these variables can be controlled:

- Aerodynamics
- Equipment composition
- Equipment set-up
- Diet
- Cycling technology
- Cycling apparel fiber technology
- Cycling technique

Essentially, Armstrong, his team, and his sponsors were defining the key elements of knowledge management in professional cycling. Thousands of hours were spent in wind tunnels, testing elements of the sport like rider equipment, position, and set-up. These tests revealed the ideal variables that help improve performance. Collected data was analyzed, and this information was then successfully applied to his training regimen in preparation for the tour.

In an April 2004 *New York Times* article[4], Armstrong offered candid insight into the knowledge-management systems he employed. He discussed the computer software rigged to him during wind-tunnel testing that gave him instant feedback on how minute changes to his position on the bike affected his aerodynamic drag and his power output. Collected data helped Armstrong know exactly what position he should take on his bike to be optimally efficient. The testing information also told Armstrong that his set-up for the 2003 tour could be improved for time trials, which he successfully implemented in 2004. This applied knowledge was so successful Armstrong "flew past his teammates"[4] during training camp in preparation for the upcoming Tour de France.

Armstrong also worked diligently with his apparel supplier, *Nike*, to use the same knowledge-management techniques to design superior apparel. In 2003 Armstrong became dehydrated during one stage of the tour and lost 90 seconds to his main adversary, Jan Ullrich. Both *Nike* and Armstrong worked hard to close that gap in performance through their *Nike Swift Suit* apparel, giving Armstrong a significant edge in 2004. "This is a mathematical model,"[4] said Rick MacDonald, one of *Nike's* designers, indicating the complex science behind their knowledge-management approach.

Armstrong and his team went to great lengths in their pursuit of knowledge. He was not satisfied merely with winning multiple tours. He wanted more. MacDonald's suggestion that the work was a 'mathematical model' reflected the scientific dimension the sport had moved into. The best rider, with the best knowledge, was using applied science to utilize the same knowledge-power principles used by other great leaders from different fields. The results ultimately speak for themselves. Armstrong has publicly acknowledged the critical importance of his approach and its impact on his success.

12.3 NFL Knowledge-Power

Professional football is by far the most popular sport in America. The popularity and money within the league is nothing short of staggering. The National Football League (NFL) was formed in 1922, and its general popularity started to take off in the 1960s. Today, each of the 32 teams in the league is worth hundreds of millions of dollars, and many players are household names. The culmination of the NFL season is the Super Bowl; the first one was played in 1967, and today it's the single most-watched annual sporting event in the U.S.—with an average of 80 to 90 million television viewers. The NFL is a major industry, with the teams and players creating their own brands. Marketing and media within the NFL are as strong as in any sport in the world, injecting billions of dollars into the industry.

Similar to PGA revenues, money in the football industry has skyrocketed during the last two decades. The success of teams and individuals translates beyond just glory; it also dictates where the flow of money is channeled. Gone are the days when players and teams trained hard, reviewed basic strategies, and went out and played on Sunday. With so much money at stake, nothing is left to chance by the people involved within the game. NFL franchises are the most competitive, organized, well-drilled, efficient exponents of methodology and employers of expert personnel than any other business organization in any industry! But with all 32 teams vying for success there is great emphasis placed on strong fundamentals and acquiring the latest information about rivals and their methods. If football is likened to a war on the field of sport, then the lessons of Sun Tzu become applicable. And we know the cornerstone of Sun Tzu's principles depends upon acquiring the very best information.

The premium placed on knowledge by teams, coaches, and players has steadily grown over the years. It is clear the knowledge-power paradigm is fully understood and adopted. Knowing about yourself and your rival is critical in modern football. It's the ultimate game of strategy acted out on a playing field. The knowledge-management process for NFL teams can essentially be broken into two categories, and they are described as follows:

1. Game Time: During a game it's essential for teams to have the capability to capture and evaluate game data, communicate information to the right personnel, and make changes to game strategy on the fly. Even the best-laid plans require adjustment, as unanticipated events cannot be foreseen.

THE KNOWLEDGE-POWER PARADIGM

Watching a game on TV, you notice assistant coaches running through plays while also making critical adjustments with their players. The assistant offensive and defensive coaches often sit high above the field calling plays from within a sealed-off booth. These vantage points give them an aerial advantage, with the added benefit of being surrounded by technology that allows them the option to review previous plays. Multiple phone sets are also found on the sidelines, where they provide direct lines of communication to the coaches up in the booths calling plays. If these coaches see something they want to communicate to certain players, they can do so via the phones. Head coaches all wear headphones and microphones on the touchline, allowing them to communicate with players and assistant coaches and to listen in on the play calling. Technology has had a strong hand in allowing teams, coaches, and players to be better equipped for efficient decision-making and communication. While these methods have been around for many years, the teams who mange the technology for optimum data collection, processing, and communication often attain a decisive adage.

2. Pre and Post-Game: Arguably, the information captured and evaluated before and after each game is one of the biggest factors determining success in football, especially where parity exists between competing teams. What you know about yourself and your opposition should help form strategies for success. Sun Tzu said, "Know the enemy and know yourself...when you are ignorant of the enemy, but know yourself, your chances of winning or losing are equal. If ignorant both of your enemy and yourself, you are certain in every battle to be in peril."[5] This is the mantra coaches and players have adopted in the NFL. Coaches and players now spend more time poring over pre- and post-game information than they do in the weights room. They diligently review game film over and over again, looking over play calling, internal performance, and virtually anything that may give them an edge over their opponents. Today's players build theaters into their homes so that when they leave their training facilities they can go straight home to watch play films into the night, building up knowledge and information about rival teams. They are working harder and smarter.

In December 2004, CBS's *60 Minutes*[6] aired an insightful report on new knowledge-power methods adopted by NFL coaches. The program featured interviews with two of the most successful coaches in the NFL, John Fox

(Carolina Panthers) and Bill Belichick (New England Patriots). Both coaches admitted to using the latest technology and outlined how information and knowledge gave them a crucial edge in preparation for each game.

Both coaches also admitted to being "detail freaks." They confessed that decisions regarding all aspects of football ultimately crossed their desks, outlining the leadership role each plays within his organization. The crux of the report centered around how both coaches have enjoyed longevity in their positions where others haven't fared so well, and how they have attained success through the use of technology, i.e. computers and information databases. *60 Minutes* reported, "NFL teams have more software engineers today than water boys. The Patriots, the Panthers—every team spends millions on special video player-super-computers that allow every coach to scout every opponent's every move."[6] Fox pointed out in the report that the computer database he employs can spit out the details for every game played by every team in the league for the past three years. The system can also highlight minute details down to each player and every play he was involved in. Talk about cutting-edge knowledge management!

Belichick, like Fox, is in at 5 a.m. every day during the season—and the first thing he does is fire up his computer system to pore over data and information. The system is a crucial part of his planning, decision-making, and execution process. This type of knowledge-management system is a direct result of the limitations imposed upon teams through player free agency.

Another preparation issue coaches have to contend with is the short time period between football games. Coaches have less than seven days after completing a game to effectively prepare for the next one. Furthermore, on average, games in the NFL are won by 6 points or less. According to Fox, "Coming up with that little edge is coaching."[6] Understanding parity among teams forces coaches to look for an edge beyond traditional methods. For Fox and Belichick, that edge comes from employing knowledge-management systems including information databases that help them get a better understanding of their opponent's game plan, thus helping them to form theirs. Teams are also hiring a new breed of coach called Quality Control Coaches; they do not coach, per se, but spend time entering and analyzing data. They are the knowledge management foot soldiers, critical to head coach generals.

Essentially, both Belichick and Fox are charting for predictable patterns

THE KNOWLEDGE-POWER PARADIGM

and trends shown by rival coaches in certain situations, "so your team knows what to expect,"[6] said Fox. The *60 Minutes* report is powerful stuff—and so are its implications to football. Two of the most respected and successful coaches in the modern era recognize there is only so much money available to acquire players, and that most games are decided by a very small margin (less than one score). This has led them and their colleagues to seek out new methods to gain the upper hand. What they have done is apply the principles of the knowledge-power paradigm and effectively use technology to get a better understanding of themselves and their competitors. Furthermore, successful leaders like Belichick and Fox, who have the vision and the drive to succeed, have bucked the trend and embraced new ways of working, with the primary goal to improve performance and attain success.

The NFL is a good example of progressive leadership that places great emphasis on knowledge management. There are leaders within the corporate business world who face the same problems and have the same hopes and dreams for success. What can these leaders learn from NFL coaches? Amid all of this evidence, why would leaders be hesitant to employ new knowledge-management methods and technologies to improve performance?

12.4 Nascar and Formula 1 - Management by Information

Nascar is the most popular motor racing brand in the U.S., and Formula 1 is one of the most-watched sporting events in the world—and arguably the most glamorous. Together they generate billions of dollars of corporate sponsorship and marketing. Just like the NFL, the teams in each of these two motor racing circuits must attain success to command a bigger financial draw. Success in Nascar and Formula 1 is highly dependent on achieving a delicate balance between developing competitive cars and recruiting talented drivers and support personnel for the overall effort. Technology has always been at the forefront of Nascar and Formula 1, mainly due to the nature of the business. We are going to explore how Nascar and Formula 1, before many other modern sports, embraced the principles of the knowledge-power paradigm.

Technology in Formula 1 translates to a laundry list of innovation and invention. Formula 1 is often seen as a development ground for the motor vehicle technologies of tomorrow. Technological innovations attributed to Formula 1 racing include active suspension, turbo-chargers, ground-effect aerodynamics, anti-locking brakes, and numerous other tire and engine breakthroughs. Nascar and Formula 1 advance engineering and scientific knowledge through sporting competition, challenging teams to innovate for success.

Computer telemetry is the foundation upon which racing technology is based. Computer telemetry offers racing teams the ability to remotely measure and evaluate various operating systems within the car. The basic road-going car that you and I drive also contains basic telemetry, but it only offers the driver rudimentary information about various systems, e.g. the fuel gauge and oil temperature, and various performance alarms. The average racing car, on the other hand, is a very complex, sensitive, and fragile piece of equipment, with thousands of systems working in synchronicity to determine performance. Teams that initially adopted computer telemetry in the 1980s found that they could acquire vital performance data. It was the first major step in acquiring real-time information from the motor car itself. Having this information offered a significant advantage over teams who did not adopt this new technology.

Every team in motor racing today depends heavily on computer telemetry. It forms an integral part of problem identification, decision-making, and problem resolution. Nascar viewers can now see basic telemetry on their TV screens. Furthermore, during a race, computer telemetry has the capability to automatically and semi-automatically manage systems within the car to improve performance. This is also known as two-way telemetry. It allows racing engineers to adjust vital systems within the car from remote locations, e.g. the pits. A good example of this is the fuel mixture content in Formula 1 racing cars, which can be adjusted by two-way telemetry, on the fly, to improve vehicle performance.

Computer telemetry systems in motor racing are the cutting edge of knowledge management. Telemetry truly epitomizes the principles of the knowledge-power paradigm because it satisfies all the necessary requirements for quality and performance improvement. While motor racing is a business, it still represents a good metaphor that can be held up to other organizations in the corporate world. If winning and success are of paramount importance to racing teams, and they recognize the vital importance of the knowledge-power paradigm, then shouldn't those same principles be important to regular organizations across all industries? Motor racing and business organizations share a common language, with synonymous terms like performance, success, efficiency, quality and leadership. Therefore, what lessons can leaders in the business world learn from the leaders in motor racing?

12.5 The Tiger Effect

Tiger Woods is said to be the most recognizable sporting figure in the world. He is a modern day sporting icon, and by the time his career is over he's likely to be acknowledged as the most successful golfer ever to have played the game. Woods' affect on the game of golf is immeasurable. Not only has he been able to increase the popularity of the game, but he has been able to break down barriers and bring the game to a wider audience. His incredible talent and marketability is a potent combination which has helped to thrust him and golf into the public spotlight.

What Michael Jordan was to basketball, Tiger Woods is to golf. Rather than being "*like Mike,*" kids of this generation proclaim "*I am Tiger Woods!*" The financial stakes have increased considerably for Woods, his rivals, and the golfing industry in the last 10 years. Not only has the prize money significantly improved, but the endorsements often bring in more money than a tournament prize—in Tiger's case a whopping $100 million contract with *Nike*. But success is a prerequisite, and success has to endure. Flash-in-the-pan success is fleeting and does not translate to long-term financial viability or credibility. This principle also applies to leaders in business: Attaining success is tough, but keeping it going is even tougher.

Woods in many ways is similar to Lance Armstrong; he has a voracious will to succeed, and he wants to be top dog in his chosen field. This does not come easily, and there is method behind the talent which allows him to consistently out-perform every other golfer in the world. Woods' talent, preparation, and attention to detail are a large part of the platform that allows him to succeed. He leaves nothing to chance. He's a fine example of a leader who adheres to the principles of the knowledge-power paradigm.

In 1997 Tiger Woods won his first Masters' green jacket, decimating the field and the Augusta golf course along the way. He metaphorically shook the golfing world to the core, and he followed that win with many memorable victories. Woods is a self-proclaimed perfectionist. He is also someone who puts long-term success ahead of short-term gains. He was determined to make changes to the one thing that most golfers at the top of their game would not even consider: rebuilding his swing–twice, between the ages of 21 and 30. He knew that if he stood still he would never be able to achieve his full potential. So with the help of his then-coach, Butch Harmon, they reconstructed his swing.

The technology most modern-day golfers employs are classic knowledge-management tools. Back in the days of Nicklaus, Palmer, Trevino, and Player, there was little by way of technology to help players perfect their swing. Today's players enjoy an arsenal of technological tools that measure data and offer immediate information to coaches. A good golf coach knows what every part of the body should be doing during each stage of a golf swing–the head, shoulders, arms, hands, torso, and legs. The problem with analyzing the golf swing from start to finish, however, is the rapid speed of the whole process; the swing is completed in just over a second, and there are numerous minute things that can result in a bad shot. If any of these elements is slightly unaligned, the result can easily be a hook or even a push, which is disastrous for a professional golfer. Paraphrasing the great golf legend Ben Hogan, most golf shots are miss-hits, and the only difference between a professional golfer and an average club golfer is the margin of error of the miss-hit. The amplification of a professional's miss-hit is far lower than that of an average club golfer.

Swing analyzers help coaches pinpoint areas which are out of sync and quickly correct the problem with the player. Swing analyzers are essentially a purposeful arrangement of high-speed cameras that capture every sequence of a swing, frame by frame. This technology is crucial to Tiger Woods; it captures and analyzes vital swing data, allowing Woods and his coach to review every aspect and angle of the swing, and then compare it to his swing from previous years. But why is this needed and even important? Anybody who has played golf will attest that golfers get into bad habits which eventually lead to poor results. If a golfer like Woods knows what his optimum swing is, he can always go back to the analyzer to check for kinks and make necessary adjustments.

In principle, this knowledge-management tool is no different from any business quality measurement and improvement tool. Swing analyzers are like Six Sigma measuring devices for golfers. In the past it took a golfer longer to figure out where his swing was going wrong, and the adjustment time depended on the talent and trained eye of the coach. Modern technology has changed all of that, affording golfers the ability to measure and analyze critical swing information.

Swing analyzers are just one of numerous golf instruments that can be considered knowledge-management technology. The golf industry is flooded with all sorts of other data analysis and evaluation tools for knowledge management. Their principles are all aligned with the knowledge-power paradigm, using accurate and timely information to improve performance. I can only imagine what the likes of Jack Nicklaus and Arnold Palmer think of such advances; I bet they wish they had had access to such knowledge management tools in their prime. Perhaps Nicklaus would have won more than his record-setting 18 majors!

From a business standpoint, we learn important lessons from professionals in the world of sport, including the ability to leverage the principles of the knowledge-power paradigm to achieve success. Tiger Woods is incredibly blessed with talent, but he works hard at his game to be the best in the world. As a leader in his sport he recognizes that even that is not enough, so he turns to obtaining important knowledge to give him the edge that often makes the difference between success and failure.

12.6 Lessons To Learn From Professional Sports

In professional sports, performance is measured by time, points or even strokes (as in golf). The ultimate performance yardstick for Armstrong is having a quicker time. For Belichick it is scoring more points, and for Woods it is taking fewer strokes. These are the elements that ultimately determine levels of success and failure within the crucible of competition. What we have learned from them are valuable insights into how they have made the leap from good to great. These individuals are recognized as leaders in their chosen sports; their drive, passion, mental fortitude, and commitment to excellence are unquestioned. They have not reached the top of the mountain by pure luck or ability alone; rather, they are testament to merging talent with careful process management. They effectively manage interrelated process variables which contribute to performance. Therefore, by analyzing interrelated processes and controlling them, there is a better chance of attaining success. This is the science of modern-day sports through knowledge management.

In an organization, a leader is in the same position as Tiger Woods, Lance Armstrong, and Bill Belichick. The leader is the master whose will determines the direction and methods employed by the organization to attain success. The success of an organization in many ways is a reflection of the leader's ability, talent, and vision to do what these stars do in their respective disciplines. For a leader to be like Tiger Woods, he needs to recognize and implement the same principle methods. In business, Jack Welch is akin to Woods. Leaders, regardless of organizational size, can be like Jack and Tiger, but they need to possess understanding, firm commitment, and the ability to execute.

So where does a leader begin to attain benefit from the knowledge-power paradigm? There are certain principles we can review to get started:

Understand Your Role in the Equation. Leaders play a specific role with regard to the success of organizations and divisions. Their vision, passion, and decision-making are the key factors in resource allocation and strategy. Bill Belichick and John Fox are the leaders of their teams: They set the tone, expectations, and levels of commitment for others to follow. What they do is reflected in their teams' performance. Both know the buck stops with them and with their methods. Organizational leaders have the same capacity as these two men, but do they have a good understanding of what their role constitutes, and do they have the desire to reach for elevated levels of excellence? If the answer is "no," then the rest of the following need not apply.

Understanding the Science of Business. Tiger Woods fully understands that large parts of his job can be viewed as interrelated processes, whether his golf swing, putting motion, or preparation for major tournaments. If something is a process, then it can be measured, analyzed, and improved. So rather than view his occupation as a recreational activity, like most weekend golfers do, he understands it in terms of science—a science that gives him the platform to continuously improve. A good leader will often see functions within her organization as processes that determine performance. Much in the same way as Tiger Woods, a leader must consciously understand the scientific principles of measuring, monitoring, · analyzing, and controlling processes. The starting point in trying to improve any process is having information and knowledge; without it, how does a leader know what needs improving? Tiger Woods is not going to try to improve his swing unless he knows specifically what 's wrong with it.

Performance and Control. Lance Armstrong recognized that winning the Tour de France comprised a series of hundreds of processes he needed to manage effectively. His knowledge of processes put him on a higher footing than his rivals; what they did not know hurt them. Information gleaned from wind-tunnel testing, fiber technology, composite materials for his bike, and numerous other elements gave him a distinct advantage through the ability to control performance. This same principle applies to leaders in organizations. Obtaining accurate information, knowledge, and understanding provides a platform from which effective control decisions can be made to positively impact performance. But as a leader, how are you breaking down processes and measuring performance to obtain information? Once you have the information, are you able to employ it effectively to control and make decisions for improved performance?

Informed Decision-Making. Leaders who put a premium on information to control performance are likely basing much of their decision-making upon that information. Bill Belichick openly admits to poring over gathered information and building up his knowledge, which allows him to be a better coach for improved team performance. In business, the best leaders make informed decisions based on accurate information; that is often what separates the good from the great. As a leader, how far are you prepared to go to obtain the information that allows you make informed decisions? Do you have the right metrics and measurements to scientifically distinguish what your customers like or dislike about your product or service? Are your processes working efficiently? How can they be more efficient? What are the problems you should be aware of right now? These are the questions effective leaders can answer instantly. High levels of performance, just like Belichick's, do not occur by accident.

Tools of the Trade. The common thread running throughout this book, with regard to the knowledge-power paradigm, is the use of technology. From the Romans to the Rothschilds through to Roush Racing, the ability to obtain information and attain success is largely attributed to the application of technology as a critical tool. Leaders need to put aside their fear of technology and proactively search out the technologies which can help them make better decisions. Your competitors may be doing it, so can you afford not to?

Commitment to the Cause. If Lance Armstrong decided to give up his commitment to improve performance after his third Tour de France victory, would he have managed to eventually win seven straight? Probably not, because every time he won his rivals upped the ante and copied his methods. Armstrong had to stay a step ahead, and he did so through his commitment to attaining information and knowledge to help improve performance. This is similar to the way leaders in business experience success, but it's only fleeting if they stand still, because environments are dynamic and the competition is restless. Therefore, adherence to knowledge management and the principles of the knowledge-power paradigm is a long-term commitment. It is a tried and tested methodology with proven success.

A Vision for Quality Improvement. Winning takes vision and a drive to always want to improve. That is what powers the Jordans and Armstrongs of this world. Quality and performance improvement is a planned outcome that results from method. The vision is the base upon which success takes form. If the vision is to attain growth through customer satisfaction, then it is vital for leaders to have a plan, the necessary tools, the information, and the skills set to make the right decisions.

Passion and Drive to Succeed. This is an attribute that cannot be taught; you either have it or you don't. Successful leaders have this attribute in abundance, and they find ways to channel it in a constructive manner that translates into positive results. But do not mistake this as simply working harder than the next guy. Instead, it is working smarter than the next guy. Woods, Armstrong and Belichick do work hard, but what makes them the best at what they do is their ability to marry their talent with working smart. Their drive to succeed has led them to find smart methods to be better than the next guy.

The professional sporting world and the corporate world are convergent, in principle, to the point where there is little difference between the two. Professional sports is essentially a business in every sense, and leaders in all industries face the same challenges, whether the leader happens to be Tiger Woods or a CEO of an organization. Still, achievers and performers from the sporting world can teach the leaders of corporate America a powerful lesson about the workings of the knowledge-power paradigm. In many instances, having knowledge, and then effectively being able to use it to your advantage, is what separates success and failure. But reaching that point requires a scientific understanding of processes, knowledge-management techniques, an appreciation of the latest technology, and a desire to apply those elements to improve performance.

13

THE QUALITY IMPROVEMENT CONTINUUM

*Everyone doing his best is not the answer. Everyone **is** doing his best. It is necessary that people understand the reason for the transformation that is necessary for survival. Moreover, there must be consistency of understanding and of effort. There is no substitute for knowledge.[1]*
- W. EDWARDS DEMING

I HAVE BEEN FORTUNATE IN MY CAREER to have worked with some quite brilliant people who have imparted useful knowledge and insights, and I am grateful to one and all. I'd imagine that this is the case for most people, to a varying degree; we all pick up good–and bad–habits on our career journeys. I had one mentor in particular who influenced me in my early sales and marketing career, and much of what he taught me I will never forget. John Esposito was a New Zealander with a thick accent and a positive attitude towards life and work. A short, resourceful fellow with Italian good looks and a sharp brain for marketing, his energy and optimism were contagious. His ability to train and develop raw sales talent was legendary within Xerox corporation circles, and it was my good fortune that much of my early training was under his tutelage. I was young and brash; heaven knows what he made of me and my attitude. I guess he saw something in me. Otherwise, why even bother being a teacher and a mentor?

THE KNOWLEDGE-POWER PARADIGM

Nonetheless, he was a disciple of value-added sales and the quality movement. We spent considerable time together, refining my skills during the first year of my sales career. He taught and I listened. John would always say, "If you are going to do something, then do it well, because at the end of the day only quality matters." I didn't have the chance to develop bad marketing habits before meeting John, and that was the advantage of not having much marketing experience in the first place. Working with him was the first time I was exposed to the importance of quality improvement.

Knowledge-power paradigm fingerprints can be found all over quality-improvement methodologies, whether it's the work of Deming, Juran, Crosby, Peters, or Six Sigma. This is only natural, because the principles which govern the knowledge-power paradigm also directly affect quality-improvement methodologies. It is impossible to improve the quality of a product, service, or process unless you have information regarding what needs to be improved and measurements which help to quantify it. Therefore, both quality and the knowledge-power paradigm are complementary and highly dependent on each other.

In this chapter we will dig deeper into the various disciplines of quality improvement, how the knowledge-power paradigm affects it, and why it is critical to leadership and performance. Quality improvement is imperative to the long-term well-being of all organizations. It does not happen by accident, and it requires consistent method and application. So let's start with the basics of quality.

13.1 The Quality Improvement Revolution

Why is quality improvement and measurement important to organizations? From a business standpoint, it really does not need too much explanation; quality improvement and measurement offers a distinct business advantage, from the ability to offer a better product to the opportunity to reduce overheads through the elimination of inefficiencies. However, there are organizations out there that believe they are doing an excellent job because profits are up, so why should they care about quality improvement? A good example of such a situation might be a physician whose book is consistently full of patients. Should he care about quality?

Measuring quality levels can be compared to gauges found on the dashboard of a car. Data from gauges gives the driver vital information about essential functions and levels. Without gauges showing vital information relating to fuel level, oil temperature, service light, vehicle speed, and revolutions per minute, the car would eventually break down. Essentially, the driver would be driving blind without knowing trouble was brewing. In the same way, even when leaders think things are going well, because business is booming, they may not fully recognize that things change rapidly—especially when quality levels are not monitored sufficiently. Furthermore, leaders should want to know what performance levels they are reaching, beyond just financials. Financial numbers are a reflection of historically attained business, but quality indicators outline elements that govern future performance. By constantly monitoring against benchmarks, leaders can establish whether the organization is on the right improvement path. Quality indicators highlight whether problems exist, whether they are likely to grow into major issues, and whether the organization is performing to expectations. The implementation of quality indicators and their constant monitoring is what separates the good from the great.

Following World War II, many organizations did not worry about quality levels or measurement, because the U.S. was the only major manufacturing nation and provided most of the needs for the rest of the world. Virtually every other nation was too ravaged even to compete, so many American firms enjoyed a monopoly. Talk about shooting fish in a barrel! Neither excellence nor quality, in an environment bereft of competition, is likely to prevail. Leaders were not being challenged to worry about quality levels or quality products. Why should they? Profits were high and business was good. Business environments constantly change, however, and leadership arrogance was the central cause for the downfall. By the 1970s and 1980s, previously ravaged economies came to the fore and pulled the proverbial rugs from under the feet of inefficient American organizations. Many manufacturing industries were threatened, their flaws exposed. Japanese and German organizations were producing better and cheaper products than their American counterparts, and consumers voted with their feet. American and British manufacturing was in a tailspin, and in some cases it took over a decade for some companies to find their balance again; others never recovered. How could this happen—and who allowed it to happen?

The Japanese were arguably the most devastated after World War II, but with aid from allies they eventually found their feet. The Japanese are a resourceful, proud people, and their determination to rise again was key in the regeneration of their nation. Ironically, the economic rise of Japanese organizations was fueled by two American quality gurus: W. Edwards Deming and Joseph Juran. Both of these men were early pioneers of the quality-improvement revolution, even though they worked independently of each other.

W. Edwards Deming helped American organizations to improve production during World War II, and with an American manufacturing monopoly following the war, his progressive, quality-centered thinking was largely ignored in the U.S. Instead, Deming took his quality-improvement ideas for product design, service, and sales to Japan, where he worked closely with industry leaders in the 1950s. Deming was a statistician by trade, so numbers and measurements came naturally to him. But numbers weren't the only important factor; it was what he did with these numbers that created a revolution in Japanese management thinking and manufacturing. Deming trained and influenced hundreds of manufacturing engineers in 'statistical process control' (SPC) and quality-based thinking. SPC is essentially statistical analysis, using mathematical theorems, which achieves quality control over vital processes. It gave Japanese organizations the ability to reduce process inefficiencies, which allowed them to produce better products at a lower cost. In other words, by obtaining information through measurement, monitoring, and application, the Japanese became far more competitive than their American counterparts. They possessed powerful tools to make significant manufacturing improvements and reduce costs. This is also the cornerstone of the knowledge-power paradigm–the ability to attain success through effectively applying information and knowledge.

Joseph Juran worked in Japan during the same period as Deming, but rather than focusing on the statistical analysis, Juran was an expert in the field of quality management. While Deming trained and influenced engineers through process improvement, Juran had a similar influence on Japanese managers. He worked closely with top- and middle-level managers to train them in understanding and executing quality-management roles. This was not an easy task, as Japanese managers took some time to get a complete understanding of quality-based initiatives.

Some American organizations had the foresight to counteract the Japanese quality manufacturing onslaught. How? By 'fighting fire with fire.' American organizations, in the midst of the Japanese quality offensive, had to take a long, hard look at every aspect of organizational design, ideology, processes, systems, and execution. If they had any chance to stop the bleeding and become competitive again, they had to change the fundamental way things were done within their own organizations. One of the architects of the American fight-back was Phil Crosby. Crosby championed the cause of the "zero defects" program and also the policy of "doing it right first time." He authored *Quality is Free*, a book in which he outlined the rationale and plan for American manufacturers to implement their own quality drive. Interestingly enough, by the 1980s Deming was back in the U.S. as a prominent figure in the American quality revolution, influencing the likes of Ford Motor Company, Honeywell, and AT&T.

By the late 1980s, companies like Ford, and Xerox in particular, had successfully implemented quality principles. Xerox became the first American company to successfully regain market share from the Japanese. The quality lesson was a difficult one for many American organizations. Many fell by the wayside because they could not come to terms with quality management and measurement processes, or they simply stayed ignorant to their predicament.

13.2 Rationale and Implications of Quality Improvement and Measurement

The impact of the work conducted by Deming, Juran, and Crosby was stunning. The damaging impact on American manufacturing to produce better and cheaper products was wholly unexpected. But that same macro principle of competitors offering better products and using better processes (hence a cheaper processing cost) still applies to all organizations, regardless of industry or organization size. The reality is that we operate in a world where the business environment is more dynamic now than ever before. Things are changing at a very rapid rate. Therefore, the pressure on leaders to gauge fundamental quality levels is acute, even when leaders perceive that success already is being attained.

As a statistician, Deming knew the importance of the knowledge-power relationship, especially when applied correctly. What he was doing, in principle, was no different from the time-motion studies by Fredrick Winslow Taylor, or the first assembly lines developed by Henry Ford. The difference was that Deming, Juran, and Crosby developed theories which expanded on earlier principles, including management buy-in to their quality ideologies. So, if all the historic and latter day lessons are not enough to convince a leader of the importance of quality improvement and

THE KNOWLEDGE-POWER PARADIGM

the knowledge-power paradigm, what can?

The importance of quality improvement to a sharp leader is clear, but to the untrained and uninitiated the concept can be an unfound treasure. Leaders and managers who are inherently reluctant to change or to explore different, better avenues are unlikely to stray from their predictable habits. For leaders who search like rabid explorers for better ways to improve operations, whether successful or unsuccessful, there is always a way. All it takes is an open mind and astute vision.

Deming was just as direct when addressing industry and organizational leaders to rationalize the need for quality measurements and improvements. Deming's Chain Reaction model outlines the broad rationale for quality improvement for organizations, as highlighted in figure 13.1.

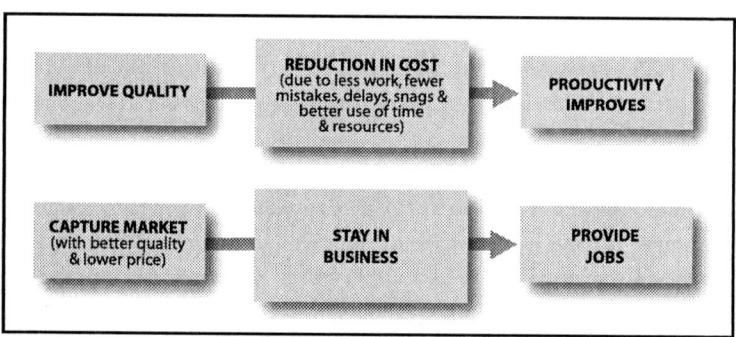

Figure 13.1 - The Deming Chain Reaction Model[2]

His model was not based on theory; instead, it was a working model based on the results achieved during his time in Japan. The ability to improve quality, when implemented correctly, can result in a significant reduction in cost. Cost can be viewed purely in financial terms, but it can also be viewed in non-financial terms, e.g. the cost of losing business/customers, the cost of time due to inefficiencies, and the cost of customer dissatisfaction.

Other broad rationale for continuous quality improvement, which Deming proposed, was competitive advantage. Organizations adept at improving system and process quality are likely to enjoy competitive advantages. If it takes an organization less time, or fewer people, than it takes a rival to complete essentially the same task, then it's clearly more efficient in the process. Similarly, if an organization has more knowledge and can translate that into being more productive in doing its business, that also gives rise to a distinct competitive advantage.

It's vital to set benchmarks and measurements for effective quality improvement. For example, if a physician is concerned about his patients' wait time and seeks to improve that particular area of performance, then he is going to have to establish a baseline. The baseline, in this case, is the average current time patients wait before seeing the physician. The baseline is critical information, setting a benchmark that must be improved upon, and also giving the physician an entry point from which he can investigate the patient processing system to iron out inefficiencies. Once he has established a revised process, he can go back to measure the wait time to ascertain whether the average wait time has been reduced.

The other essential point to explore regarding this type of quality improvement is the relationship between quality benchmarks. If the same physician, for example, knew satisfaction levels were far lower among patients who had to wait more than 30 minutes than among those who only had to wait 15 minutes, he could infer the justification for patient dissatisfaction by the process of rational deduction. Essentially, he has the power to improve the quality of service offered to his patients because he has more information from them. This same principle can be applied to any organization by uncovering sources of performance measurement through information correlation and data mining.

Quality gurus like Deming also place a great deal of emphasis on getting customer feedback information, i.e. what customers think. Deming states, "Do you know your customer? Do you know what he needs? Almost nobody does ...What must be done about it? And don't tell me you can't do anything about it. You can...Everybody here has a job in improvement... You can show your top management what to do. And if you can't show your top management what to do, he's not worth working for..."[1] Strong words indeed, but Deming makes a critical point: Improvements can be attained from what customers tell you about what they experience, want, and need. Often, organizations, especially small and medium-sized ones, assume they know what customers want without formally asking them. Basing important decisions on assumptions is a flawed and ignorant strategy. Having accurate and timely information about customer needs is a good base upon which management decisions are made. And the collection of this information on a regular basis is critical, as

THE KNOWLEDGE-POWER PARADIGM

customer needs are dynamic and often can change over time.

In competitive markets where leaders embrace continuous quality-improvement methods, a great emphasis is placed on acquiring customer knowledge. Your customers will tell you what they need and expect; all you need to do is effectively ask the right questions, and collect and evaluate the resulting data. Until recently, something this simple was not systematically easy for small and medium-sized companies to execute. Since the emergence of IT systems, small and medium-sized companies now have the opportunity to gather crucial data. Organizations that ask basic questions to a small customer base now have the ability to ask specific questions to a large customer base to attain extremely accurate data. Methods and techniques to capture and monitor data have advanced, paving the way for superior quality-improvement measures. Such methods and techniques are illustrated in figure 13.2.

Prior to recent innovations in technology which enable customer-centric quality improvements, organizations often based quality-improvement plans on extremely small sample data and anecdotal observations. Such methods are wholly flawed, as they are almost always been based on statistically invalid and inaccurate data. Conversely, having accurate data

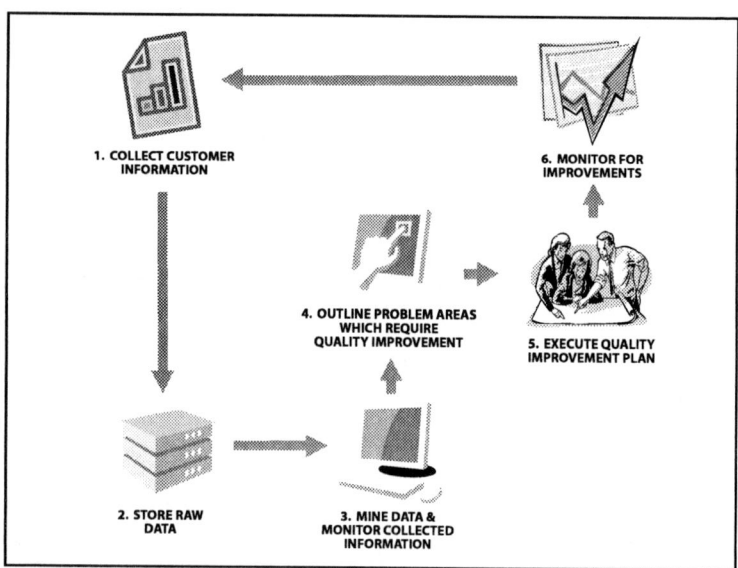

Figure 13.2 - The Customer Centric Quality Improvement Process

from a larger sample size to uncover crucial relationships aids quality-improvement processes by addressing known problem areas, as opposed to assumed problem areas, thereby appreciably raising the prospect of improving quality, reducing inefficiencies, and increasing productivity.

In simple terms, when Deming was asked how to improve quality and productivity he responded, "By everyone doing his best...is wrong. The system is such that almost nobody can do his best. You have to know what to do, then do your best."[1] And the only way of knowing what to do is to have accurate information, by systematically collecting and monitoring data on a regular basis.

13.3 Essential Attributes of Modern Quality Improvement Methodologies

Business and management thinking evolves over time, and the same applies to quality improvement methodologies. Even quality-improvement methods can benefit from quality improvement! The quality revolution has greatly evolved since the 1940s, and methodologies like Six Sigma have yielded some excellent results for organizations across many different industries worldwide. Other well-known methodologies like *Total Quality Management* (TQM) and *In Search of Excellence*, promoted by Tom Peters, offer differing yet effective methods for continuous quality improvement.

Successful leaders like Jack Welch firmly believe in quality improvement—but even he had a preferred methodology. His weapon of choice was Six Sigma. He felt that "earlier quality programs were too heavy on slogans and light on results,"[3] whereas other organizations preferred the TQM or the Excellence methods. In reality there is no wrong answer, as long as the performance improvements of the quality program employed exceed the cost of undertaking them. There are certain common characteristics that quality methodologies adhere to, however, which converge with the knowledge-power paradigm. These essential characteristics can be classified as follows:

Involvement and Buy-In: For quality-improvement processes to be successful they require involvement and buy-in from various levels within the organization, from process managers, to executors, to leaders. Methodologies can only work if all parties that influence decision-making and execution are on the same page and share a common goal. Quality-improvement methodologies frequently fail to attain full potential because of a lack of involvement and buy-in at leadership level.

A Sense of Purpose: Each quality-improvement methodology must have a sense of purpose. Why has it been undertaken? How is it going to be executed? What does the organization hope to achieve? A sense of purpose also connects the various parties involved in the quality-improvement process, as long as the sense of purpose is commonly shared.

Methodology: Which methodology is going to be used for quality improvement? While information gathering and analysis are common among quality-improvement methodologies, there are different processes within each one that take the organization from a current to a desired state. Leaders are normally tasked to identify a preferred methodology that best suits the way the organization works and the desired results.

Quality Improvement Measurement: Quality improvement often leads to financial gain, from the reduction in cost to an increase in revenue. But quality improvement can also lead to efficiencies that cannot easily be measured in purely financial terms. For example, an organization can improve its quality levels by improving the lead time for product delivery, resulting in greater customer satisfaction and an increase in repeat business volume. In such circumstances quality measurement can reflect a reduction in physical process time and customer satisfaction levels. While a method may not easily measure how quality improvement translates to cold, hard financials, it can make the correlation between quality improvement and the impact on the organizational bottom line in the mid- and long-term.

Customer is King: All quality gurus agree upon the importance of the customer within their quality-improvement processes. Deming went as far as to outline the customer as the most important part of the production line. Improving the quality of a system is only worthwhile if it directly—and indirectly—impacts the customer in a positive way; otherwise, don't do it. Leaders often forget the importance of the customer and take them for granted. But modern consumers are very sophisticated and are accustomed to receiving quality service wherever they go, so they are patently aware when they experience below-par service. The impression a customer has of an organization is something that cannot be bought; it has to be earned, and that can only happen through quality processes, products, and service. It's estimated that a dissatisfied customer will tell 11 to 20 people about the experience. Furthermore, only about 4% of all dissatisfied customers voluntarily tell the vendor about their bad experience–which means a whopping 96% never inform the vendor! Ignore the needs of your customer at your own peril; the only way to know their needs effectively is by asking them.

Effective Decision-Making: Quality-improvement methodologies are essentially processes that allow leaders the ability to make accurate decisions for resource allocation, process flow, and strategy. Trusting that process can help leaders move from current to desired state. Decisions cannot ever have any degree of certainty in an informational vacuum, but with accurate information uncertainty can greatly be reduced. Therefore, regardless of which quality-improvement methodology is chosen, the basis of each one is in the ability to acquire information upon which sound decision-making can take place. This characteristic is found in all quality-improvement models advocated by Deming, Juran, Crosby, and Peters, including TQM and Six Sigma.

Data Capture & Measurement: This provides the precursor to effective decision-making, and initial benchmarks help establish a baseline for improvement. For quality improvement to work, organizations must know the levels they are trying to achieve. For example, if a car dealership is trying to improve upon its current level of repeat business, it has to establish precisely what that current level is. Therefore, data capture and measurement processes must be strong in order to yield accurate results. Quality gurus all advocate tried and tested methods over a sustained time period; only then can the full power of quality improvement take hold.

Information Monitoring: This is the second step of the knowledge-management process, and it refers to the evaluation and monitoring of captured data. Measured and captured data is useless unless it can be evaluated successfully to glean pertinent information and knowledge. Monitoring allows decision-makers to pinpoint inefficiencies, requirements, and areas for improvement. This type of information also shapes the planning and execution of quality improvements.

THE KNOWLEDGE-POWER PARADIGM

Long-Termism: All quality-improvement methodologies are set up for long-term benefit. Quality improvement has been described as "a race without a finish line!" No matter how good your product or service, it can always be improved upon. Constantly changing business environments dictate the challenges organizations face over time. Leaders who adopt quality-improvement strategies must be prepared to commit to the long-term nature of the program. Seldom, if ever, do consistent quality-improvement methodologies succeed during a short period of time.

Strategic Thinking: Acute strategic thinking and decision-making by leaders is required for quality-improvement success. Strategic thinking must be congruent to macro and micro processes, with special attention paid to change management implications and resource allocation. Strategic decisions often are made by leaders alone; therefore, the need for buy-in at the highest levels within an organization is critical.

Operational Excellence: Quality-improvement methodologies strive for operational excellence. Regardless of the process or system the quality-improvement methodology is addressing, the overall goal is to strive for excellence. Essentially, isn't that what leaders are tasked to do? The better they are with organizational processes, the closer they come to achieving their goals.

The knowledge-power paradigm goes hand in hand with quality-improvement thinking and process. Many of the principles which apply to one also apply to the other. The quality-improvement movement was greatly influenced by the likes of Deming, Juran, Crosby, and Peters. Their work is not based on theory alone; for evidence, one need only look at the thousands of successful examples of organizations which, by wanting to achieve excellence, have taken a leadership position and improved organizational performance. Quality improvement, and the knowledge-power paradigm for that matter, is not for all leaders. It's for those who are concerned with and strive to elevate practice and performance. They are the ones who want to break free from the average and endeavor to be among the best—if not the best. Quality improvement can be a significant investment, and the return on that investment can be great. But nothing that is worth doing is ever easy, and neither is the quality-improvement continuum.

14

STEPPING UP TO THE STARTING LINE

*It is no good to try to stop knowledge from going forward.
Ignorance is never better than knowledge.*
- ENRICO FERMI

WE HAVE DISCUSSED THE knowledge-power paradigm extensively, and you may now be ready to explore how you can benefit from its principles. So where do you start and what can you do next? The first thing to recognize is the importance of making a conscious decision to explore how the paradigm can be put into practice. The key to applying the knowledge-power paradigm is to understand the workings of knowledge management. That is, actively using gathered and evaluated data to identify improvement opportunities and execute decisions for quality improvement. In this chapter we will outline practical steps leaders can take to implement the knowledge-power paradigm, and we will outline tools to assist in leveraging benefits. Other aspects covered in this chapter include how to use information once it is acquired, and the best method to foster an environment for effective communication.

Figure 14.1 illustrates the six essential stages successful leaders progress through when designing effective knowledge-management systems. We will discuss the contents and workings of each one of these stages

THE KNOWLEDGE-POWER PARADIGM

separately, and outline essential factors leaders should take into consideration when successfully navigating through the maze.

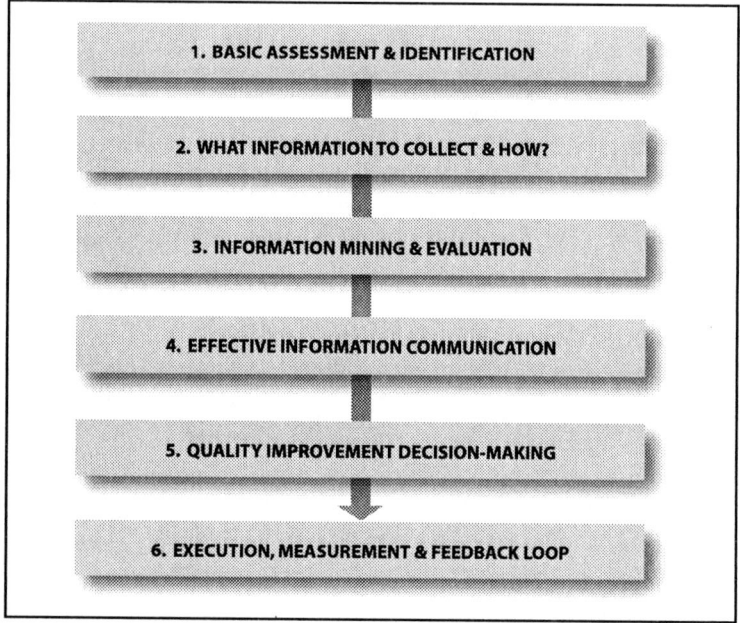

Figure 14.1 - The 6 Stages of Knowledge Management Design

14.1 Basic Assessment and Identification

All quality-improvement processes require initial systems assessment for improvement. There are literally hundreds of processes that can be improved upon within organizations. But which ones should be tackled first? Leaders can employ many criteria to come to an assertion; outlined below are some of the most commonly employed during the assessment and identification stage:

Need: Leaders already may have a good idea, based on their daily activities, which process or system most requires improvement. It could be an area where business is consistently performing below expectations, or an area which is not financially producing.

Impact: This refers to a process where improvement, through better knowledge management, can significantly impact and advance performance. The process in question could be simple or complex, and the level of knowledge management required will depend on this factor.

Ease: Certain processes are easier to improve upon, as identifying problems and executing strategy for them is relatively straightforward. Leaders sometimes prefer to tackle the easiest problem, which require simple fixes, and then move on to the more complex ones.

Cost: This identification criteria is based on a resource-limiting factor, i.e. where resource constraints determine which process is earmarked for improvement. For example, a leader may identify a process which requires quality improvement, but the financial requirement to successfully undertake the quality improvement prohibits the completion of the project. The reverse can also apply, if the cost of potentially improving a process fits into the leader's budget, allowing the project to move forward.

Financial Rate of Return: This is often an attractive criterion for process-improvement identification, as it relates directly to improving the financial rate of return. Undertaking an improvement project can be justified only if the cost of the knowledge-management process is less than the incremental financial rate of return. The financial impact can be two-fold; improvements in the process or system can result in significant reduction to cost, and/or a significant increase in revenue. For example, having better information for a certain process allows the leader to make better decisions about resource allocation and customer service, which in turn reduces cost and increases revenue beyond the cost of the project itself.

Leaders can probably easily identify numerous processes and systems that can be improved upon through better knowledge management and communication. Upon closer assessment they can probably whittle those down to several key areas they want to tackle first. Once improvement processes have been identified, the leader will have to set out distinct parameters for data and information collection.

THE KNOWLEDGE-POWER PARADIGM

14.2 What Information to Collect and How?

Knowing what data and information to collect is critical within the knowledge-management process. If collected data is inappropriate to the identified system, then the paradigm is not likely to yield suitable results. One of the key assumptions of the knowledge-power paradigm is the ability to acquire accurate and appropriate knowledge. Therefore, what is being measured has to be congruent with what needs to be improved.

It's critical to collect data in quantitative form. For example, a leader may decide to collect customer satisfaction data with respect to a specific operational process he aims to improve. For the data to be useful, there has to be a method that allows it to be quantified, e.g. the percentage of people who were satisfied or dissatisfied. Alternatively, if the process in question happens to be an assembly line, and the leader wishes to reduce the amount of defective 'widgets' produced, she could quantify data collection by measuring the number of defective 'widgets' per 100, per 1,000, per 10,000, etc.

Quantifiable data is easier to absorb in quality-improvement terms, as it can be used as a benchmark. So when the leader makes decisions to improve process performance, the following round of data gathering (measurement) can reveal whether there has indeed been an improvement. But this cannot be possible without having the ability to gather quantifiable data in the first place.

So far we have identified how a leader identifies what processes to improve and what data to collect. The next logical step is to establish an appropriate method for data collection. There are numerous factors that go into deciding an appropriate methodology for data collection, and the factors that affect this decision include:

1. Budget: How much budget is available to invest into a data-collection system? Remember, if the cost of acquiring knowledge is greater than the benefit gained from the knowledge, then the program is not worthwhile.

2. Time: How long will it take to collect data? A labor-intensive data-collection process will invariably take longer and cost more in financial terms. Additionally, the longer data collection takes, the more mistakes are likely to occur.

3. Technology: How can modern technology assist with data gathering and measurement? Organizations are turning to the use of technology to save time and money in acquiring invaluable information to help with decision-making and process quality improvement.

4. Ease of Data Collection: How easy is it to collect data? For example, if data collection involves manual polling of people, such as customers, then the measurement and data-gathering process has to be easy to understand, administer, and use. Otherwise the measurement process becomes inconvenient, even though the intentions are praiseworthy.

5. Integrity: Data-collection methods must have integrity with respect to what's being collected and communicated. Furthermore, the method must be consistent in measurement. Using the same measurement method helps to ensure the data collected has integrity. Data variances due to inconsistent measurement methods can lead to evaluation discrepancies.

6. Usability: Data-collection systems must be easy to use and apply. If the system forms part of an existing process, then the system should dovetail into the process without causing too much disturbance.

By now the leader should have a good idea of the information he wants to collect, and he should have established an appropriate data-collection method. The next step is to evaluate collected data, including data segmentation and garnering of valuable information.

14.3 Data Segmentation, Evaluation, and Next Steps

The ability to effectively evaluate and segment data for knowledge is the key to any successful knowledge-management system. As previously mentioned, the knowledge-management process has two sides: data gathering and evaluation. Its effectiveness is largely dependent on the ability to successfully complete both of these tasks on a regular and consistent basis. Leaders can be efficient in collecting data but still fall short in their ability to evaluate data successfully. Acquired data is often unstructured; it has little value unless it can be aggregated and quantified. Furthermore, the data-evaluation process should be straightforward and relatively easy to navigate.

If the process improvement is an easy fix, then the data-evaluation process should logically be a quick one for the leader. Conversely, a leader is more likely to spend far more time poring over and evaluating data for critical and complex operations. It's relative, but the effectiveness of data evaluation should be uniform, regardless of complexity.

The importance Deming placed upon keeping tabs on customer needs for quality improvement is a classic example when exploring the subject of knowledge evaluation. GE places the same emphasis on knowing exactly what their customers are thinking. GE openly states, "Customers are the center of the GE universe: they define quality. They expect performance, reliability, competitive prices, on-time delivery, service, clear and correct transaction processing and more. In every attribute that influences customer perception, we know that just being good is not enough. Delighting our customers is a necessity. Because if we don't do it, someone else will! Quality requires us to look at our business from the customer's perspective, not ours. In other words, we must look at our processes from the outside-in. By understanding the transaction lifecycle from the customer's needs and processes, we can discover what they are seeing and feeling. With this knowledge, we can identify areas where we can add significant value or improvement from their perspective."[1]

All successful leaders place customer knowledge high on their priority list of 'must-have' information. But very few have established a system proactively that allows for the effective capture and analysis of this information. The acid test is to ask simple questions, such as: "Can you quantify what the current satisfaction level is among your customers?" "Can you quantify what aspects of your product/service your customers like/dislike?" "Can you quantify whether most of your customers are male or female?" The list of answers draws out essential information that aids improved performance—and the list can be extremely long. If leaders cannot easily obtain answers to such basic questions, then there is a lot of room to improve their knowledge-management process.

Data collection is easier to undertake, arguably, than the ability to effectively evaluate it. Earlier we cited the example of physicians who collect patient-satisfaction data through hard-copy surveys. By the end of a given month the physician may have been efficient enough to collect a couple of hundred surveys. But to evaluate this information effectively, the physician must have a system that allows him to input the collected data into a database, and then analyze it in order to establish meaningful understanding. This is where many knowledge-management problems begin for leaders. The physician realizes that he would like to acquire certain information to help monitor performance, with the goal of offering the best service possible. The knowledge-management system he employs, however, is effective at collecting data but ineffective for data evaluation, unless he pays someone to physically input raw data into a database. Therefore, invariably the data is evaluated piecemeal via the physician, reviewing a small sample to get a handle on what is being communicated by patients–a wholly unsatisfactory method of garnering knowledge and understanding.

The same can be applied to the example of car dealership managers, but for different reasons. Previously, we discussed the traditional system used by car manufacturers and dealerships that collect customer experience surveys after a sale has been made. Because the survey is often sent out several weeks after the sale, six to eight weeks can easily pass before the dealership or manufacturer receives the completed survey and communicates the evaluated information. Such time-lags are a huge hindrance for leaders who want to know immediately as problems arise. Furthermore, the data being collected and evaluated represents customers who go on to make a purchase. What about collecting information from customers who decided not to make a purchase? If the dealership conversion rate is one in every ten customers, then the company is getting critical customer information from less than 10% of the people who walk through the doors! Would it not be valuable for the dealership manager to know why the majority of potential customers did not buy their product? Leaders also should want to get their hands on customer feedback from other divisions of the dealership, such as used car sales and the vehicle service department.

So how can organizational leaders, from physicians to car dealership managers, effectively evaluate collected data? It's impossible for the average human mind to evaluate and process mass data. Therefore, technology is the key to effective data evaluation. In fact, technology is also the key to helping measure data. If customer information and feedback is important to organizations, and there is not a logical argument to suggest it's not, then such knowledge can effectively be collected and evaluated through technology. Browser-based collection and evaluation devices allow the mass collection of customer feedback data, which can then be stored in a database for later monitoring and evaluation. Leaders access the database at a convenient time to review critical information about various operating procedures and performance. The database can be programmed automatically to quantify collected data, allowing benchmarking. Furthermore, depending on the type of information collected, the leader should also be able to segment data and acquire knowledge based on certain selected categories, e.g. age, sex, time of service, and also the type of answer given to a specific question. This type of knowledge-management system can be incredibly powerful in the hands of leaders. If applied properly, it can supply vital information to help strategic decision-making for quality improvement.

Technology also can be employed for data evaluation where it has a specific function in capturing process data. For example, leaders can employ systems to check whether critical items, within processes, are being completed within set parameters. That is, systems gather data on the completion of essential and repetitive tasks, allowing managers to monitor process quality on the fly. The leader can also set goals, such as a 99% completion rate, and if the software reflects anything lower than the desired level the leader can perform corrective action. If the leader does not have the ability to capture data and monitor these levels, then he will not have the ability to make informed and purposeful decisions to improve quality. Examples of such systems include internal employee appraisals and exit interview processes.

Effective knowledge-management systems assist leaders with problem-solving and decision-making processes. Information supply and better understanding allow for problem identification, maintenance, and improvement opportunities within organizations. This helps to complete the essential loop within the knowledge-power success model, where acquired knowledge is the precursor to goal setting, action planning, and execution. Essentially, the knowledge-management process becomes the eyes and ears of quality-improvement endeavors.

14.4 Communication

Information gleaned from knowledge-management processes offers the leader the option to take necessary actions and/or communicate findings to other parties. In most organizations, sharing information, especially information pertaining to critical processes, requires effective communication.

This allows for better decision-making, improvements across different divisions, and benchmarking for best practices.

Effective knowledge-management systems must assist information communication processes because organizations depend on the flow and transfer of information. Today, communication options are wide and varied, from e-mail, to the Internet, to wireless devices. Not only is it important for the knowledge-management system to be able to communicate data and information, but it should also be secure, ensuring that only the intended recipients receive the information.

Information can often have a limited shelf-life, and it can become outdated if it doesn't make it into the right hands within a certain time frame. This is another benefit of employing a technologically based knowledge-management system, as it allows for 'real-time' communication. For example, online stock-trading organizations offer what they call 'real-time' stock quotes. While there is still a small time-lag between the actual quote and the quote given to the user, it's about as close as the user will ever come to absolute 'real-time.' This type of knowledge-management system highlights how the right information, in the hands of the right person, at the right time, helps the leader make an informed decision.

Speed of communication has a major impact on organizational performance; it can make all the difference. Regardless of size and industry, organizations must have the intrinsic ability to identify issues and opportunities, make decisions, and take action. The ability to do this is tied into the effectiveness of the knowledge-management and communication system being employed. Leaders who choose to ignore such systems should recognize that their competitors may not choose to ignore the same systems, therefore gaining an edge.

Many of the long-term competitive advantages, e.g. innovation, price, barriers to entry, channels, and economies of scale, have been eroded away. Having information in its place, and the ability to communicate it, is a supreme advantage that has come to the fore. This differentiator has always existed, but its importance was often overshadowed by other, more traditional, advantages. There will never be a time when knowledge and communication will not create a significant competitive advantage, because there will never come a time when everything that needs to be known is actually known!

14.5 Quality Improvement Planning and Execution

The knowledge-power success model, as illustrated in figure 14.2, outlines the various stages often found in different quality-improvement methodologies. The 'data collection measurement' and 'data evaluation' stages comprise the knowledge-management part of the improvement cycle. Once leaders garner a better understanding and quantify process performance, strategies can be executed for improved performance. Therefore, the importance of knowledge management within the process of managerial decision-making cannot be overstated.

To help illustrate the impact knowledge-management systems have on goal-setting, strategic planning, and execution, let's examine their effect on the ability to measure and understand customer satisfaction levels. If a leader can pinpoint a specific area of business operation that customers have highlighted as an issue, then he is enjoying the power of knowledge—as he has the ability to constructively do something about it. But not having this information does not mean that he may not come by the information at a later date. The cost implications can be significant, and any delay can prolong inefficiencies. By identifying problems early, power is attained from the ability to effectively do something about it, assuming that the course of action taken is a correct one.

The quality-improvement planning and execution stage is not used exclusively to identify problems. For example, a multi-location organization can use a knowledge-management system to identify over-performing areas. Knowing why a process is over-performing, especially if it is validated by customer feedback and not just financial performance, allows leaders to know what the organization is doing right and why. Conscious understanding presents an opportunity to mandate best practices across all locations. Understanding valuable information allows leaders to make effective decisions for future processes; knowing what has worked in the past can be a good indicator for future success.

Finally, environmental disturbances can impact the effect of the quality improvement planning and execution process. Leaders should be aware that knowledge management helps to set the table for informed decision-making, but there are many known and unknown external factors which determine obtained results. In the next section we will talk about the important role of identifying performance and performance-related factors within the knowledge-management system.

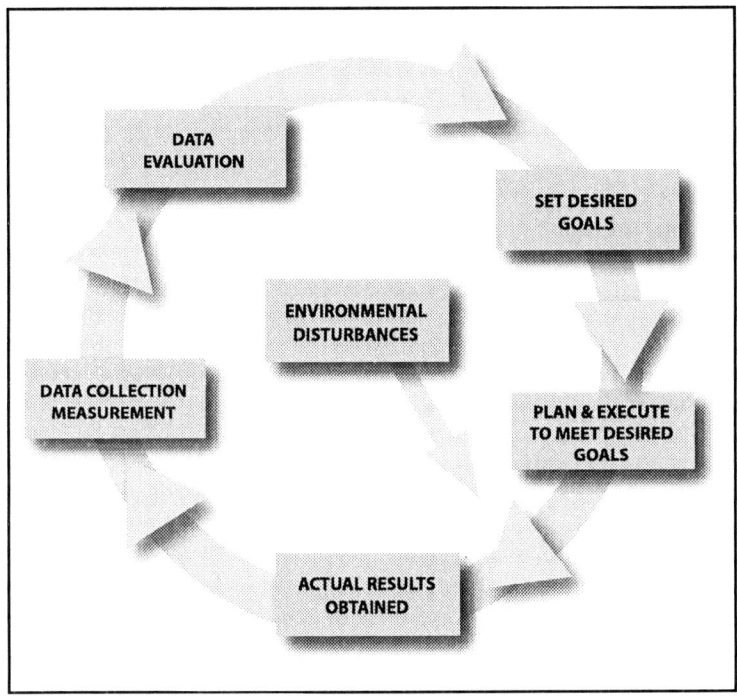

Figure 14.2 - The Knowledge-Power-Success Model

14.6 Performance and Re-measurement

In practice, the benefit of an effective knowledge-management system is the ability to measure process specifics at the front end, prior to goal setting, planning, and execution. That same knowledge-management process allows re-measurement after strategy execution, giving the leader the ability to gauge variations in performance output. If the goal of strategy execution is performance improvement, then knowledge-management systems should offer information on whether the strategy has been successful. The system will also output vital information outlining the variance between actual and desired performance.

All quality-improvement methodologies state the importance of re-measuring and feeding information back to the process manager. This is very much the case for both the Six Sigma and Total Quality Management (TQM). According to Motorola University, "the Six Sigma Management System drives clarity around the business strategy and the metrics that most reflect success with that strategy. It provides the framework to prioritize resources for projects that will improve the metrics, and it leverages leaders who will manage the efforts for rapid, sustainable, and improved business results."[2]

The key to the success, according to Motorola University, are "the metrics that most reflect success with that strategy."[2] Metrics are the result of conscious measurement and quantification of performance, prioritization of resources (strategy), and then re-measurement to evaluate metrics again. Without the ability to measure, and then re-measure, it's impossible for any quality-improvement process to succeed.

The final point to make regarding performance and re-measurement processes is the importance of consistently employing the same knowledge-management methods for data collection and evaluation. Scientifically, measurement methods can have an effect on the results of what is being measured. Therefore, differing methods may produce inconsistent results. Stating this does not and should not preclude the use of improved knowledge-measurement systems, but leaders should not change the system unless there is a clear rationale for potential benefits.

Leaders who are serious about continuous improvement should establish effective knowledge-management programs to help capture and quantify data and allow leaders an opportunity to analyze it. A critical responsibility of all leaders is to identify process improvements and also decide upon the method used to execute process improvement. The same knowledge-management system will re-measure the results obtained after strategy execution, outlining actual performance. The quality-improvement process can be cycled over and over again for continuous improvement. This approach has been employed by organizations in many industries and of varying sizes. The advantage that modern technology affords smaller organizations is the ability to benefit from the aforementioned without the need to invest significant resources. Leaders striving for a critical competitive advantage no longer have an excuse for ignoring the benefits of the knowledge-power paradigm and continuous quality improvement.

15

ONE PARABLE & TEN TEXT MESSAGES

If we could first know where we are, and whither we are tending, we could then better judge what to do, and how to do it.
- ABRAHAM LINCOLN

IN THIS BOOK WE HAVE OUTLINED the importance of attaining accurate knowledge, getting it to the right person at the right time, and how to use it in a constructive way to attain success. These are the fundamentals of the knowledge-power paradigm. We have briefly reviewed some of the teachings of Sun Tzu and outlined the importance of knowledge in his treatise, *The Art of War*. Therefore, it only seems appropriate that we revisit the lessons of Sun Tzu to evaluate all that has been discussed, and bring it together in the context of leaders looking to improve and succeed. While there have been many books and papers written about Sun Tzu's impact on business strategy, this book has steered more toward the importance of knowledge and its impact on organizational performance in the context of his stanza.

If Sun Tzu were alive today, he would undoubtedly be a great leader in his field of choosing—perhaps a coach in the business or sporting world. Either way, his principles from centuries ago still apply. If he were to send us only ten critical teachings, via text message, what would they be

THE KNOWLEDGE-POWER PARADIGM

and how would they apply to you and me? Furthermore, how do the great modern leaders and teachers match up against the teachings of Sun Tzu? Finally, what can we take away from historical and modern lessons taught with the knowledge-power paradigm?

15.1 Ten Text Messages[1]

Many of Sun Tzu's teachings reflected the critical need for knowledge and the subsequent use of knowledge to determine strategy and success. So what were the ten most important teachings from Sun Tzu, in the context of the knowledge-power paradigm? If I were Sun Tzu text messaging one of my generals with advice, these are the ten I would pick:

Text Message #1:
"*In respect of military method, we have, firstly, Measurement; secondly, Estimation of quantity; thirdly, Calculation; fourthly, Balancing of chances; fifthly, Victory.*"

Going back to the knowledge-power success model, what Sun Tzu outlines above is the essence of the model–the importance of knowledge management (measurement and quantity), planning (calculation and balancing), and execution (victory). These elements are very similar to quality improvement methods, like Six Sigma and TQM.

Text Message #2:
"*The Commander stands for the virtues of wisdom, sincerely, benevolence, courage and strictness…Thus it may be known that the leader of armies is the arbiter of the people's fate, the man on whom it depends whether the nation shall be in peace or in peril.*"

Sun Tzu fully understood the importance of the leader's role. In modern organizations that role is filled by managers, executives and entrepreneurs. They are the generals who determine the course taken, and their understanding and grasp of the knowledge-power paradigm often determines whether success is attained and to what level. The Six Sigma quality-improvement program recognizes this very aspect. One of the critical requirements is buy-in from executive leadership and upper management (also known as champions). Therefore, the knowledge-power paradigm has to be a top-down approach.

> *Text Message #3:*
> "Now the general who wins a battle makes many calculations in his temple ere the battle is fought. The general who loses a battle makes but few calculations beforehand. Thus do many calculations lead to victory, and few calculations to defeat: how much more no calculation at all! It is by attention to this point that I can foresee who is likely to win or lose."

In this verse from *The Art of War*, Sun Tzu outlines the importance of making calculations. In modern business, 'calculations,' in Sun Tzu's terms, refers to the ability to evaluate information and knowledge. This is a critical part of the knowledge-management process, allowing for knowledge to be gleaned from data and information. Sun Tzu is outlining the need for leaders to evaluate information, because evaluations help to formulate strategy and execution. As discussed in Chapter 12, leaders in the sporting world have become very adept at adhering to this principle; athletes like Lance Armstrong, Tiger Woods and Bill Belichick embody this lesson, and much of their success is influenced by their ability to evaluate and leverage collected data.

> *Text Message #4:*
> "Thus, though we have heard of stupid haste in war, cleverness has never been seen associated with long delays."

Going to war is an execution of a battle plan. In business terms, that translates to strategy followed by action to attain desired goals. The lesson here is not to be hasty to act, but also not to procrastinate. There is a fine line with regard to timing, determined by the leader/manager. The duty is to be efficient in the formulation and execution of strategy. This implies that knowledge management, in the decision-making process, must be efficient as well as effective. Is the knowledge-management part of your decision-

THE KNOWLEDGE-POWER PARADIGM

making too efficient to be effective? Is it not efficient enough so that it is paralyzing the decision-making process?

> **Text Message #5:**
> "Now in order to kill the enemy, our men must be roused to anger; that there may be advantage from defeating the enemy, they must have their rewards."

This lesson focuses purely on motivation: There has to be motivation to defeat the enemy. Great leaders not only are self-motivated for success, but they also have the ability to motivate others, i.e. their troops. Management techniques such as quality improvement and knowledge management require motivation and the desire to succeed. The reward is improved performance and elevated business results. Motivation, however, has to start at the top and cascade down. If leaders do not have motivation to attain the results, neither will their troops.

> **Text Message #6:**
> "If you know the enemy and know yourself, you need not fear the result of a hundred battles. If you know yourself but not the enemy, for every victory gained you will also suffer a defeat. If you know neither the enemy nor yourself, you will succumb in every battle."

This is the central point of Sun Tzu's message of knowledge. Without knowledge it is difficult to strategize effectively, and, therefore, the result of actions is unlikely to be effective. Results will be 50-50 if you have limited knowledge, i.e. about yourself and your competition. Accurate knowledge about yourself, your business environment and also your competitors is a good platform upon which strategies and decisions are formed. Of all of the strategies employed by your organization, how many are rooted in having current knowledge in each of the aforementioned areas? If the results of strategies employed are not satisfactory, do you know why and how to turn bad performance into good performance? Sun Tzu was clear in his strategy for success; his method was based on obtaining and employing superior knowledge.

> **Text Message #7:**
> *"Security against defeat implies defensive tactics;
> ability to defeat the enemy means taking the offensive...
> The general who is skilled in defense hides in the most secret
> recesses of the earth; he who is skilled in attack flashes forth
> from the topmost heights of heaven. Thus on the one hand we
> have ability to protect ourselves; on the other, a victory that is complete."*

Organizational system and process strategies significantly impact the performance of the whole company. Effective strategy implementation is one of the many critical factors which determine organizational performance. Strategy can be categorized into two groups: defensive and offensive. A defensive strategy implies a willingness not to lose, whereas an offensive strategy implies a passionate enthusiasm to win. Most successful leaders share the common trait of implementing an offensive type of strategy. Great leaders, like Rothschild and Welch, took the proverbial *"bull by the horns"* and wrestled it to the ground. They could have been good, but they wanted to be great. Great strategies are founded on having supreme knowledge and then effectively using it. The question every leader and manager needs to ask is, "What kind of leader do I want to be?" The answer will reveal itself through the choice and performance of the strategies employed.

> **Text Message #8:**
> *"The consummate leader cultivates the moral law, and strictly
> adheres to method and discipline; thus it is in his power to control success."*

This message relates to the broad doctrine for quality improvement and control. All quality-improvement methodologies, like TQM and Six Sigma, allow for performance improvement (success) through adherence to method and discipline. These processes do not require external factors to influence performance; instead they are internally self-reliant to attain improved performance. This lesson from Sun Tzu once again highlights the essential role played by the leader within the process.

> **Text Message #9:**
> *"The quality of decision is like the well-timed swoop of a falcon which enables it to strike and destroy its victim."*

On the field of battle, quality decision-making affects outcome. In business, quality decision-making impacts performance. If a leader is satisfied with her level of performance she only needs to compare and contrast it against other successful leaders to measure true success. While decisions made by a leader may result in some success, she must always reflect upon the quality of those decisions to learn whether she could have achieved better results. Leadership decision-making is one of the most influential factors that determine performance, and knowledge management is a function of quality decision-making. Therefore, knowledge management becomes a direct function of performance.

> **Text Message #10:**
> *"Therefore the clever combatant imposes his will on the enemy, but does not allow the enemy's will to be imposed on him."*

This lesson is related to lesson #7, in that imposing the will on the enemy is an offensive position to take: It's proactive. The enemy in this case does not necessarily have to be a competitor. It can also be a system or process that organizations wish to control and improve upon. The search for improved performance is eternal, but a proactive approach is always recommended over a reactive approach. Are you waiting for something to go wrong before deciding to act, or are you going to act for continuous improvement, regardless of outcome?

15.2 The Parable of the Obstacle in Our Path

"In ancient times, a King had a boulder placed on a roadway. Then he hid himself and watched to see if anyone would remove the huge rock. Some of the king's wealthiest merchants and courtiers came by and simply walked around it. Many loudly blamed the king for not keeping the roads clear, but none did anything about getting the stone out of the way. Then a peasant came along carrying a load of vegetables. Upon approaching the boulder, the peasant laid down his burden and

tried to move the stone to the side of the road. After much pushing and straining, he finally succeeded. After the peasant picked up his load of vegetables, he noticed a purse lying in the road where the boulder had been. The purse contained many gold coins and a note from the king indicating that the gold was for the person who removed the boulder from the roadway. The peasant learned what many of us never understand. Every obstacle presents an opportunity to improve our condition."

One of the most important roles played by leaders in organizations is to remove obstacles from the proverbial path. Obstacles, often referred to as bottlenecks, create inefficiencies and hinder performance. The role of the leader is to recognize where these obstacles are, assess their size, gauge the impact they are having on performance, decide whether they should be removed, plan how to remove them, and then execute that plan. Obstacles come in many sizes, shapes and forms, and they often give leaders problems as they hamper performance. Just as in the parable above, however, when the obstacles are removed, the prize often presents itself.

In this book, the importance of effective knowledge management has been put forward with plenty of well-known examples. Fundamentally, it is up to leaders and managers to choose which path they take and how much attention to pay to this essential part of strategic decision-making. Donald Trump is another big advocate of knowledge management. He admits that much of what he has achieved comes down to having more knowledge than his rivals, which gives him the vital competitive edge to succeed. Trump states, "Rudyard Kipling wrote something I read in college and have never forgotten: 'I keep six honest serving men, they taught me all I knew—their names are What and Why and When and How and Where and Who.' Finding the answers to those questions will ensure that your information is comprehensive and correct. There's really no such thing as knowing too much about what you're doing."[2]

In another example, Trump outlines how knowledge helped him to close a lucrative deal for a building on Wall Street: "I spent time studying the building and the area, and kept informed about the latest developments. When the opportunity finally came to purchase it, I was ready and knew what I was getting into. The tallest building in lower Manhattan, 40 Wall Street is a 1.3 million square foot landmark. I bought it for $1 million. You can imagine what it's worth now, considering it's hard to find a one-bedroom apartment for under $1 million these days. When I say knowledge

THE KNOWLEDGE-POWER PARADIGM

is power, I mean it. Use it to your advantage."[2]

The principles outlined by Trump are not exclusive to the 'rock star' business types and entrepreneurs of this world; they apply equally to all types: men and women, young and old, rich and poor. In fact, the Wall Street example Trump cites is one of his first ventures into New York real estate; he acquired the property very early in his career. Thus, it is never too early or too late to adhere to the principles of the knowledge-power paradigm. Review your current processes, identify problems, and make sound decisions to improve. Also look into the various data-gathering, analysis and communication solutions available in the market. Rapid development of technology has created access for firms of all sizes, across all industries, to aid knowledge-management techniques. Leaders who take advantage of such tools benefit greatly from enhanced performance and greater competitive advantage.

A 2003 article ('Knowledge is Power') in *The Economist* states, "One area to start catching up on is knowledge. This is true both personally, as executives work out whether or not they are staying on top of internal or external developments, but also at the level of companies. A survey of knowledge management, *'Knowledge Unplugged,'* published in 2001 by McKinsey, found that the best-performing companies were far more likely than the worst-performing ones to use creative techniques for acquiring, processing and distributing knowledge-everything from emphasizing teamwork in product development to holding 'idea contests' and trying to avoid boring daily routines."[3]

If the McKinsey study is right, there is more evidence pointing to effective knowledge-management process as beneficial to organizational performance. The article continues, "But creating an atmosphere in which knowledge can be shared, can be almost as challenging as obtaining it in the first place."[3] In this book we have outlined the what, the why, the who, the how and the when of the knowledge-power paradigm. The sharing of knowledge within an organization goes down to the very root of the culture that is cultivated within. Organizational culture is an area that itself would fill a book; suffice to say that culture also stems from leadership. Once the leadership of an organization chooses to implement and improve its knowledge-management techniques, it is essential to focus on cultivating and developing a culture which encourages performance through knowledge management.

15.3 Final Analysis

The argument advocating the principles of the knowledge-power paradigm are strong. Many may choose to ignore them and carry on with their status quo, while many will succeed by applying them. We know this because history is a good indicator: What has happened in the past often points to what is likely to occur in the future. But a new breed of leader, younger and technologically savvy, is emerging within organizations, part of the new technological generation. This leader has matured through the IT revolution and is open to employing technology to help lead more effectively and efficiently. This new breed is not stuck in the mire of "*this is how things are done around here.*" They are challenging stereotypes and convention. This is where the new competition is coming from.

John Fox, head coach of the Carolina Panthers, fully appreciates the erosion of traditional footballing advantages, resulting in greater parity across the NFL. This makes his job more challenging, but at the same time it makes his role more clear. He understands that the "…average game is won by six points or less, so if all of them are close, coming up with that little edge is coaching."[4] This same meticulous preparation and approach is shared by Bill Belichick, head coach of the New England Patriots. The on-field performance of their teams reflects knowledge-management success resulting in quality improvement. They are also leaders who have embraced technology to help them and their subordinates perform more effectively at their jobs.

The role and responsibilities of leadership have essentially remained the same through history, but the way the leader works constantly develops and evolves. Organizations that perform always progress, while the ones that do not tend to stagnate. Organizational leaders and aspiring leaders essentially face the same scenario: They are competing with each other, and performance is the ultimate measure of leadership ability. The principles of the knowledge-power paradigm and knowledge management have emerged as key tools in offering a crucial competitive edge for leaders. These principles have always been used effectively by great leaders, but thanks to technological development, knowledge management is accessible and available to all.

For a leader, the choice is clear: Change is inevitable and adaptation is necessary if one is going to progress and improve performance in a dynamic environment. The new generation of leaders already is applying these

THE KNOWLEDGE-POWER PARADIGM

philosophical arguments, and they are succeeding. How are you going to manage the knowledge revolution to give you the edge that others don't have? Are you ready to take the step toward employing technology to gather vital data? Are you willing to evaluate information to be more knowledgeable, and therefore more effective, as a leader?

NOTES

Preface -

1. *Report to the President - By the Presidential Commission on the Space Shuttle Challenger Accident*, June 6, 1986 - Washington, D.C.

2. *Columbia Accident Investigation Board (CAIB) Final Report*, Volumes I - VI, August 2003.

Chapter 1 -

1. The Holy Bible (New International Version), Passage 1 Kings 3:9.

Chapter 2 -

1. *Winning the War for Talent*, Knowledge@Wharton Article, August 1999.

2. Edwin L Godkin Lecture at Harvard University's John F Kennedy School of Government in 1994.

3. *The Art of War*, Sun Tzu, Chapter 3, 6th Century BC, China.

4. *Wall Street*, Oliver Stone and Stanley Weiser, CBS/Fox, December 1987.

Chapter 3 -

1. *Jack - Straight From the Gut*, Jack Welch With John A. Byrne, Warner Business Books, 2003.

Chapter 5 -

1. *Philosophiæ Naturalis Principia Mathematica*, Laws of Motion III, Isaac Newton, July 5, 1687.

2. *Iraq Study Group Report*, James A. Baker and Lee H. Hamilton, March 2006.

3. *Review of Intelligence on Weapons of Mass Destruction*, Report of a Committee of Privy Counsellors, The Rt Hon The Lord Butler of Brockwell, Ordered by the House of Commons, 14 July, 2004.

4. *Commentariolus*, Nicolaus Copernicus, 1514.

Chapter 6 -

1. *Strategic Management - Concepts and Experiences*, Leslie W. Rue and Phyllis G. Holland, Decond Edition, McGraw Hill, 1989.

2. Speech to Special Joint Session of Congress, John F. Kennedy, Washington D.C., 25 May, 1961.

Chapter 7 -
1. www.riotinto.com

Chapter 8 -
1. Einstein Archives, 31-101, Unpublished translation by Aaron Wiener, circa 1932.
2. *The Three Ways of Great Leaders*, Fast Company Magazine, Issue 98, Bill Breen, Page 50, September 2005.
3. House, R. J. (2004) *Culture, Leadership, and Organizations: The GLOBE Study of 62 Societies*, SAGE Publications, Thousand Oaks, 2004.
4. *Foreign Relations of the United States*, 1961-1963, Volume XI, Cuban Missile Crisis and Aftermath, Department of State, Washington D.C.
5. Commission on Presidential Debates, General Election Presidential Debate, September 26, 1960. Chicago, IL, ABC, CBS, NBC.
6. *Jack - Straight From the Gut*, Jack Welch With John A. Byrne, Warner Business Books, 2003.
7. *The Twenty Most Influential Businessmen of All Time*, Forbes Magazine, Michael Noer, July 2005.

Chapter 9 -
1. *Essential Tenants of Organizational Behavior*, Joseph E. Champoux, Thomson South-Western, 2003.
2. *Patricia Dunn Resigns from HP Board*, Press Release, Hewlett-Packard Development Company, Palo Alto, CA. September, 2006.
3. *HP Execs on Spying: It Wasn't Me*, USA Today, Michelle Kessler, Jon Swartz and Sue Kirchhoff. September 2006.

Chapter 10 -
1. *Medical Malpractice Briefing Book*, published by Public Citizen, Congress Watch (2004).
2. *The "Crisis" in Medical Malpractice Insurance*, Patricia M. Danzon, Andrew J. Epstein and Scott Johnson, The Wharton School - University of Pennsylvania. December 2003.
3. *Medical Malpractice, Implications of Rising Premiums on Access to Health Care*, Report to Congressional Requesters, United States General Accounting Office. August 2003.
4. *Doctors Earn MBAs to Tackle Ills of Health System*, Julie Appleby, USAToday (Money Section), July 5, 2002.
5. The 2007 Florida Statutes, Title XLV (Torts), Chapter 766 (Medical Malpractice and Related Matters); 766.102 (4).

Chapter 11 -

1. U.S. Department of Labor, Bureau of Labor Statistics.
2. Radio Address of the President George W. Bush to the Nation. Camp David. September 15, 2001.
3. *Government Increasingly Turning to Data Mining*, Arshad Mohammed and Sara Kehaulani Goo, The Washington Post, June 15, 2006.
4. *Karl Rove's Split Personality*, Todd S. Purdum, Vanity Fair, December 2006.
5. www.google.com
6. Reasons For Resisting Technology, www.fhwa.dot.gov.
7. H.M. Warner, Warner Brothers, 1927.

Chapter 12 -

1. The PGA of America, Palm Beach Gardens, FL.
2. *The Tiger Effect*, Hank Gola, New York Daily News, April 2, 2007.
3. *It's Not About the Bike - My Journey Back to Life*, Lance Armstrong with Sally Jenkins, Berkley Books, 2001.
4. *Overhauling Lance Armstrong*, John Markoff, The New York Times, April 19, 2004.
5. *The Art of War*, Sun Tzu, Chapter 3, 6th Century BC, China.
6. *The Secret of their NFL Success*, Lesley Stahl, 60 Minutes, CBS News, September 19, 2004.

Chapter 13 -

1. *The Deming Management Method*, Mary Walton, Perigee Books, 1986.
2. *Out of the Crisis*, W. Edwards Deming, The MIT Press, 2000.
3. *Jack - Straight From the Gut*, Jack Welch With John A. Byrne, Warner Business Books, 2003.

Chapter 14 -

1. The General Electric Company (GE), www.ge.com
2. Motorola University, www.motorola.com

Chapter 15 -

1. *The Art of War*, Sun Tzu, Chapter 1 - 13, 6th Century BC, China.
2. *Use Knowledge to Your Advantage*, Donald J. Trump, Trump University. Issue 4: June 21, 2006.
3. *Knowledge is Power - But Only if You Knew How to Acquire It*, The Economist Global Executive, May 8, 2003.
4. *The Secret of their NFL Success*, Lesley Stahl, 60 Minutes, CBS News, September 19, 2004.